SHERIDAN

RICHARD BRINSLEY SHERIDAN
After the Portrait by Sir Joshua Reynolds.

SHERIDAN

Lewis Gibbs

Illustrated with
16 pages of half-tones

KENNIKAT PRESS
Port Washington, N. Y./London

SHERIDAN

First published in 1947
Reissued in 1970 by Kennikat Press
Library of Congress Catalog Card No: 75-103189
SBN 8046-0826-1

Manufactured by Taylor Publishing Company   Dallas, Texas

CONTENTS

ILLUSTRATIONS

CHAPTER ONE

A General View

O N THE THIRTEENTH of July 1816 Richard Brinsley
Sheridan was buried in Westminster Abbey—this is to begin
with an instructive glance at his latter end. The pall-bearers
were the Duke of Bedford, the Earl of Lauderdale, Earl Mulgrave, the Bishop of London, Lord Holland, and Lord Spencer.
In addition, an impressive and numerous train of mourners
attended, including three dukes (two of them—York and Sussex
—royal); marquises, earls, and other members of the nobility to
the number of fifteen; the Lord Mayor; a goodly array of
honourables, right honourables, baronets, and mere knights,
tailing off into a score of Mr.s and reverends, two doctors, and
nearly the whole of the principal performers of Covent Garden
and Drury Lane.

Now a funeral in Westminster Abbey with such an attendance
suggests very strongly the proper conclusion to a story of success;
and yet every one has heard that Sheridan's story, though doubtless
edifying in its way, is chiefly so because it affords a striking
example of the kind of conduct which makes the greatest talents
useless, leads to misery and ruin, and is thus to be carefully
avoided by the prudent, and especially by such as wish to die
solvent. His was a career, as the third Lord Holland (who
appears above among the pall-bearers) judiciously observed, *To
point a moral or adorn a tale.* Lord Eldon likewise, before whom,
as Chancellor, Sheridan once appeared in connection with the
debts of Drury Lane, took occasion to point out—quoting also
from Dr. Johnson—that 'negligence and irregularity, long continued, will make knowledge useless, wit ridiculous, and genius
contemptible.' 'Poor Sheridan,' was the Prince Regent's expression to Croker in 1817; and indeed, even before Sheridan's
death, 'Poor Sheridan' had begun to be the tune. 'Poor
Brinsley!' exclaimed Byron; and again, 'Poor dear Sherry.
What a wreck is that man!'

I

We remind ourselves, therefore, that the funeral was not a state one, and that the memorial stone, with its simple inscription, was not the tribute of a grateful country, or of any of the crowd of distinguished and aristocratic mourners, but of 'an attached friend,' that is to say, Peter Moore, whose name makes a comparatively humble figure among those of that brilliant assembly. He had, however, done more than one friendly office for Sheridan. During the Westminster election of 1806, as one of Sheridan's supporters, he had offered a reward of £100 for the capture of two ruffians who had violently assaulted Mr. Sheridan as he was going to the hustings; and in 1808, he, with Sir R. Berkeley and Mr. Homan, undertook the arduous task of investigating Sheridan's affairs with a view to getting them straightened out and the debts paid—a consummation which was not achieved. He was also a member of the Drury Lane Committee which was formed after the burning of the theatre in 1809. Like Sheridan, he was a Whig. He represented Coventry in Parliament for twenty-one years, and then, having lost the considerable fortune he had originally made in the service of the East India Company, fled to France to escape arrest—which reminds us somewhat of the case of Sheridan's father, and might conceivably have been Sheridan's own case.

However, when all is said, the funeral and the grave in the Abbey speak plainly enough of a career and of achievement; and the more so if we consider in what circumstances the career began. When Sheridan wrote *The Rivals*, and thus succeeded in presenting himself for the first time to the public eye as someone to be noticed, he had no useful friends or family connections, no money, no influence, and no profession. As his first biographer put it, concisely and not inaccurately, he had neither property nor pedigree. He had a wife, however, who was celebrated for her beauty and her voice, but it is well to remember, in estimating the progress made by Sheridan in the subsequent course of his life, that before her marriage she was a professional singer —a situation which was regarded in the eighteenth century with very little of the favour which it enjoys to-day. As Thomas Moore (who, by the time he came to write Sheridan's life, had left the unregenerate 'Thomas Little' far behind him) delicately observed, a woman was bound to lose, by frequent exhibitions before the public, 'that fine glow of feminine modesty, for whose absence not all the talents and accomplishments of the whole sex can atone.'

The inscription in Westminster Abbey makes no mention of Sheridan's career, either because Peter Moore thought any such information unnecessary, or because, possibly, he was not quite sure how that career ought to be described. To tell the truth, it would not have been easy for him to find a satisfactory description; for what, after all, was Sheridan's career? He is buried in Poets' Corner, which seems to settle the matter out of hand. Moreover, to the passer-by, his name invariably suggests his plays, though, very likely, not much else. This points to the conclusion that his fame rests chiefly on his best plays, which, having by this time endured some hundred and seventy years, may be reckoned far advanced on the road to immortality.

But in setting Sheridan down as a dramatist we are faced at once with a difficulty. Of the forty years and upwards over which his career stretched he gave no more than five to the writing of his plays. *The Rivals* came out in January 1775 and *The Critic* in October 1779. Between these two dates lies all that matters of Sheridan's career as a dramatist. His political career, on the other hand, lasted thirty-two years, which seems to show that, far from feeling any overmastering impulse to write plays, or any consuming desire for literary fame, he gave his best hopes and efforts, as well as the greater part of his active life, to politics. And indeed, it is certain that he would rather have been buried among the statesmen than among the poets. He told Creevey in 1805 that the happiest day of his life was the one on which he was elected, for the first time, as a member of Parliament for Stafford. After dinner he could not resist the impulse to steal away by himself to speculate to his heart's content on the prospects of distinction which were now opened to him—prospects which, if in some respects they were to prove painfully deceptive, were in others to turn out sufficiently brilliant, though not very profitable, realities. And yet, when he indulged in these speculations, *The School for Scandal* was barely three years old, and the applause which greeted it was still ringing in his ears.

The aristocratic company which gathered at Sheridan's grave did not think of him as a dramatist, though, like every one else, they were well acquainted with his plays, which were still favourite pieces in the repertoire. But the writing of those plays belonged to a bygone age—to an age when the king, now old, blind, and mad, was remarkably hale and active, and had Lord North for his first minister and the Americans for his enemies; to an age when the French Revolution still lay ten years in the future, and Napoleon, now safely in custody at Saint Helena, was a child in Corsica. Besides, if Sheridan had been a dramatist and nothing else—even if he had written a score of plays each as brilliant as *The School for Scandal*—not one of the dukes, earls, marquises, and so forth, would have been present at his funeral. They knew him as the follower of Fox, the enemy of Pitt, the friend and adviser (as far as that exalted personage could have a friend) of the Prince of Wales, the orator whom they had always heard with attention, generally with pleasure, and often with delight. They remembered him as a social companion, whose wit and charm had lit up many a party and added a relish to many a dinner. They remembered him as one of themselves— not, perhaps, without an occasional stray thought that it was odd that he should have been so. For Sheridan, though one of themselves in so many essential respects, was manifestly not so in others: there was something in it that seemed to demand, and at the same time to defy, explanation.

As to the principal performers of Covent Garden and Drury Lane theatres, who saw Sheridan laid to rest in the Abbey, they remembered him chiefly as the manager of Drury Lane; and some of them, perhaps, recalled the all too frequent occasions when the affairs of that celebrated house were sadly embarrassed; when salaries were not forthcoming at the end of the week: when the furnishers of theatrical properties were clamouring for payment and the scene painters at a stand for want of colours; when business was not attended to and Mr. Sheridan could not be seen. It is unlikely that they bore any grudge on these scores, for Sheridan was Sheridan and it was impossible to resist him. Not very long ago he had come to the new theatre—the one built in place of his own, which had been burnt to the ground. He had no theatre any longer to manage or mismanage. He was old and his legs were inclined to be swollen and his face was blotched and discoloured, though his eyes were as fine as ever. He had come into the green-room and was soon as pleasant and charming as only he could be; and every one wished him to come again.

Altogether, he had been manager of Drury Lane for thirty-three years, that is to say, he had the control of the property and directed its policy. The stage management he left to others. For a time his father had undertaken it, and after that one or other of the actors performed the duties—under Richard Brinsley's rule they were apt to prove singularly trying.

To be manager of Drury Lane was something: it was to be a public figure of a kind. But socially it was not a particularly elevated or dignified position, and it might have been felt that there was no essential difference between Mr. Sheridan of Drury Lane and Mr. Harris of Covent Garden, who had brought out *The Rivals* and *The Duenna* before their aspiring and impecunious author had acquired the smallest share in any theatre.

In 1781 Horace Walpole, taking a glance at the parliamentary scene, noted that the young men in opposition were making a considerable figure, and mentioned particularly John Townshend (second son to the viscount) and Sheridan (manager of the theatre). The parentheses have the air of comments and the contrast between them cannot be altogether ignored. More than one person thought that Parliament was not the proper place for 'the manager of a public theatre,' and as Sheridan's political career progressed and his importance to his party increased, the incongruity was likely to become still more striking. It was occasionally the subject of pointed and ungenerous comment, and the situation was hardly improved by the fact that Sheridan's management involved the theatre in highly complicated financial troubles, which, like his own, were matters of public notoriety. Yet Sheridan—and it is not the least of his achievements—got all this accepted, and it is strange to think of him, meanwhile, negotiating with Thurlow concerning the position of Lord Chancellor; advising the Prince of Wales *on the subject of His Royal Highness's debts*; staying with the Duke and Duchess of Devonshire at Chatsworth; visiting the Duke of Atholl in Scotland and acquiring a strong liking for his grace's Atholl brose; and obliging Lord and Lady Holland by getting the wording of the Public Debtors Bill altered so that it clearly had no retrospective effect—a matter of considerable importance to that family, who still owed the Government £53,000.

If Sheridan clung to Drury Lane so long—until, in fact, the fire of 1809 deprived him of it for good—it was not so much from choice as from necessity. It was vitally important to him. For twenty-five years it was his only source of income, and on it depended, not merely his fortunes, but his actual livelihood. This being so, it is not altogether surprising to find his connection with the theatre constantly presenting itself as a matter, not so much of the drama, as of money—which, indeed, was, more often than not, his own way of looking at it.

§

It appears, therefore, that Sheridan had not one career, but three; which is a matter of some concern to his biographers. He was a dramatist, the manager of a theatre, and a politician. The writing of plays and the managing of a theatre are not wholly unrelated, but neither of them has any obvious connection with politics. Nevertheless, the three are connected in Sheridan's life. If he had not written plays he would not have become the manager of Drury Lane, and if he had not been the manager of Drury Lane he would, in all probability, never have been able to enter Parliament. Two of the careers ran side by side for nearly thirty years, and all three are highly remarkable and raise very curious questions.

In the first place, Sheridan's achievement as a dramatist was of an extremely rare kind. *The School for Scandal*, for instance, remains with us in a double sense, having not only a secure place in our literature, but also a hold on the stage. Between the early

years of the eighteenth century and the last decade of the nine-
teenth, vast numbers of plays were written, and writers of the
highest eminence turned their attention at one time or another
to the drama. But among them all Sheridan's only rival was
Goldsmith.

Yet Sheridan gave up this career, though he had not been tried
and embittered by having to wait long for success: on the contrary, he had enjoyed the most flattering and complete theatrical
triumphs. It was in the full flush of them that he laid down his
pen. His success, as Boaden says,[1] was 'so *prodigious* that one
must have personally known Mr. Sheridan to be able to conceive
how he could so suddenly abandon a course of equal profit and
fame for another to which his nature seemed unsuited.'

Secondly, his long and (to him) highly important connection
with Drury Lane presents a number of curious and characteristic
features. All that need be said here is that he originally bought
a share worth £10,000 from Garrick, and two years afterwards
the half of the property still belonging to Garrick's partner.
This half he bought for £45,000. The only capital he ever
embarked in this enterprise was the modest sum of £1,300, and
it is not altogether impossible that even this was borrowed. In
any case he got it back after the second transaction by disposing
of his original share. Thus he became the owner, to the extent
of £45,000, of a theatre worth £80,000 without paying a penny
of ready money. These dealings mystified people a good deal at
the time, for it was well known that he had nothing except what
he got from his plays. He declined to satisfy curiosity on the
subject, and generally turned the matter off with a laugh or a
joke. The mystery has been cleared up since then, but without
making the affair much less surprising.

The capital value of the theatre increased later to about
£150,000, and the property was so nearly indestructible that
even after the fire, when nothing but the patent remained, that
patent was valued at £48,000. It was on this valuation that
Sheridan (who then owned half of it) was to be paid. He was
also to get £4,000 for the 'fruit offices' and the reversion of

[1] James Boaden (1762–1839), *Memoirs of the Life of John Philip Kemble.*

boxes and shares. Yet both he and the theatre were perpetually encumbered with debts, and when the building of the new theatre was undertaken, it was considered essential that he should have nothing to do with it. And accordingly he, who had been manager for thirty-three years, and had brought out *The School for Scandal* and *The Critic* there when Garrick's theatre stood on the site, had nothing to do with it, and was not even present on the night when it was opened with a prologue containing a handsome reference to the great days 'ere Brinsley ceased to write.'

Thirdly there is his political career, which bulks so largely— even formidably—in his life. When it began, the war of American Independence was still in progress. When it ended, Napoleon was invading Russia, the Prince of Wales was Prince Regent, and Burke, Pitt, and Fox were dead.

It was this parliamentary stage, with its long succession of striking scenes, that the author of *The School for Scandal* (who, before he was twenty-one, had run away to France with Elizabeth Linley, and fought two duels) trod for more than thirty years. In that extensive historical drama he is to be seen plainly enough, for he is generally conspicuous, and has an air of assurance, of consequence, of success. He speaks, and is heard with the greatest admiration and applause. And yet his name is not to be found opposite any of the leading parts. Those, it appears, have been entrusted to Mr. Pitt, Mr. Fox, and a score of lesser performers. As for Mr. Sheridan, it is almost as if he were only one of the *lords, gentlemen, and attendants* lumped together, according to custom, at the end of the list of *dramatis personae*.

Nevertheless, during nearly the whole of that time, he was a notable figure in Parliament and a man to be reckoned with. His talents were the admiration of friends and foes alike, even when, as happened not infrequently, his character was being abused. It was generally agreed that his abilities would have entitled him to the highest position. Wraxall,[1] who was not a friend of his either personally or politically, hardly ever speaks

---

[1] Sir Nathaniel William Wraxall. He sat in Parliament from 1780 to 1794 as a supporter first of Lord North and afterwards of Pitt, and makes frequent mention of Sheridan in his memoirs.

of him without expressions of admiration which sometimes verge on the extravagant. In his opinion, if Sheridan had cared to imitate Burke, Windham, Sir Gilbert Elliot, and others who went over to Pitt during the French Revolution, he might have named his price. Yet Wraxall was well aware of Sheridan's failings: he speaks of his 'excesses of wine' which in later life covered his face with 'disgusting eruptions,' mentions his unfaithfulness to his wife, remarks that his whole life formed a tissue of inventions and subterfuges to avoid the payment of his debts, and is quite willing to give currency to any scandal about him.

Lady Holland, who was too shrewd to be blind to Sheridan's shortcomings, and not prevented by any excess of good nature from remarking on them with perfect candour, was obliged to admit that, as far as ability was concerned, he deserved the first rank—which, in that particular case, meant the leadership of the Whig party in the House of Commons. Creevey's boundless devotion to Fox made him suspicious of Sheridan, whose conduct he once characterized as *diabolical*, but he could not help paying tribute to his extraordinary talents, any more than he could help enjoying the charm of his company. Lawrence, the painter, told Joseph Farington that Sheridan had the best talents of the political men of the day, and Farington, who had no love for the Whigs, agreed that if Sheridan had used his talents prudently, nothing could have prevented him from being at the head of affairs.[1] Lady Hester Stanhope declared that Pitt had a high admiration for Sheridan's abilities, and it was even said that he rated Sheridan above Fox. Sheridan had been employing those abilities for twenty years in remorseless attacks on Pitt.

As for oratory, which was then conducted in the grand manner, Sheridan's won unbounded applause at a time when Burke, Fox, and Pitt were at the height of their powers. The fame of it has not yet altogether died away, though it is muffled and distorted by the medium of imperfect reports, and rendered faint by its passage across a century and a half. The very subjects of his speeches seem remote now, and almost unreal. Fashions in

[1] *The Farington Diary*, ed. Greig (Hutchinson); first published 1922–8. Joseph Farington (1747–1821) was an artist, and a member of the Royal Academy.

eloquence, as in other things, change, and those of the past often appear odd and even a trifle ridiculous. Gentlemen who present themselves to the Speaker's eye no longer apostrophize him at effective points with a 'Good God, sir!' or adorn their remarks with Latin. But change has no power over wit, and Sheridan, like Sir John Vanbrugh, though he may have wanted grace, never wanted wit.

His speeches on the impeachment of Warren Hastings are still well known by report. The first of them, delivered in the House of Commons, lasted five and a half hours and produced an effect which can hardly have been equalled before or since. Long afterwards Fox judged it to have been the best speech ever made within the walls of Parliament. The Earl of Chatham, in a letter to the Duke of Rutland, declared that it was one of the most wonderful performances he had ever heard, and almost the greatest imaginable exertion of the human mind. Sir Gilbert Elliot, afterwards first Earl of Minto, writing an account of it to his wife, told her that it was impossible to describe the feelings Sheridan excited. When the speech ended—which it did at midnight—the House was worked up to an incredible pitch of enthusiasm and admiration. There was a shout of applause, or, according to Wraxall, a general involuntary hum of admiration, which went on for several minutes. Sir Gilbert himself had been frequently moved to tears, and, to use his own odd expression, the *bone* rose repeatedly in his throat.

Nowadays, an honourable member may be confident that his eloquence will be transmitted intact to posterity—which will not often be grateful for it. It was otherwise in Sheridan's time, but even then the orator could correct his speeches for the press. Sheridan rarely gave himself this trouble.[1] Still, there can be no doubt of his merit: it rests on abundant and undeniable evidence. Burke was a greater man than Sheridan, but he was often heard with reluctance and sometimes coughed down. Sheridan could obtain a hearing at any time, and was nearly always listened to with eagerness.

[1] The edition of his speeches (1816) claims, however, that *several* were corrected by himself. This is probably an overstatement.

Parliamentary talents are marketable commodities: how was it, then, that Sheridan got no better return for his? Far less distinguished ones gained other men government offices, lucrative places, pensions, and titles. But Sheridan was never at the head of an administration—he never even sat in a Cabinet, and his name is not associated with any public measure. He was thirty-two years in Parliament, and a prominent member of it during nearly the whole of that time. But for thirty of those years he was in opposition. He was in office three times, but the three together cover only about two years, and the highest place he ever got was that of Treasurer of the Navy. He was once returned for Westminster, and he became a right honourable. And that was all. He left Parliament in 1812, not because he was tired of it, or had acquired, like Fox, a longing for a tranquil domestic life in the country, but because he could not find a seat. He died at well past sixty. If he had died at fifty his fame would have been higher, and if he had died at forty it would have been higher still. Of all the problems which his parliamentary career presents to a biographer, by far the greatest is that of doing justice to it without losing the reader in the wandering mazes of thirty years of political history. The play—to return to the former metaphor—has to be described from the point of view of a character who, though always on the stage, never has a leading part.

§

A man's career is, in the widest sense of the word, his whole life. But Sheridan was a public figure: he became so on the night when *The Rivals* succeeded, and he remained so to the day of his death. Like every one else he had a private life, but for various reasons he had less of it than most people, and though he married twice and had children, it was never of the steady and settled domestic sort. From the house in Orchard Street where he began his career, to the house in Savile Row, which Lord Wellesley lent him, and in which he died, he had upwards of a score of residences. When William Smyth called on him he found that Sheridan's town house was in Grosvenor Street.

His son Tom, however, to whom Smyth was to be tutor, was running wild in his father's mansion at Isleworth; and as for the house which the tutor and his pupil were to occupy, it was at Wanstead. Sheridan himself turned out to be living at none of these places, but at Nerot's Hotel.

During the summer, when Parliament had risen (which it did in June or July) and the two winter theatres were shut, he was often to be found staying at one or other of the great country houses of his political friends, such as Chatsworth, Althorp, Stanmore Priory, Wynnstay, and Crewe Hall. In winter, Parliament would be sitting (and it frequently sat very late); Drury Lane must, of course, be attended to; and there was the social life of the town. All this left little enough room for the quiet scenes of family life—even supposing him to have had any taste for them.

He had numerous friends and acquaintances who enjoyed the charm of his company, a charm of whose exceptional quality there can be no doubt at all. After the success of *The Rivals* he met Fox at a small party arranged by John Townshend. Fox afterwards declared that he had always thought Hare, next to Townshend's uncle—Charles Townshend—the wittiest man he had ever met, but that Sheridan infinitely surpassed them both. At the other end of his life, Byron, who often met him in society, said he was *superb*. Lady Holland confided to her Journal that though she knew very well that Sheridan ought to be despised for his private life and suspected for his political conduct, her impulse was too much for her, and whenever she saw him, even if only for a few minutes, all these reasonable prejudices were at once put to flight.

But though Sheridan had so many friends, it does not appear that he ever had a friend in the full sense of the word. Tickell and Richardson were both intimate with him, but neither they nor anybody else had his full confidence. At the time of Fox's death he was heard to say that he had only two friends—Fox and the Prince of Wales. If this were to be taken seriously it would mean that he never had a friend at all. There was something elusive about Sheridan—something almost secretive. He loved to make a mystery of his doings. He is often mentioned in the memoirs and diaries of the time, but the references, however valuable, are only too frequently tantalizing rather than satisfying. Besides, they are sometimes unreliable and occasionally contradictory. He himself kept no diary and wrote no memoirs—a fact which would not have surprised any one who knew him. It was a letter-writing age, but he had no love for writing letters, and those written to him lay only too often and too long unopened on his table or in his letter-bag. He was one of those men to whom anecdotes cling naturally; but anecdotes, however entertaining, are untrustworthy material for biography. He had no Boswell, and not even a Lockhart or a Forster. John Watkins,[1] who wrote the first life of Sheridan, had little personal knowledge of him, and his work, though published as early as 1817, has hardly any value. Thomas Moore, who wrote what may be called the official biography, was never on intimate terms with Sheridan, and did not meet him until after 1800. As for the octogenarian 'who stood by his knee in youth and sat at his table in manhood,' he did not produce his two volumes until 1859, and even if we could feel much confidence in his memory or his veracity, what he has to say would not be particularly enlightening. The case of the inquirer into Sheridan's private life bears a certain resemblance to that of the crowd of duns who used to wait for him of a morning. At last he appears—and with a smile and a wave of the hand he is out of doors and gone.

§

Finally there is the question of his debts. The career of a man who has no money of his own has a bread-and-butter aspect— he must make a living. Pitt had only a small patrimony, but he was not altogether unprovided for; and he had a profession which he was prepared, if necessary, to follow. He also had a great name and valuable family connections. During his lifetime the sum of £11,700 was raised by a private subscription

---

[1] John Watkins, LL.D., produced a *Universal Biography and Historical Dictionary*, and other biographical works. Byron described him as dealing 'in the life and libel line.'

towards the payment of his debts, though he had enjoyed for many years not only an official salary of £6,000 a year, but also £3,000 as Lord Warden of the Cinque Ports. Fox, who squandered a fortune in early life, was eventually made easy by a subscription which gave him £3,000 a year. Sheridan had not a shilling of his own, and neither profession nor family influence; and nobody ever took up a subscription for him.

These things make it less surprising that the question of money should have figured so prominently in his life. His debts were as well known as his drinking, and the fame of his borrowings has descended as a sort of legend to our own day. There was also a widespread belief that very large sums of money passed through his hands. 'He was always in want of money,' wrote Hazlitt, eleven years after Sheridan's death, 'though he received vast sums which he must have disbursed, and yet nobody can tell what became of them, for he paid nobody.' Byron, having heard him lament the fact that he never had any money of his own, expressed his sympathy, but added the reflection that, to be sure, he had had a good deal of other people's. Moore remarked in his Journal that Sheridan was said to have drawn, at one time and another, £330,000 from Drury Lane. This was untrue, but the report is significant. Sheridan himself, drawing up an account for the encouragement of Kemble, who at one time thought of buying a share in Drury Lane, wrote: 'I bought of Mr. Garrick at the rate of £70,000 for the whole theatre,' and went on to say that his subsequent purchases from Mr. Lacy and Dr. Ford were at the rate of £94,000 and £86,000 respectively. These are imposing figures: they make the 'vast sums' of which Hazlitt spoke seem more than probable. We remember with an effort that Sheridan began with nothing; that the transactions referred to were almost wholly paper ones; and that Kemble (who, according to Sheridan, might expect an income of not less than £4,690) could hardly have forgotten that his ordinary salary was very often not forthcoming in full. Indeed, only four years earlier, Sheridan owed him nearly £1,400 for back salary, and the best he could do was to give him a bond for £500 in payment of part of it.

At the time of Sheridan's second marriage, the lady's family, it appears, made inquiries into his financial position and came to the conclusion that he could reckon on a steady income of £10,000 a year. If Sheridan convinced them of this it is more than likely that he convinced himself also. But where he is concerned the word 'income' is apt to be misleading, for his income was invariably saddled with numerous and complicated liabilities. He himself, always optimistic, was only too inclined to overlook the uncomfortable fact that he had, properly speaking, nothing but his clear income to dispose of. There was at all times something *deceivable* about the appearance of Sheridan's finances, and whether his debts were, as the Prince Regent thought, *la mer à boire*, or whether, as Lord Holland considered, not so enormous as was generally supposed, though so involved that no third party could hope to straighten them out, there, at any rate, they everlastingly were.

Now debts may be the result of extravagance or carelessness, but they may also be the result of the failure of expectations, in themselves, very likely, not unreasonable. A man may get into debt by spending too much, or—to take another point of view— by having too little. It must not be forgotten that one of Sheridan's careers turned out to be not only unremunerative, but also expensive, both directly and indirectly. To be sure, there is a proverb about cutting one's coat according to one's cloth, but homely wisdom was never much in Sheridan's way. If he had a singular facility in the matter of borrowing, and could charm the ears of creditors, and even of bankers and attorneys; if, as Michael Kelly[1] said, 'to-morrow was always his favourite pay-day,' these things might conceivably be due to necessity, quite as much as to inclination and want of principle. 'Could some enchanter's wand,' said Richardson[2] (who had seen his own money disappear in the bottomless pit of Drury Lane), 'touch him into

[1] The singer and composer. Owing to his work at Drury Lane he had a good deal to do with Sheridan. At one time he had a connection, real or fancied, with the wine trade, which led Sheridan to say that he should describe himself as a 'composer of wines and importer of tunes.' His *Reminiscences* (1826) were actually written by Theodore Hook, but Kelly supplied the information.

[2] Joseph Richardson (1755–1803), mentioned on page 12, with Sheridan's brother-in-law, Richard Tickell.

the possession of fortune, he would instantly convert him into a being of the nicest honour and most unimpeachable moral excellence.'

This is handsome, and may seem exaggerated, but there is a kernel of truth in it. It is not a question of justifying Sheridan, but of understanding him. If his career was worked out in perpetual difficulties over money, that was bound to influence his conduct, though it was not likely to console his creditors—with which reflection these preliminaries may be brought to an end.

CHAPTER TWO

The Family—Harrow and Bath

SHERIDAN WAS BORN in 1751 at 12 Dorset Street, Dublin. The entry in the register of St. Mary's Church, which is dated 4th November, gives his first name, by an odd mistake, as Thomas. He had three Christian names: Richard Brinsley Butler, but he himself always dropped the 'Butler.'

The question of his ancestry was settled in one sense—and a very important one—briefly and without any difficulty, by his contemporaries. Lord Holland calls his extraction 'low'; to Lady Holland it was 'mean'; Moore speaks of his 'disadvantages of birth and station'; to Horace Walpole he is merely 'the son of the Irish player'; and John Watkins describes him, at the time of his first marriage, as 'a man possessing neither pedigree nor property.'

Alicia Lefanu, in her Memoirs of the life and writings of Mrs. Frances Sheridan (her grandmother, and the mother of Richard Brinsley) took dignified exception to this remark of Watkins. 'If,' she wrote, 'an unbroken descent from a family of equal antiquity and respectability in Ireland . . . which, though at the beginning of the last century it no longer possessed the large estates that the ancient geographers of the kingdom assigned to the Sheridans, yet never fell from its rank among the respectable gentry of the county of Cavan . . .' if, in short, all this did not entitle Sheridan's pedigree to be spoken of with respect, then it was hard to say what could possibly do so. But Lord Holland and the rest understood the case perfectly, and knew very well what they were saying. What they meant was that unless a man's family gave him property, rank, or influential connections, and thus unlocked for him the gates of privilege and conferred on him the right to enter good society on equal terms it could expect no consideration. Sheridan's family gave him none of these things: he was born in that middle region of society from which so many great men have sprung—among them his countryman and contemporary, Burke.

There is a story that the Sheridans came from Spain, and that the first of them founded, by the Pope's order (and not altogether inappropriately) a school on Trinity Island. Hardly less legendary, perhaps, are the stories of the bygone importance of the family, and the extensive lands it possessed. The genealogical table drawn up by Walter Sichel in his *Sheridan* shows the figure, dimly seen, of an O'Sheridan of Cloughoughter (or Longhoughter) Castle, and later, such precise personages as the Bishops of Kilmore and Cloyne, and a private secretary to James II in exile. With these we arrive at the end of the seventeenth century and are within easy reach of Sheridan himself. The Bishop of Kilmore was William Sheridan, who was deprived of his bishopric because he would not take the oath of allegiance when William III came to the throne. The Bishop of Cloyne and the private secretary were his brothers, and all three were uncles of the Thomas Sheridan who was Richard Brinsley's grandfather. ·

This Thomas Sheridan is very well known as the friend and correspondent of Swift, who gave him much-needed advice (often in an exceedingly peremptory style), stayed at his house at Quilca, and rated him without tenderness or ceremony for his shortcomings. He was a good scholar and an excellent school-master—by Swift's account the best in the three kingdoms. His character was pleasant and easy going, and he was not much troubled by ambition. Any one might impose on him: he had no worldly wisdom and never could be brought to attend to his own affairs and interests. It is hardly necessary to add that he was poor. As a clergyman, he 'preached himself out of his preferment' by delivering, in sheer thoughtlessness, on the anniversary of the Hanoverian succession, a sermon which had the exquisitely inopportune text: 'Sufficient unto the day is the evil thereof.' The preferment had been given him, at Swift's suggestion, by Carteret, who was then Lord Lieutenant. He eventually lost Swift's friendship by fulfilling, with entirely characteristic simplicity and candour, the dean's request to be told whenever avarice seemed to be growing on him.

The Prince Regent, having been looking through Scott's edition of Swift, told Croker that he was astonished to find what a resemblance there was between *poor Sheridan* (who had died a year ago) and his grandfather.

His second son, Thomas—Richard Brinsley's father—bore very little resemblance to either. He was born in 1719, and had Swift for his godfather. He was sent to school at Westminster, where he did well enough to win a king's scholarship, but the family poverty prevented him from going on to the university. However, he graduated at Trinity College, Dublin, and then, having to make his living, turned actor instead of schoolmaster. He had already tried his hand at play-writing.

It is at this point that the theatre first makes its appearance in the history of the Sheridans—it was to figure in it more or less conspicuously for seventy years to come. In 1743 the bills at the Theatre Royal, Smock Alley, announced 'a young gentleman' in the part of Richard III; very much as, two years earlier, those of Goodman's Fields had announced the real beginning of Garrick's career: 'Richard III by a gentleman who never appeared on any stage.' Foote, similarly, made his first appearance, at the little theatre in the Haymarket, in the part of Othello, under the description of 'a gentleman.' Thomas Sheridan's success, without equalling that of Garrick, was quite enough to justify him in appearing subsequently under his own name, and he thus fitted himself for Horace Walpole's phrase, 'an Irish player.' By 1745 he had progressed so far as to be manager of the theatre.

There was nothing luxurious about Smock Alley, and the management of it was an arduous, not to say hazardous, business. Many years later, Kemble, coming there from provincial theatres in England, complained that there was no scenery worth the name, and very little of anything else except dirt and drunkenness. When Thomas Sheridan took charge, the audience, as he afterwards told Windham, used to crowd on to the stage so that there was hardly any room for the actors. The pit would be sparsely occupied and the boxes empty, but the upper gallery, which cost twopence, was always full. The mob there squabbled and fought with the footmen, and insisted on having any tune played which they chose to call for. If their demands were disregarded they were in the habit of signifying their displeasure by throwing bottles and stones. When Peg Woffington was acting Cordelia to Garrick's Lear, one of the gentlemen on the stage took the opportunity of putting his hand into her bosom as Lear's head was resting on her lap. Afterwards he searched everywhere for Garrick with the intention of thrashing him, because he had heard that Garrick had ventured to look displeased.

Thomas Sheridan, himself the most precise and respectable of men, set to work to remedy these disorders. He had to face a riot. One of his first measures was to forbid admission behind the scenes, whereupon a Mr. Kelly, a young gentleman from Connaught (another account gives Galway the honour of his origin) climbed over the spiked railings of the orchestra, made his way to the dressing-room, and there attacked George Ann Bellamy—an actress whose life, by her own story, was freely studded with exciting adventures. The manager behaved, on this critical occasion, with equal resolution and dignity; and, in the legal proceedings which followed (in which Kelly was fined £500 and sentenced to three months' imprisonment) with such magnanimity that he won general approval. He might be a player, but he upheld his character as a gentleman. It was during these troubles that he met the gifted lady who became his wife. She was Frances Chamberlaine, daughter of Dr. Philip Chamberlaine, Prebend of Rathmichael, Archdeacon of Glendalough, and Rector of St. Nicholas Without.

For the next eight years Thomas Sheridan managed his theatre very successfully, and it was during this prosperous time that Richard Brinsley was born. There were six children altogether, but two died in infancy, leaving two sons and two daughters. The elder of the boys was Charles Francis, and the daughters were Alicia and Elizabeth.

Theatrical management, as Richard Brinsley himself might have reflected in years to come, is a precarious undertaking and subject to a great variety of accidents. How precarious it was in the eighteenth century, and above all in Dublin, his father now had excellent reason to know. In 1754 the good years came to a disastrous end. It happened that some lines in the play *Mahomet the Impostor* had the appearance, extremely gratifying to an Irish audience, of being a reflection on the Government. Political feeling ran high at the time, and Sheridan, who had nothing to gain and a good deal to lose by it, warned the actor Digges, in whose part the passage occurred, that he would do well to keep clear of politics. The warning was given in general terms, but when the audience clamoured for the lines in question, Digges thought fit to say that Mr. Sheridan had forbidden him to repeat them; whereupon a riot began and the theatre was wrecked.

In consideration of the cause in which he had suffered—however unintentionally—Sheridan was offered a government pension of £300, which, as things turned out, he would, perhaps, have done wisely to accept. He refused it, however, not so much out of high-mindedness or in a spirit of independence, as because he knew very well that, if he accepted it, the calumnies circulated about him would be generally believed, and the hostility of the tyrannical audience would force him out of the theatre altogether. After all, Smock Alley was his livelihood. He let it for the time being and went to England, where he made his appearance with some success as an actor. But among actors the first place was already Garrick's, and nothing better than the second was available to Thomas Sheridan or any one else. 'Second only to Garrick' was the phrase applied to him more than once, and perhaps justly—but without any mention of the distance between them. He was an able and conscientious actor, though somewhat stiff and pedantic. Indeed, there was a touch of pedantry about him at all times, and as he grew older it became more marked.

After being away two years he came back to Dublin and took up management again. But the high-spirited patrons of Smock Alley, who had kept the quarrel in mind, insisted on his making an apology from the stage. As Alicia Lefanu puts it, with great delicacy: 'It was thought necessary to address the audience with a few words of apology and explanation.' The manager—a proud man—was obliged to swallow this draught, and it must have been a bitter one. He got little good by it. The theatre was in a wretched condition and he could not make it prosper. Moreover, there was now a rival in Crow Street to contend with. Nothing would go right, and after two years he gave up the struggle and returned to England. He was thirty-nine years old, and it was a little late to go seeking his fortune.

From this time onwards his life was a wandering one and filled with a remarkable variety of activities, none of which brought him much reward. He lectured on elocution at the Pewterers' Hall in London, at Bristol, at Bath, at Edinburgh, at Oxford, at Cambridge; he took pupils; he produced a number of books, including a General Dictionary of the English Language, and an edition of Swift's works, with a Life, in eighteen volumes; he acted; he gave 'Attic Entertainments'; he projected an academy for the purpose of instructing young gentlemen in the art of reading and reciting. There was no want of energy in Thomas Sheridan: he was always busy with some scheme or other, and always on the point of succeeding. But he was one of those men whose abilities and efforts, however estimable, never seem to meet with success. Every one admitted that he was 'a very worthy man'; but then he was also pompous, dull, and irritating. For all his dignity there was a distinct touch of the ridiculous about him. Leigh Hunt's father, who was a clergyman (he had been advised to go on the stage, but was 'too proud for that'), used to read the church services with an admirable delivery. One Sunday Thomas Sheridan came round to the vestry and complimented him heartily on having profited so greatly from his *Treatise on Reading the Liturgy*—which Hunt had never seen. Johnson's remark is well known: 'Why sir, Sherry is dull, naturally dull; but it must have taken him a great deal of pains to become what we now see him. Such an excess of stupidity, sir, is not in nature.'

His abilities did not go altogether unappreciated, however. Both Oxford and Cambridge gave him the degree of Master of Arts, and he had the reputation of being an excellent teacher of elocution. Among his pupils was Alexander Wedderburn, afterwards Lord Loughborough and Earl of Rosslyn, whose Scotch

Mʳ SHERIDAN *in the Character of* BRUTUS

"It must be by his Death:

Burney Collection, British Museum.

THOMAS SHERIDAN
(Father of Richard Brinsley.)

accent was thus corrected by an Irishman. It was Wedderburn who was instrumental in getting Johnson his pension, and it was Thomas Sheridan, more than anybody else, who suggested it to him: 'he rang the bell,' as Wedderburn told Boswell. When, later, Sheridan was also given one, Johnson exclaimed in wrath that if Sheridan was to have a pension it was time to think of giving up his. 'However,' he added after a pause, during which his better nature struggled for the upper hand, 'I am glad that Mr. Sheridan has a pension, for he is a very good man.'

The £200 a year which Sheridan got in this way was a much-needed relief. It was, at least, a settled income, and that was what he sorely needed. It was not enough, however, to keep him out of debt. In the meanwhile, to help matters, his wife had put her literary talents to work, and in 1761, when the second visit to England had lasted three years without producing any fortune, her successful novel, *Memoirs of Miss Sidney Biddulph*, was published in three volumes by Dodsley. It was inscribed to 'the author of *Clarissa* and *Sir Charles Grandison*,' who had arranged for the publication and was as well qualified as any man to appreciate the book, which was long read and praised. It contains, as Boswell says, 'an excellent moral, while it inculcates a future state of retribution. . . . The amiable and pious heroine goes to the grave unrelieved, but resigned, and full of hope of "heaven's mercy."'

Besides this, two of Mrs. Sheridan's plays were produced by Garrick at Drury Lane in 1763, and the first was such a decided success that it was still a stock piece at that house more than a dozen years later. But authorship, though a very good staff, was not to be depended on as a crutch. The unpaid bills mounted up, and in 1764 Sheridan thought it best to retire to France with his wife, his daughters, and his elder son. In France living was cheap and he was out of the reach of his creditors. They stayed at Blois, where Mrs. Sheridan wrote her 'oriental tale of Nourjahad,' and where, in 1766, she died. The family did not come back to England until 1769, by which time Richard Brinsley was a youth of seventeen.

§

When Thomas Sheridan went to England for the second time he left his younger son and the two girls in Dublin, where they were sent to school at Sam Whyte's 'Seminary for the Instruction of Youth' in Grafton Street. Sam Whyte was a relative of Mrs. Sheridan: his bills were still unpaid many years afterwards.

In England the Sheridans made the acquaintance of Dr. Sumner, then a master at Eton. He subsequently became headmaster of Harrow, and it was arranged that Richard Brinsley should go there. Accordingly he entered the school in 1762, and when the family departed for Blois, less than two years later, he was left behind.

By his own account he was unhappy at Harrow. He told Lord Holland that he had to put up with many a slight there as the son of a poor player, and that this gave him such a bitter dislike to the stage that he had never in his life seen a performance through from beginning to end. This last statement Lord Holland thought incredible, but it is probable that there is at least an imaginative truth in it. Boys are very often sensitive about the circumstances of their parents, and such things as poverty and lack of social importance are well understood to be excellent subjects for taunts. Sheridan told Creevey, likewise, that he was low-spirited at school. He felt neglected there; he was left without money; he was not taken home for the holidays; the school bills were unpaid; he did not distinguish himself at all as a scholar, and got all his learning during the two years after he left. It is obvious that there is a good deal of truth in all this, and he would hardly have told Creevey about it more than thirty-five years afterwards if the memory had not rankled. Still, it is not necessary to suppose that he was continuously unhappy during those seven years, though if he was low-spirited and unsure of himself it is not very surprising that he should have done no better at his lessons.

Harrow had a good reputation at this time. Sumner, and Thackeray who preceded him, were capable men and good scholars. Under Thackeray the numbers had increased to a hundred and thirty, and under Sumner they went up to two hundred and fifty. When Sheridan came to the school Parr was a senior boy: five years later he came back as a master. He and Sumner agreed that Dick Sheridan was slovenly in construing and defective in Greek grammar, though not deficient in ability. Accordingly they decided that he should be called up more often and made to work harder. He had to stand at the master's table, where no compassionate friend could prompt him, and in this way he improved at last to the point of learning some grammatical rules. In his somewhat pompous description of Sheridan's scholarship Parr declared that 'he had read and he had understood the four orations of Demosthenes read and taught in our public schools. He was at home in Virgil and in Horace. . . .' He was less positive about Homer. To tell the truth, all this amounts to very little. It is evidence of the same order as that of Charles Brinsley (Sheridan's son by his second marriage) who said that he had seen his father with a copy of Lucan's *Pharsalia* on his bed of a morning—from which it has sometimes been inferred that his spare moments were commonly devoted to this sort of reading.

He was not a scholar. In the opinion of Lord Holland he had less learning than the ordinary well-educated English gentleman; and Lady Holland thought it very odd indeed that he should know no French. But then, the ordinary well-educated English gentleman could not write like Sheridan or deliver such speeches as his. He got from his education a taste for reading and a sense of style which he improved to extraordinarily good purpose, and he possessed the faculty of making the most of whatever learning he had. He kept enough odds and ends of it in his mind to be able to correct a Greek quotation on which Lord Belgrave ventured in the House of Commons, and to make an apt remark in Latin. Kemble said he loved Spenser and had whole cantos of *The Faerie Queene* by heart—he certainly quoted a stanza during his concluding speech at the trial of Warren Hastings. According to Michael Kelly he could repeat long passages from Dryden, who was his favourite poet.

Altogether, there is no reason why Harrow should not take

B

credit for him. In Byron's day they used to show his name—
R. B. Sheridan 1765—and consider it did honour to the walls.
Moore, it is true, remarks that his spelling was inclined to be
erratic. In his earlier days *thing* sometimes appeared as *think*, and
to the end of his life he was apt to use one 'm' and one 's'
where it is more usual to find two. Moore had the use of
Sheridan's papers and was in a position to know the truth of
these things; but they are of very little consequence, and any
one who takes them too seriously may perhaps end by believing
the report that the true author of *The School for Scandal* was not
the manager of Drury Lane, but 'a young lady, the daughter of
a merchant in Thames Street.'

When he left Harrow—in 1768 or 1769—his regular education
ended. Thomas Sheridan could reflect with satisfaction that he
held the degree of M.A. at three seats of learning: Richard
Brinsley never had the smallest connection with any university.
The family, now without a mother, came back from France and
settled in Frith Street, Soho—though 'settled' is hardly a word
which applies to its domestic arrangements. The two sons now
had lessons from a Mr. Lewis Ker, 'an Irish gentleman,' and, as
Moore says, 'attended the fencing and riding schools of Mr.
Angelo.' Their father taught them English grammar and oratory
—subjects which were very dear to his heart. Their education
was thus, to all appearance, handsomely provided for, but it may
be doubted whether the lessons were as regular or as effective as
could have been wished; and in any case, they did not last long.
As to Angelo, he was a neighbour and a friend.

Thomas Sheridan continued to pursue success industriously,
and it continued to elude him. In 1770 the family moved to
Bath, where he gave Attic Entertainments diversified with music,
and tried to establish an academy for the purpose of giving young
gentlemen regular instruction in grammar and the art of reading
and reciting. An advertisement to this effect duly appeared in
the *Bath Chronicle*, but the young gentlemen of Bath proved
indifferent to the advantages afforded by this kind of instruction,
and the project failed. Long afterwards Richard Brinsley told
Creevey that he and his brother were to have acted as assistants

in this academy, and that the post designed for himself was the exalted one of 'rhetorical usher.'

He was happy at Bath. To be sure, his position was not particularly brilliant: he was still the poor player's son, and, the academy having failed (no doubt to his great relief), his future was dubious. Nevertheless, he felt free; his quality began to show itself, and a certain vanity (frequently remarked on afterwards by those who knew him) merged into a desire for distinction —a desire quite strong enough to be called ambition. It was accompanied, as it was throughout his life, by a curious and characteristic pride. He found the society at Bath very agreeable. He wrote verses to the ladies, and recommended himself to their favour—never a matter of indifference to him—by his dancing and his wit. He dropped poetical contributions into Lady Miller's vase at Bath Easton, and no doubt they were worthy of the company they found in that elegant receptacle. He complimented Lady Margaret Fordyce, then the reigning belle of Bath,[1] by addressing to her the lines entitled *Clio's Protest, or, the Picture Varnished,* in answer to *The Bath Picture,* by Mr. Andrews, who was thought to have done Lady Margaret much less than justice. He did his best to appear in the character of a young man of fashion, though, being entirely dependent on what his father allowed him, he must have been cruelly hampered by want of money, and could hardly have commanded much credit. It is easy to fancy him strolling about the town in his cocked hat and scarlet waistcoat after the style of a buck of the period, but not quite so sure of himself as he wished to appear. He was still very young—a young man with some education, excellent spirits, and no discernible prospects.

Whatever his natural bent may have been, it is certain at least that he had his full share of that general kind of ambition common to aspiring young men who are poor and find themselves not very favourably placed; and who are desperately anxious to distinguish themselves, without knowing very well what particular sort of distinction to aim at. Young Richard Brinsley wanted to distinguish himself, to make a figure in the world, to be a person

[1] She was the sister of Lady Anne Lindsay, who wrote *Auld Robin Gray.*

of consequence, and have the entry into good society, and money to spend—he never had any desire to accumulate it. He may not have wanted to be a man of letters; he may even have found literary composition an arduous and distasteful business—there is good reason, in fact, to believe that he very often did find it so. It was he who wrote at this very time: 'But easy writing's vile hard reading.' Nevertheless, he would still have been likely to take to literature, as so many others in such circumstances have done, because it was the only field open to him. No doubt it was crowded and the rewards were uncertain, but it offered a chance of success, and, above all, was free to everybody.

After leaving Harrow he corresponded with a friend he had made there, Nathaniel Brassey Halhed, who was now at Christ Church, Oxford. The two adventured into authorship and wrote a farce in three acts, called *Jupiter*, or, as Sheridan named it after revision, *Ixion*. It has a certain interest as containing a faint suggestion of *The Critic*. 'The thoughts of £200 shared between us,' wrote Halhed fervently, 'are enough to bring the tears into one's eyes.' The farce did not appear on any stage, however, and the £200 remained visionary. After this they projected a 'periodical miscellany,' to which Sheridan gave the improbable title of *Hernan's Miscellany*, though Halhed preferred *The Reformer*. One number was actually written, but not printed. They also contemplated a collection of occasional poems and translations, and a volume of *Crazy Tales*.

Finally they settled upon a translation and cast about for an author sufficiently out of the way to have an air of novelty, and a subject which would lend itself to the warm sentiments of love. These requirements, which they very reasonably considered would add greatly to the attractions of the work, were met by Aristae-netus, an obscure Greek writer of the fifth or sixth century A.D., to whom two books of love stories in the form of letters are ascribed.[1] The translations, or paraphrases, were in metre, and were finished (Sheridan's with the aid of a Greek grammar) and the verses polished by the end of 1770. The book came out in

[1] English translations had already appeared in 1701 and 1715. The version by Sheridan and Halhed was subsequently included in Bohn's Classical Library.

the following August in a small edition which went off slowly. A second appeared two years later, but the work brought the hopeful authors neither fame nor fortune, which is not altogether surprising, though Mr. Lewis Ker, the tutor, wrote to Sheridan that one critic had 'fathered the book on Mr. Johnson, author of the English Dictionary, etc.'

With these *Love Epistles of Aristaenetus* the literary partnership came to an end. Halhed went to Calcutta as a writer in the East India Company's service. His career was sufficiently curious. He became a distinguished orientalist, translated the Gentoo Code from the Persian, wrote a Bengali grammar, and on his return to England went into Parliament as member for Lymington. He was a zealous believer in the fantastic revelations of Richard Brothers,[1] published imitations of some of the epigrams of Martial (no doubt with an odd thought or two of the Aristaenetus of twenty-five years ago), and outlived Sheridan by fourteen years.

Sheridan himself, left behind at Bath, could hardly be said to have achieved even the beginnings of any career as yet—unless a share in a metrical translation which had attracted no interest, some attempts in manuscript, and some verses in the *Bath Chronicle*[2] can be so described. However, he was only twenty. Before anything further could be done his fortunes became involved in those of the youthful and lovely Elizabeth Ann Linley, whose singing helped to 'diversify' Thomas Sheridan's Entertainments, and was, in all human probability, a much greater attraction than his own reciting, or even the discourse on oratory with which he was accustomed to open the proceedings.

---

[1] Richard Brothers (1757–1824) was to be 'revealed' in 1795 as the prince who was to rule the world. He was arrested in that year, however, for 'treasonable practices'—the Government being sensitive then on such points. Halhed raised the matter in the House of Commons but could get no support.

[2] *Clio's Protest*, mentioned above, and *The Ridotto of Bath*.

CHAPTER THREE

Miss Linley

FOR MANY YEARS Thomas Linley had been established at Bath as a teacher of music. The Sheridans had made his acquaintance as long ago as 1763, when they were at Bath and Richard Brinsley's mother took lessons from him. He also directed the concerts at the Assembly Rooms, and in general, according to the common lot of music masters, was obliged to make his living by looking about for pupils and getting whatever musical engagements he could. He was helped by his wife, who was an economical housekeeper and a notable saver of fires and candle-ends—qualities for which she found full scope in years to come, when she superintended the wardrobe at Drury Lane. Linley was a talented musician and had an excellent reputation as a capable and conscientious teacher. His father was a carpenter who contrived in later life to acquire some house property. One star differs from another in glory: Thomas Sheridan, though professionally associated with the Linleys, nevertheless considered them beneath him and not very desirable acquaintances for his family.

Linley was a handsome man with a grave, reserved air. His children—there were twelve in all—inherited his good looks and were also exceptionally gifted. The eldest daughter, Elizabeth Ann, though only sixteen when Richard Brinsley first knew her, was already becoming widely celebrated for her extraordinary beauty and her singing. Her sister, Mary, appeared in the following year, at the age of thirteen, at the Three Choirs Festival at Hereford; and her brother, Thomas, had first performed in public six years ago, when he was eight. The children, in fact, were part of their father's livelihood, and Elizabeth Ann was bound apprentice to him until she reached the age of twenty-one —a somewhat drastic arrangement; but then he might have argued that she owed her training to him and that the family

ELIZABETH ANN LINLEY AND HER BROTHER, THOMAS
After the Painting by Gainsborough.

welfare was his object. When she sang at the Queen's Concert at Buckingham House in 1773, both their majesties were greatly impressed, and the king, a lover of music, told Linley that his daughter was a great credit to him, and that he had never heard a finer voice. He presented the gratified father with a bank-note for £100.

But Miss Linley's situation, however flattering, was not altogether an agreeable one. She excited the liveliest admiration wherever she went, but as a professional singer she was exposed to the attentions of numbers of men for whom she cared nothing, and whose devotion, however extreme, was, for one reason or another, not very likely to lead to marriage. When she appeared in the oratorio at Drury Lane, Fanny Burney remarked that she met with as much applause and admiration as Garrick ever got, and that the whole town was distracted about her. She also noted that Miss Linley had met with numerous adventures— this was in 1773—and that no other young lady of the time had had so many lovers and admirers. Men of all ranks had paid their addresses to her, but whether these addresses were of the honourable kind or not was more than Miss Burney (in whom there was always a decided strain of prudishness) would undertake to say.

Elizabeth's beauty was of an unusual and ethereal kind. The seeds of consumption were scattered in the Linleys: it was of this disease that she herself was to die, and it is not impossible that the touch of it helped to give her features their special quality. She was called Saint Cecilia, and it was in this character that Sir Joshua Reynolds painted her. The name was apt enough, but it has had the defect of concealing the fact that she was a warm-hearted girl, much in need of affection. A happy, or even a contented marriage, however, was not among the gifts that fortune, so bountiful in other respects, had placed within easy reach of her.

Nevertheless, a marriage had actually been arranged, when she was only sixteen, with a Mr. Walter Long, whom Moore describes as 'an old gentleman of considerable fortune in Wiltshire.' She was not in love with him, and, according to Moore, on learning this he was generous enough to take the blame of breaking the engagement, and to settle £3,000 on her in order to satisfy her father, who threatened to bring the case into court. He certainly did settle £3,000 on her, and allowed her to keep jewels to the value of £1,000 besides, but gossip was not inclined to ascribe this to pure generosity. Indeed, the affair was talked of enough to set Foote writing a comedy on the subject, and on 26th June 1771 *The Maid of Bath* was brought out successfully at the little theatre in the Haymarket. 'This,' notes Genest in his account of the English stage, 'is a very good comedy—it is founded on fact.' It was also an unwarrantable intrusion on the private lives of people who were certain to be pained by such a proceeding, but no such consideration ever deterred Foote, who dealt largely in personalities. He had exhibited Thomas Sheridan as a highly ludicrous figure in *The Orators*, and ridiculed his lectures unmercifully. Public opinion saw nothing to object to in the practice, and it is worth while observing that the prologue to *The Maid of Bath* was written by Garrick, and the epilogue by Cumberland.

In this play Mr. Long appears as 'Flint,'[1] and Miss Linley under the transparent disguise of 'Miss Linnet.' 'Major Racket,' having designs of his own on Miss Linnet, plans to break off the match between her and Flint, by persuading the latter that the marriage would be extremely unwise. Flint, therefore, concluding that seduction would, after all, be a more desirable arrangement, proposes to Miss Linnet that she should spend the night with him, promising, in accordance with the time-honoured formula of deception, to marry her in the morning. Miss Linnet, however, is proof against this, and likewise demurs to an offer of marriage which 'Major Racket' is induced to make her. She objects that he has seduced a milliner's apprentice,[2] and declares her intention of supporting herself by her music.

Foote himself played the part of Flint, who appears throughout in a most unfavourable light. According to Genest, Long survived until 1807, 'and was latterly as famous for his stinginess

[1] 'Last winter,' says Lady Catherine Coldstream in the play, 'I got acquainted with Master Foote, the play-actor—I will get him to bring the filthy loon on the stage.'
[2] 'Miss Patty Prim from the Grove.'

as he had been in youth for his amours.' If the date is correct he can hardly have been more than fifty at the time of the engagement; though, to be sure, between fifty and sixteen lies most of the distance between crabbed age and youth.[1]

In the story of Elizabeth Linley, the 'Major Racket' of the play was a leading figure. He was Thomas Mathews, generally known as Captain Mathews, though he had left the army with the rank of ensign. It was long supposed that he originally paid court to Miss Linley as a single man, but Mr. R. Crompton Rhodes has shown that he married Miss Diana Jones as far back as 1763. His addresses to Elizabeth, therefore, were never of the honourable kind, though, as we have seen, there was nothing particularly surprising in this fact. It is certain that his importunities had the power to cause her the greatest distress of mind, and it is not easy to see why they should have been able to do so unless he had at one time had reason to think himself a favoured lover; nor is there any other obvious explanation of his subsequent behaviour to Sheridan. Elizabeth's distress may therefore have arisen from a conflict between love and duty, or from some almost innocent but compromising indiscretion due to a momentary affection which she conquered or outgrew. It is also possible that Mathews's passion may have been strong and genuine in its way, though unlawful, and not the mere desire of a libertine. The story has always been told from Sheridan's side, and Mathews, accordingly, makes a thoroughly discreditable appearance in it. He was, however, 'a most agreeable companion, though of libertine habits,' and an excellent whist player—he wrote a book on the subject. He died, very well respected, at Bath in 1820.

Whatever the relations between him and Elizabeth actually were, they undeniably ended by causing her so much suffering that she resolved on the desperate course of running away. Several of the details with which the story has been embellished are matters of doubt—according to one account she made her

---

[1] In his edition of Foote's plays, 'Jon Bee' (John Badcock) says that Long died at Bath, 2nd February 1807, aged ninety-five, a bachelor worth nearly a quarter of a million sterling. This would make his age at the time of his proposals to Miss Linley fifty-seven. Badcock accepts Foote's version of the affair as substantially true.

* B

will and tried to kill herself by taking laudanum—and the
plainest narrative of the affair has an inevitable air of melodrama. Having no one in her own family to whom she could
turn for help, she took Sheridan's sister Alicia, and Sheridan
himself, into her confidence, and it was settled that she should
go to France, a country of which the Sheridans (though not
Richard Brinsley) had some experience. There she might take
refuge in a convent which would receive her as a guest. As to
her father, who would lose money by her flight, he could be
compensated out of the £3,000 which she had had from Long.
Of the parties to this plan, only one had reached the mature
age of twenty.

It was hardly possible for Elizabeth to carry out such an undertaking alone, and here Sheridan's services were needed. It is
doubtful what his feelings for her were at this time. His
brother had fallen in love with her and had prudently retired
from Bath in order to be out of the reach of her attraction.
Halhed, likewise, had seen her at Oxford and fallen a victim to
her charms. It is quite certain, however, that she herself had
never thought of Richard Brinsley as a lover, and that he did not
become her escort in any such character. Altogether, there is no
reason to deny him the credit of disinterested and chivalrous
motives, at the outset, at any rate. As she reminded him afterwards, when the reminder had to be coupled with reproaches,
she regarded him at this time only as a friend, and it was his
delicacy and compassion which subsequently won her heart.
The escapade was not, in fact, an elopement in the ordinary
sense of the word, though it is often called so.

As the protector of a young lady of eighteen, bent on flight
from her home, Sheridan had some obvious defects. He himself was only twenty, and had no money and very little experience
of the world. He had never been abroad and could not speak
French. He had plenty of confidence and resourcefulness, however. On 18th March 1772, Miss Linley pleaded illness and
did not sing at the concert. With the romantic adjuncts of a
sedan chair and a post-chaise the pair left Bath and went to
London. Sheridan is said to have been careful to provide a maid

to keep his charge in countenance and preserve her reputation, but what became of the maid subsequently is not known.

In London he introduced Elizabeth as an heiress who was to marry him in France, and appeared with her, according to the account in *My First Play*, at Charles Lamb's godfather, F[ield]'s, who 'kept the oil shop (now Davies's) at the corner of Feather-stone-buildings in Holborn. . . . It was to his house in Holborn,' says Lamb, 'that young Brinsley brought his first wife on her elopement with him from a boarding school at Bath—the beautiful Maria Linley. My parents were present (over a quadrille table) when he arrived in the evening with his harmonious charge.' This was written in 1821, and serves to show what may happen to the details of a story in fifty years. The youthful pair got a passage to Dunkirk, and were married in a village near Calais by a priest 'well known for his services on such occasions.' For this not entirely surprising sequel, Moore accounts regretfully by observing that the protector had now degenerated into a mere selfish lover.

Like much else in the adventure, this marriage raises difficulties. It was invalid, in any case. Both parties were under age; it was not consummated, and the qualifications of the priest are open to doubt. The lovers did not behave afterwards as they might have been expected to do if they considered the ceremony binding; and their parents, if they had any suspicion of its having taken place, seem to have ignored it. According to Sheridan's sister Alicia, whose account is the only evidence of it, he pressed Elizabeth to marry him, saying that he had long been in love with her and that after what had happened she could not appear in England again except as his wife. A few weeks later, however, she did reappear there, and not as his wife.

The journey ended at Lille, where Elizabeth got an apartment in a convent, but afterwards, being ill, was taken care of by an English doctor and his lady, Sheridan, meanwhile, being accommodated at a hotel on the Grande Place. He wrote to his brother assuring him that he had never departed, even in thought, from the 'honour and consistency which engaged him at first'; but he made no mention of the marriage. When the pair had been absent about a month Mr. Linley arrived and persuaded his daughter to return home with him. He appears to have been satisfied with whatever explanation was given him, and to have behaved calmly. Elizabeth had engagements in England to fulfil.[1]

In the meantime, Sheridan's conduct had been viewed in some quarters with not altogether unnatural suspicion and disapproval. His brother was angry with him, and Mathews, having written to Richard Brinsley and received no answer, took the strong course of posting him in the *Bath Chronicle* as 'a L[iar] and a treacherous S[coundrel].' Sheridan returned to England, and sat up all night at Canterbury, as he said, in order not to break a high-spirited and boyish resolve that he would not sleep until he had called Mathews to account. Reaching London, he roused that gentleman in his lodging at Crutched Friars at an unseasonable hour of the night. The story of these proceedings is his own—a fact which it is proper to bear in mind. According to it Mathews behaved 'perfectly dastardly,' and far from showing any inclination to fight, entered into explanations and threw the blame on Charles Sheridan and 'another gentleman' at Bath. Of Sheridan's own courage, not to say pugnacity, there can be no doubt at all, and Mathews may very well have regretted that he had ever given provocation to such an adversary.

Going on to Bath, Sheridan saw his brother, and as Mathews's story was discredited and he had made no satisfactory amends, the two went to town and called him out. Mathews had been in the army, and may have had the rank of captain, as has been suggested, in the militia. He could not refuse to fight, but, by Sheridan's account, he showed a remarkable degree of reluctance. After much going back and forth in Hyde Park, the party repaired to the 'Hercules' Pillars,' whence they proceeded to the Bedford Coffee-house, and finally to the Castle Tavern in Henrietta Street, where the duel was fought. It was a brief encounter and ended without the perdition of souls. Sheridan, having mastered his adversary's sword, held the point of his own at his

---

[1] A careful examination of the details of this curious story will be found in *Harlequin Sheridan*, by R. Crompton Rhodes.

breast, whereupon Mathews begged his life. A good deal of argument followed, in the course of which Sheridan took his opponent's sword and broke it. Mathews protested bitterly against this unusual conduct, and said such a thing was never done. He would not fight again, however, and matters were adjusted at last on the understanding that he should make a satisfactory and public apology, and that there should be no mention of the breaking of his sword. The apology appeared in the *Bath Chronicle* on 7th May 1772, and was entirely satisfactory. Mathews declared in it that his statements had been the effects of passion and misrepresentation, retracted what he had said about Mr. Sheridan, and 'particularly begged his pardon' for his previous advertisement in that newspaper.

Sheridan now had the high satisfaction of being victorious in love and arms, but his worldly circumstances were not otherwise improved. Married or not, he and Elizabeth Linley met as lovers, but they were obliged to meet in secret, which, perhaps, had a charm of its own. They exchanged letters and verses. She was in love with him heart and soul—her *whole soul* was devoted to him and she could never change. She longed for the time when he would be able to make her his entirely. He was her dear *Horatio*[1]—very much as William Siddons was Sarah Kemble's *Strephon*. In Sheridan's verses she appeared, after the same fashion, as *Laura*; though, to be sure, she signed her ordinary letters with a very plain Eliza Ann, and Sheridan, when they were married, wrote of her as 'Betsey.'

However, Mathews was not yet done with. He had retired to Wales, and there, meditating on the events connected with the duel, which, perhaps—including the matter of the breaking of the sword—had been talked of a little too freely, and in a a style injurious to his credit, resolved upon getting satisfaction by one means or another. He may have been urged on by a Mr. Barnett, who acted for him on this occasion. The result was a second duel, fought on the top of Kingsdown in the early hours of the morning of 1st July. As before, the weapons were swords; but this time the affair was bloody and unceremonious.

[1] He appeared later as *Silvio*.

Sheridan, running in to repeat his former manœuvre, was wounded twice. With the second thrust Mathews's sword broke, and he seized Sheridan's sword arm and threw him down. He succeeded in stabbing him on the ground a number of times with the point of his broken sword, Sheridan, his own sword first bent and then broken, continuing the struggle and refusing to beg his life. At last the seconds succeeded in stopping the fight, and Mathews, probably believing his opponent mortally wounded, went off in one of the two post-chaises in which the parties had driven to the ground. Sheridan's second appears to have left him to shift for himself, and he was eventually lifted by one of the postilions into the remaining chaise and driven back to Bath, where he was put to bed at the 'White Hart.' The details of this duel are somewhat confused, and were afterwards the subject of argument and recrimination which, at one time, seemed likely to bring on a third encounter. Thomas Sheridan said that Mathews had stabbed Richard Brinsley twenty or thirty times, but this, no doubt, was an exaggeration. His wounds, however numerous, were not mortal, though he must have run some risk of dying of fever and loss of blood. Eight days later the *Bath Chronicle* was able to announce that he was out of danger.

§

Thus, in the short space of less than four months, and before he had reached the age of twenty-one, Sheridan had fought two duels. He had also conducted a young lady in her flight to France and won her heart—a lady who, though only eighteen, was already a celebrity, and who, to the end of her life, won boundless admiration wherever she went. This jewel among women Sheridan did not know how to prize, but he himself said she was an angel if ever there was one: Michael Kelly spoke of her 'heavenly countenance,' and Sir Gilbert Elliot told his wife that he had never seen anything alive nearer his notion of an angel, or some such half-divine creature.

As to the duels, they were the only ones Sheridan ever fought, though even political life was by no means free from them, and during his parliamentary career Fox, Pitt, and Canning—to mention no more—were all engaged in such encounters. His own nearest approach to making a third appearance on the field of honour occurred in 1804, when Adair challenged him at Woburn for damning Fox.

In this summer of 1772, after the second duel with Mathews, his romantic adventures came to an end for the time being. The sober reality of the situation was that he was a penniless younger son, still under age, and without any prospects worth the name. He was entirely dependent on what his father allowed him out of an income which was never large enough, and of which the only part that could be depended on was the £200 from his pension. Thomas Sheridan's favour was reserved almost entirely for his elder son, who, by this time, had been provided for by an appointment as secretary to the legation in Sweden. Charles was a prudent young man and might be counted upon to make the most of any opportunities that came his way. It was very unlikely that influence would extend so far as to provide the graceless Richard Brinsley with any post, though it is said that an offer had once been made to provide both sons with commissions in the army, and that their father had refused it.

Charles Sheridan blamed his brother severely for fighting a second time, and his father was angry, not only on that account, but also because the connection with Elizabeth Linley was necessarily brought to notice again, and the fact that there had been secret meetings came to light. He took vigorous measures to put an end to the affair for good; forbade all intercourse with the Linleys; made his imprudent son promise to hold no communication with Elizabeth; and having engagements for the winter in Ireland, determined to take his daughters there, give up his house at Bath, and send Richard Brinsley off to friends at Farm Hill, near Waltham Abbey, where he could set to work to study law. Linley took similar steps on his side—perhaps with even better reason—and refused to consider the possibility of any engagement between his daughter and so ill-provided a lover as young Sheridan. Thus, in the traditional manner, the two were parted.

Less than nine months later they were married, as every one knows, and it is tempting to regard the case as one more instance of the triumph of love over all the obstacles in its way, and especially the hostility of parents.

It was not altogether so, however. Sheridan duly went off to Waltham Abbey in August, and wrote a penitent, if not entirely candid, letter to his father. In this ingenious epistle he did all he could to put his undeniable disobedience in the matter of Elizabeth in the least unfavourable light. He even went so far as to attribute it solely to his desire to be able to carry out his father's wishes eventually. He declared positively that the connection was now ended, and that there need be no further anxiety on that score. In short, it appeared that he had given up all thought of Elizabeth Linley. He read Blackstone and corresponded with Thomas Grenville, whom he had met at Bath, where his brother (afterwards Marquis of Buckingham) took lessons from Thomas Sheridan. He wrote freely of Elizabeth in his letters to Grenville, and not in the style of a young man supposed to be head over heels in love. He agreed that no happiness could be expected from such an attachment. His reason told him plainly that it was undesirable, and even his feelings were only partly engaged. On the whole, he was convinced it would be better to end it, which, apparently, he was quite ready to do.

But Elizabeth saw matters otherwise. She contrived to send him letters full of the most ardent affection, and entreated him to reply. He was surprised at this. He thought she had been sincere in agreeing with him that there should be no correspondence between them. Very likely she was so at the time, but then she could still see him and letters seemed unimportant. It was different now that they were separated. He flirted meanwhile, and not altogether innocently, with a 'Mrs. L——' and a 'Miss C——,' and she heard of it and reproached him bitterly. She demanded the return of her letters, but he would not give them up unless she assured him that she loved someone else. He heard that she was to marry Sir Thomas Clarges, and she wrote that she had refused him and other eligible gentlemen. She had done this for his sake, and now she would never love again. She was within reach of him, for in the spring of 1773 she sang in oratorios in London, where, according to Horace Walpole, the king admired her and ogled her as much as he dared to do on such a solemn occasion. But Sheridan professed indifference as to the place where she happened to be, though Moore relates the fanciful story of his disguising himself more than once as a hackney coachman in order to be able to drive her home from the theatre.

From all this it is plain enough that one of the two was entirely in love. As to the other, it may be said that Cupid had clapped him on the shoulder. It was easy to be in love with Elizabeth Linley—it was even difficult not to be so. But between that and loving her with a wholehearted and constant devotion there is a notable difference, and it hardly seems that Sheridan's affection for her was of the latter kind. The love and resolution that brought about the marriage in the face of so many difficulties were really hers. For Sheridan it may be admitted that the attachment was imprudent, and that any reasonable person would have advised him to put an end to it. He was in no position to marry. He was very young and had just begun to think of a profession: on 6th April 1773 he was entered at the Middle Temple. He had no money, and Elizabeth was not an heiress. But when did love ever reason in such a fashion?

In the end Linley's consent to the marriage was given. Thomas Sheridan's was not, but that, perhaps, made no great difference. Richard Brinsley, whose circumstances had not changed in the past nine months, except that he was now of age, could hardly have been the husband that Linley would have chosen for his daughter. However, her heart was given and there was no likelihood that she would listen to reason. Her career had been sufficiently chequered already to make it desirable on general grounds that she should be married, and it is probable that her father was influenced by being allowed to keep a considerable part of the sum which Long had settled on her. The remainder served as her dowry and was the sole capital with which the youthful pair embarked on matrimony. According to Sichel it amounted to £1,050 in Consols.

The *Gentleman's Magazine* recorded the marriage, on 13th April 1773, of 'Mr. Sheridan of the Temple to the celebrated Miss Linley of Bath.' The honeymoon was spent in a cottage at East Burnham, and Richard Brinsley, himself quite undistinguished, but with a celebrated wife, was now under the necessity, for more reasons than one, of making a career by whatever means he could find.

CHAPTER FOUR

'The Rivals' and 'The Duenna'—The Drury Lane Venture

SHERIDAN AND HIS WIFE, eventually established in a house in Orchard Street, Portman Square, which Linley furnished for them, need not have been particularly short of money, for Elizabeth could earn large sums by her singing. This, however, Sheridan, to the general surprise, firmly refused to allow her to do. He had, of course, no more objection to living on his wife's money than Bassanio had to living on Portia's. To marry an heiress—which amounted to the same thing—was a reputable means of getting a fortune or mending a broken one, and the Archers, Aimwells, and Tom Fashions of comedy did not greatly depart in that respect from the usages of ordinary life. According to Horace Walpole, Charles Fox himself, overwhelmed with debt, contemplated about this time a marriage with a Miss Phipps from the West Indies with a fortune of £80,000, though he had never set eyes on the lady. The match was to have been arranged by the 'Honourable Mrs. Grieve,' subsequently arrested for fraud. Fox's only comment on the affair was that she had had no money from him.[1] Sheridan's objection was to allowing his wife to appear on a public stage to be stared at and applauded by any one who cared to pay the price of a seat, and it was on this ground that Johnson heartily approved of his decision. The point of delicacy in this matter has shifted since then.

The Sheridans, therefore, were poor. To a friend who asked him how he found the means to keep up a house and entertain guests, Richard Brinsley is said to have replied: 'My dear sir, they *are* my means.' The story may not be true, but it serves well enough to illustrate the position of the young couple at this time. They gave private concerts at their house. 'It was,' says Alicia Lefanu, 'the least expensive form of entertainment they could give.' The performers consisted entirely of Mrs. Sheridan's family—herself, her father, her sisters, and her brother Thomas. These concerts were an undeniable attraction, especially since

[1] The story may owe something to invention, but it will serve as an example.

Elizabeth could no longer be heard in public, and gained the youthful hosts a number of acquaintances. According to the information of Lord Broughton (Byron's Hobhouse) it was Lady Cork who first introduced them to Devonshire House, but the duchess, though very willing to receive Elizabeth, was not by any means so sure about her obscure husband, who, besides being of no consequence himself, was only the son of a player. His position, in fact, was not at all a flattering one at this period, though he had youth on his side, and a pleasant, animated air. He was not regularly handsome, but his dark hazel eyes were, as they remained to his dying day, unusually large and brilliant. As to his charm and wit, they were much relished later on, but not so easily perceived while he was still poor and unknown. Altogether, he must have been spurred on to activity, not only by the want of money, but also by an even more pressing need to distinguish himself. The only ready way of bringing wit and talent to market was, as he had already discovered, to turn author. Law, which he could hardly be said to have begun to study, was now out of the question, its delays being as grievous to the budding lawyer as to the client. Literature gaped for him: it was almost inevitable that he should try his fortune again among the crowd who jostled along that way in search of fame—or bread.

It is quite possible, all things considered, that he would rather have kept clear of the theatre. Long afterwards he told Lord Holland that he wrote *The Duenna*, not out of any love for the drama, but solely for money. It is certain, at any rate, that comedy was only one of the lines he now attempted. He tried his hand at periodical writing, began an essay on the recently published letters of Lord Chesterfield, and planned a pamphlet on the unexpected subject of the education of women, which he thought of inscribing to the queen. In 1775 he meditated an answer, among the numbers that appeared in newspapers and pamphlets, to Johnson's *Taxation no Tyranny*. In short, he was quite uncertain of the direction in which his talents lay, and as ready as young writers in general to enlighten the public upon any question whatever.

Something definite emerged out of all this. In November 1774 he wrote to his father-in-law that he had been very seriously at work on a book which he was just then sending to the press; and went on to mention a 'profitable affair' of another nature: 'There will be a comedy of mine in rehearsal at Covent Garden within a few days. . . . I have done it at Mr. Harris's own request.' He added that, except for a scene or two, he had not written a line of it two months ago; and gave the comfortable news that, according to Harris, the least shilling he would get by it—if it succeeded—would be £600.

As to the book, in spite of the positiveness of Sheridan's statement, it never got as far as the press; but the comedy was a very different matter—it was *The Rivals*. Harris's suggestion that it should be written was not much out of the ordinary way of business, and though his interest in it was good-natured, he risked very little. If the piece failed, Sheridan would get nothing whatever; and if he got £600 the profits of the theatre would be far greater. It was put into rehearsal before the end of the year, and the hopes and excitement of the family ran high. 'We are all in the greatest anxiety about Sheridan's play,' wrote Elizabeth's sister Mary. . . . 'I am told he will get at least £700 for it.' The day of trial for Richard Brinsley's fortune and the hopes that attended it came early in the new year. On 17th January 1775 the audience assembled at Covent Garden to see the new comedy. In the boxes people chattered and laughed; the patrons in the upper galleries sang, whistled, ate oranges, and tossed the peel down on to the heads of the occupants of the benches in the pit; the candles flickered in the chandeliers, and in their soft, dim light the curtain rose on *The Rivals*. The prologue, spoken by Mr. Woodward (Captain Absolute) and Mr. Quick (Bob Acres), concluded with the modest couplet:

> Thus, all respecting, he appeals to all,
> And by the general voice will stand or fall.

The fate of a play was settled without much ceremony in those days, and the general voice was never reluctant to make itself heard. The hopes of success—of £700—of £600—of anything at all—began to fade very soon. Even in the early scenes there were the ominous sounds of groans and catcalls, and though the play was acted through and not damned absolutely, there could be no mistaking the verdict. The audience, says Boaden, treated it 'rather roughly.' It was given out for the next night, but only after a struggle. This should have been the end of the matter, and the disappointed author might get what consolation he could from his own line: 'His crime at worst—a bad attempt to please.' He saw it otherwise, however, and stubbornly refused to admit defeat. The comedy was withdrawn 'for alteration,' though to turn a decided failure into a success was clearly a desperate, not to say a hopeless, undertaking. Indeed, as Sheridan himself was told, it was quite unprecedented. Nevertheless, faced with the task of revising the luckless play to good purpose, reassuring Harris, and winning over an audience that might be reasonably expected to be hostile, he set to work with altogether admirable confidence, resolution, and good sense.[1]

Afterwards, when the play was printed, he gave a slightly self-conscious account of the whole business in a preface. 'The season was advanced,' he explained, 'when I first put the play into Mr. Harris's hands: it was at that time at least double the length of any acting comedy. I profited by his judgment and experience in the curtailing of it—till, I believe, his feeling for the vanity of a young author got the better of his desire for correctness, and he left many excrescences remaining because he had assisted in pruning so many more. . . . With regard to some particular passages which on the first night's representation seemed generally disliked, I confess that if I felt any emotion of surprise at the disapprobation, it was not that they were disapproved of, but that I had not before perceived that they deserved it.'

The chief criticisms were that the play was far too long; that Lee failed hopelessly as Sir Lucius; that Shuter, who played Sir Anthony Absolute, knew hardly a line of his part; and that the character of Sir Lucius was objectionable. Sheridan shortened the play and dealt with the passages which had 'seemed generally

[1] Genest's entries are, '(Jan.) 17th. Never acted, *Rivals*. 18th. After this night it was withdrawn for alteration. . . . 28th. *Rivals*, altered. . . .' However, the play was not acted on the 18th.

disliked.' No labours could make Faulkland and Julia entirely satisfactory, and the excellence of the rest had to atone for them. 'The Rivals,' remarks Genest, 'is an excellent comedy on the whole—but Faulkland is not a pleasing character.' Nobody is likely to quarrel with this reasonable verdict.

Sheridan went to work energetically and finished his alterations in a few days. Clinch replaced Lee in the part of Sir Lucius O'Trigger, and Mr. Shuter learned his lines. On the 28th the comedy was once more presented to the public, and this time the event answered the deferred hopes of the author and his warmly sympathetic family—the play succeeded so brilliantly that it was given on fifteen successive nights. 'After the first night,' wrote Elizabeth's sister, 'we were indeed all very fearful that the audience would go very much prejudiced against it.' But she was able to reflect with relief that there could be no doubt of its success now, as it had survived more difficulties than any play not actually damned on its first appearance. In due course it was performed and admired at Bath, where the scene of it is laid, and where many of the audience remembered young Mr. Sheridan, who had run off with the lovely Miss Linley—now his wife—and lain desperately wounded at the 'White Hart' after a duel.

The success of The Rivals marks a turning point in Richard Brinsley's life: he was somebody at last, and somebody, as it turned out, he was to be for the rest of his days. For all that, it is important not to misunderstand his position. To begin with, in writing a play he had done something so natural, in the circumstances, as to be almost inevitable, even if Harris had never suggested it. All sorts of people wrote for the theatre—his own father and mother had done so. The author of a play might be a gentleman of leisure, like Fanny Burney's Daddy Crisp; or a lady, like Miss Burney herself, Mrs. Cowley, and Mrs. Inchbald; or a clergyman, like the Scottish minister, John Home; or an actor, like Foote, Garrick, and John Kemble; or a man of letters, who, like Johnson and Goldsmith, tried that line as well as others; or a footman who subsequently became a bookseller, like Robert Dodsley; or a general like John Burgoyne, who brought out his first play two years before he surrendered with his army to the Americans at Saratoga.

Apart from the desire of distinction and considerations of vanity—though, as every one knows, there is something peculiarly gratifying in the applause of an audience—a successful play was a sufficiently 'profitable affair' to the author. Harris's estimate of at least £600—which, to the penniless Sheridan must have seemed very like a fortune—was not at all excessive. Holcroft, for example, made as much by his *Follies of a Day*, and Hugh Kelly got £700 from his *False Delicacy*. A play was a success if it ran nine nights, and the three nights allotted to the author, after deducting some £70 for expenses, would bring in £600 with reasonably good houses. Besides this a bookseller would pay £100 or £150 for the right to print a successful play. The chance of such profits, compared with the paltry £25 for which Lowndes bought Fanny Burney's novel *Evelina*, appealed strongly to needy and aspiring authors, and it had long since occurred to those out of suits with fortune that a successful play might get them out of their troubles. In the seventh scene of 'The Rake's Progress' Hogarth shows his hero in a debtors' prison, together with a scolding wife, a fainting woman and her child, and the jailer pointing grimly to his book of prison fees. Besides these there is a penniless enthusiast entirely absorbed in his search for the philosopher's stone, and another letting fall a paper with the inscription: 'Being a new scheme for paying the debts of the nation.' The Rake himself is seated dejectedly beside a table on which lie a bundle of manuscript and a short letter: 'Sir, I have read your play and find it will not do.—J. RICH.'

Sheridan, of course, was not in such a desperate plight when he wrote *The Rivals*, though one day he was to see the inside of a sponging-house—but that was nearly forty years later. Nevertheless, the similarity between the two cases is not altogether fanciful. Richard Brinsley's play was a notable success, but then his mother had once written a very successful play—*The Discovery* —which was, in fact, still in the repertoire. But this did not prevent her second venture, *The Dupe*, from being damned out-right, or her third, *A Journey to Bath*, from being flatly refused by Garrick on the ground that it had neither plot nor humour. Who could be sure, in this spring of 1775, that her son's case would be any different? *The Rivals* brought him money, notice, and a number of desirable acquaintances: what was even more important, it gave his self-confidence and resource the solid backing of success—and all this when he was still only twenty-three. But it did not establish him in a career 'of equal fame and profit,' or in any career at all, for a man would hardly expect to make his way in the world merely by writing plays, even if, like Richard Cumberland, he turned out upwards of fifty tragedies, comedies, musical dramas, and farces in the course of his life. Whatever we may think Sheridan's ambition in particular to have been, it is quite certain that, in general, what he wanted was to *get on*, for which purpose he was obliged to use his talents and energies as best he could. Indeed, he had to get on, if only because, to put the matter at its lowest, he had to make a living. He was married and must be able to provide for a wife and a family. Even after the success of *The Rivals*, and in spite of the fact that it was a work of exceptional merit and promise, his position was, in reality, entirely uncertain. The profits of the play exceeded the original expectations, but they were soon spent, and however long its popularity lasted, it would bring him nothing more.

For the present he followed up his fortune in the theatre. On 2nd May his farce *St. Patrick's Day, or, the Scheming Lieutenant* was acted at Clinch's benefit, in recognition, perhaps, of that actor's services in *The Rivals*. This was only a slight piece in two acts, and, though lively enough, of no particular significance. A more important business was in hand during the summer— a 'comic opera' for which Linley was to arrange the music. Sheridan had the valuable gift—so often denied to genius—of being able to hit the popular taste. Indeed, he had an instinctive popularity, both in the theatre and out of it, which, if he had lived in our own day, would have brought him a rich reward. He realized and turned to their most profitable account the attractions of this kind of opera, with its dialogue interspersed with songs. He himself was not at all musical. 'He had not the smallest idea of turning a tune,' says Michael Kelly, and the best he could do in that way was to make 'a sort of rumbling noise with his voice resembling a deep gruff *bow-wow-wow.*' However, he had a very good notion of the kind of setting his verses required, and even managed to convey it to the composer.

Linley told Garrick that, as far as the music was concerned, the opera was 'compiled'—a way of proceeding which he did not like at all. He had set some airs, and so had his son, but he would have had nothing to do with it if it had not been for the fact that his son-in-law was absolutely obliged to try to get some money by this means, since he persisted in refusing to allow his wife to sing.

The Duenna was written by the autumn, and the music was ready. On 21st November the piece was brought out at Covent Garden and proved an immediate and resounding success. It had an astonishing run for those days. 'It was acted seventy-five times in the season,' says Moore, 'the only intervals being Christmas and the Fridays in every week.' Mr. Leoni, who took the part of Don Carlos, was a Jew, and could not appear on Friday nights. The success was long continued. Nearly forty years afterwards Byron declared that *The Duenna* was the best opera ever written, and to his mind far before 'that St. Giles's lampoon *The Beggar's Opera*'—an opinion which few will be found to share nowadays.

The Duenna, in fact, is neither a strikingly original work nor particularly distinguished by wit and invention, though Hazlitt called it 'a perfect work of art' and said it had the 'utmost sweetness and point.' But if it can hardly be said to contribute much to Sheridan's enduring fame, it gave him the undeniable gratifications of popularity and profit. Thomas Sheridan was now reconciled to his erring but fortunate son; Garrick, at Drury Lane, was perturbed by the crowded audiences at the rival house; and *The Duenna* put money into Richard Brinsley's pocket, where, as usual, it was much needed. In addition to the customary gains, he sold the copyright to Harris and made handsome profits for himself out of the books of the songs which were hawked about the theatre, though the attraction of these must have been

Painted by Sir Joshua Reynolds. Publish'd Oct' 17 1792 by W. Dickinson N° 24, Old Bond Street.

S.ᵗ CECILIA.

MRS. SHERIDAN (BORN LINLEY) AS SAINT CECILIA

due at least as much to the music—freely whistled about the streets—as to the words. Two such successes as he had now won in a single year made a remarkable change in his position. He might have no security for the future, but he had good reason to trust his ability and fortune, and unquestionably he made a figure in the world at the time. There were two celebrities now in the Orchard Street house, and though Elizabeth's love for her *dear Horatio* could not by any possibility be increased, she was able to feel that her faith in him was justified.

§

Towards the end of this year Garrick contemplated retiring from the stage and giving up the management of Drury Lane, which had been in his hands since 1747. He was now getting on for sixty years old and his theatrical career had lasted upwards of thirty. With *The Duenna* still in the first flush of success, Sheridan began to negotiate with Garrick for his share of the property.

Garrick owned half the patent. His original outlay had been £8,000, but at that time a full house was only worth £200 and the theatre was in debt. It had been enlarged in 1762 and had now profited for nearly thirty years by Garrick's acting, management, and prestige. He valued his share at present, very reasonably, at £35,000, and would not take less for it. A year ago *The Rivals* had been in rehearsal and its hopeful author, now anxious to embark on such a considerable financial operation, penniless. Even at this time he had nothing that could be dignified with the name of capital. Since his marriage nearly three years ago he had received little more than £2,500, including Elizabeth's jointure and the profits of *The Duenna*; and nobody who knew him would expect to find much of this untouched, though he did in the end contrive to scrape together the sum of £1,300.

With these less than modest resources it was clearly impossible to buy anything worth £35,000, but Sheridan was not deterred by this difficulty. The affair could be managed by borrowing money and finding partners. He was anxious that Harris should not hear of the negotiations—after all, they might come to nothing, and he valued Harris's good-will, which would hardly be extended very cordially to a young man who proposed to become his rival. There was also a difficulty over Colman, who wanted to buy the patent; but since the whole of it was not to be had, he withdrew in the end and bought the patent of the Haymarket from Foote.

In the meantime Sheridan succeeded in finding two partners, and at one time had hopes of a third. One of these was his father-in-law, who had property at Bath, and had been connected to some extent for the past two years with Drury Lane, where he helped to direct the oratorios. The other was Dr. James Ford, a court physician of Albemarle Street. This somewhat odd assortment of investors was not looked upon with much confidence by some of Garrick's friends, and the lack of ready money was the subject of comment. 'What a strange jumble of people they have put in the papers as the purchasers of the patent!' wrote Kitty Clive. 'I thought I should have died with laughing when I saw a man-midwife'—this was Dr. Ford—'among them: I suppose they have taken him in to prevent *miscarriages*. I have some opinion of Mr. Sheridan, as I hear everybody say he is very sensible; then he has a divine wife, and I loved his mother dearly.'

Sheridan, the moving spirit in the enterprise, was full of eagerness and activity, and exerted all his persuasive powers. 'I have a certainty of my part,' he wrote to his father-in-law concerning the finding of the money; but he did not say what the certainty was. He discussed rates of interest and percentages of profits as if he had quite forgotten the time when £600 had the sound of wealth. He talked of examining the structural soundness of the theatre—which had to be pulled down fifteen years later—and went over the vital subject of the profits with Garrick, who, though willing to give information, would not produce any accounts, insisting that the purchase must necessarily be 'on speculation.' This was a piece of wisdom which Richard Brinsley did not, perhaps, appreciate at its proper value. He concluded, however, that a property which gave an income of ten per cent might safely be bought with money borrowed at five per cent. Linley, moreover, might come and help with the theatre, and, of course, be paid for his trouble. He himself would not be expected to undertake the management gratis, and his father could give them 'the benefit of his experience' for a time, at any rate.

It must be admitted that the enterprise, so very desirable from Sheridan's point of view, did credit to his determination and resourcefulness. It was altogether natural that he should be eager to seize the opportunity of linking his fortunes with those of Drury Lane: it gave him another source of income and would make any plays he wrote in future more profitable to him. His success so far had been won in the theatre, and if Garrick, when he undertook the management, had brought with him the advantage of his unrivalled genius as an actor, Sheridan (as Garrick fully realized) could bring something perhaps not less valuable —namely, his gift for dramatic writing. Sheridan, no doubt, thought of Garrick's handsome fortune, which, apart from his earnings as an actor, he had made largely by his share in the theatre, and partly as manager and author. Prudent economy, which his detractors called meanness, had also something to do with it, but Sheridan's talents did not lie in that direction. To be manager of a theatre was hardly to be famous or distinguished, and when, in later years, people described him as 'the theatre manager,' the words often carried an uncomplimentary intention. Nevertheless, to succeed Garrick at Drury Lane was a considerable achievement for a young man who had been so recently unknown, and if Sheridan ever reflected on his father's fortunes at Smock Alley, he probably reflected at the same time that there was a great deal of difference between Smock Alley and Garrick's Drury, and between his father and himself.

The purchase was completed eventually by means of some complicated arrangements—Sheridan's first experience of this sort of transaction, for which he afterwards showed such remarkable aptitude. His own share was £10,000, raised for the most part by mortgage; Linley took £10,000, accounting for much of it by a bond to Garrick; and Dr. Ford had £15,000, which was raised by a mortgage and guaranteed by securities. It was he, also, who had provided nearly £8,000 of Sheridan's purchase money. In the spring of 1776 Garrick brought his long and brilliant career to a close by playing a succession of his favourite parts, and on 10th June he took his farewell of the stage with a speech which drew tears from the audience, as well as from himself. In September the theatre opened for the new season under Sheridan's management: he was not yet twenty-five, and his star was in the ascendant.

This was the beginning of his long and momentous connection with Drury Lane. For more than thirty years the theatre was to support, almost alone, the weight of his ambitions and fortunes —a burden under which it was often to creak and strain ominously, though patched up and held together by all sorts of ingenious (not to say desperate) expedients. On the first Friday in Lent, 12th March 1792, he was to open a new and larger theatre— his own instead of Garrick's—on the site, with 'a sacred oratorio commencing with Handel's immortal Coronation Anthem.' This theatre, with its cut-glass chandeliers and its four tiers of boxes, was to have an iron curtain and a 'reservoir of water in case of fire.' On 24th February 1809 he was to see it burnt to the ground, and solemnly assure meanwhile (as Mathews, the actor, told Hazlitt) some astonished friends with whom he stood at the end of the Piazza in Covent Garden, that there was no evil equal to the consciousness of having done an unjust action— '*but that, thank God, I have never felt!*'

CHAPTER FIVE

' *The School for Scandal*'—*The Manager's Progress*

DRURY LANE WAS now Sheridan's responsibility, and it was his business to see that the anticipated profits were made: he had to settle, among other things, his own liabilities out of them. A theatre, in spite of its undeniable connection with the Muses, is, after all, a financial undertaking, as he had excellent reason to know, and the success of its management is not a matter of opinion, but a thing to be settled by the plain accounts of receipts and expenses. Two years ago he had been an aspiring author, dependent on the good-will of a manager: now he was a manager himself and the fate of other authors was in his hands. Their manuscripts, which he never showed much inclination to read, heaped up on his table, and the day was to come when Coleridge, exasperated beyond endurance by his endless procrastination and evasiveness over *Osorio*, would set him down as 'an unprincipled rogue.'

Elizabeth willingly helped with the reading of the manuscripts, hoping, no doubt, to find some extraordinary new attraction among their dreary pages: she also kept very neat and careful accounts, and was sometimes able to smooth over those difficulties which the temperament of theatrical people is well known to occasion only too often. The theatre meant a great deal to her: it promised to give her a settled home with a regular income: it would save her gifted husband from having to be constantly racking his brains and tiring his invention in order to please capricious audiences, and pay the tailor, the butcher, and the wine-merchant.

For some months Sheridan's management was not particularly successful. A new play from his pen was greatly to be desired, but none was forthcoming as yet. On the other hand there was trouble before the end of the year with Willoughby Lacy, the son of the James Lacy who had been Garrick's original partner. As he was the owner of half the patent he had a manifest right to interfere in the management if he thought fit. He now showed an inclination to do so, and to bring in two new partners. The prospect alarmed Linley, but Sheridan remained confident and optimistic. He was determined not to allow the intrusion. He himself owned no more than one-seventh of the property, but he and no one else was to manage it. The position was important to him. He and his father-in-law had reckoned from the beginning on Lacy's continuing to leave the direction of the theatre alone: he had no ability or experience, and would do, it was supposed, whatever Garrick advised. Unless Sheridan could have the management in his own hands, his investment and Linley's would take on a very different complexion.

In this emergency he acted with characteristic resource and not too much scruple. Actors and actresses were suddenly unable to appear; a mysterious illness seemed to afflict them whenever they were wanted; he himself left things alone, and the business of the theatre could not be carried on. This ingenious stratagem was well understood and aroused resentment in some quarters, but it answered perfectly and Lacy found himself obliged to give way. One writer in the press blamed Sheridan severely for 'seducing the actors from their duties,' and characterized his proceedings as 'an insult to the public, from whose indulgence and favour this conceited young man, with his wife and family, are to receive their daily bread.'

It was now high time for the new management to justify itself, and early in the new year—1777—Sheridan presented *The Rivals*; but *The Rivals*, though not previously seen at Drury Lane, had no other kind of novelty, being already two years old. In February he brought out *A Trip to Scarborough*, but this again, though Sheridan set his hand to it, was not a new play, being only Vanbrugh's *The Relapse, or, Virtue in Danger,* modified to suit the taste of the times and given a new title. The taste of the times, indeed, was far advanced towards the 'cautious purity' remarked on by Hazlitt as characteristic of 'modern drama.' Bawdy and blasphemy had long since gone out of fashion, and such free dealings with morality as the comic dramatists of the Restoration had permitted themselves were no longer tolerated.

The days had gone by when a lady was afraid to venture to a new play, or, if she did venture, thought it advisable to go in a mask.

The Relapse had first been performed at Drury Lane as far back as the end of 1696, Colley Cibber taking the part of Lord Foppington. It was Vanbrugh's first play, and, with the possible exception of *The Confederacy*, his best. It is characteristically full-blooded and vigorous, with a wealth of comic invention and at least three notable figures—Lord Foppington, Sir Tunbelly Clumsy, and his bouncing daughter Hoyden. It is plentifully supplied with wit, and, like its author, much less plentifully with *grace*. In his admirably impudent preface Vanbrugh coolly declared: 'I am even to this day insensible of those two shining graces in the play (which some part of the town is pleased to compliment me with) blasphemy and bawdy. For my part I cannot find them out.' He went on to assert that every woman of a real reputation in town would find the piece so innocent that she would think it no affront to her Prayer Book to lay it upon the same shelf; and bestowed a passing glance upon 'the saints . . . with skrew'd faces and wry mouths,' who were friends to nobody, and had 'too much zeal to have any charity.' Jeremy Collier's *Short View of the Immorality and Prophaneness of the English Stage* came out three months after *The Relapse,* and it was not long before the saints proved too much for the wits.

Sheridan removed the chief causes of offence. In his version Berinthia is no longer carried off by Loveless, crying: 'Help, help! I'm ravish'd, ruined, undone. O Lord, I shall never be able to bear it' (*Very softly*); nor is the virtue of Amanda in such extreme danger as it has to endure in the scene in *The Relapse* of which Vanbrugh, referring to the first night's performance, said: 'I confess I once gave Amanda for gone.' The adaptation, in fact, was carefully done and is a very skilful piece of work. It provides a new ending, which (though brought about by one of those transitions so much more common on the stage than in real life) is a good deal smoother and neater than the rough-hewn one of Vanbrugh. The alterations, however, were bound to sap the vigour and blunt the wit of the play, and give it something of the appearance of a wolf in sheep's clothing—the real animal

c

showing through here and there with an odd and disconcerting effect.

In altering an old play Sheridan was, of course, doing nothing out of the ordinary, for old plays generally were altered. Shakespeare, like others, felt the profane hand of the improver, and if he had been able to visit Drury Lane in these refined days would have seen and heard even more surprising things than a dying speech of Macbeth written for him by Garrick. Sheridan's own opinion of the kind of work he had been engaged on may be gathered from *The Critic*, where Dangle, referring to the 'nicety of the audience,' says: 'No double entendre, no smart innuendo admitted; even Vanbrugh and Congreve obliged to undergo a bungling reformation!' and Sneer replies: 'Yes, and our prudery in this respect is just on a par with the artificial bashfulness of a courtesan, who increases the blush upon her cheeks in an exact proportion to the diminution of her modesty.'

Sheridan's labours in the cause of propriety were not appreciated by the audience, who remembered *The Relapse* very well and had been led to suppose that *A Trip to Scarborough* was a new comedy by the author of *The Rivals*. Finding themselves deceived, says Mrs. Robinson ('Perdita'—though at this time she had not acquired that name or a royal lover), who played the part of Amanda, they 'expressed a considerable degree of disapprobation.' In plain English, they hissed so loudly that Berinthia (Mrs. Yates) fled from the stage, leaving the hapless Amanda to brave the storm alone. Sheridan, from the side wing, adjured her not to quit the boards, and His Royal Highness, the Duke of Cumberland, moved by the sight of beauty in distress, exhorted her from the stage-box to take courage, pointing out that they were not hissing her, but the play. Mrs. Robinson was new to the stage, having played only one part before—that of Juliet, in which, her head ornamented with white feathers, she had worn an elegant dress of pale pink satin trimmed with crape and richly spangled with silver; and had been much admired. She now stood fluttering on the stage for a while, quite uncertain what to do. Finally she tried the effect of a curtsy. The curtsy was followed by applause and the play was allowed to go on.

From the original in the Wallace Collection, by permission.
MRS. ROBINSON ('PERDITA')
Gainsborough.

The bad reception which the piece met with caused the wits to call it ' *A Relapse, or, Drury in Danger* '; but, as Genest remarks, 'in spite of all that has been said it may confidently be affirmed that we have *very* few such good alterations of old plays as this. . . . At first it experienced considerable opposition, but afterwards it was frequently represented.' Though it has no real claim to originality it is generally included in editions of Sheridan's plays.

The season was now more than half over, and still he had not found the success he needed. It was not far off, however. He had been at work on a comedy of which two separate versions had been sketched out. The fusion of these, which brought Lady Sneerwell and her circle, Charles and Joseph Surface, Maria, Sir Peter and Lady Teazle, into the same plan of action, and thus produced *The School for Scandal*, was an exacting labour; and when it was done and the scenes had been fitted together, there were the lines to be polished with extreme care and the wit to be pointed. Sheridan was never famous for regularity; he could not be relied on to keep an appointment, or to read letters, or answer them if he did read them; he was notoriously unpunctual, and much given to procrastination. But he was not by any means so idle as he allowed people to believe—a fact which had been noticed years ago by the tutor, Lewis Ker. His writing was neither hasty nor easy,[1] and if he scribbled at the end of the final page of *The School for Scandal*: 'Finished at last, thank God! R. B. Sheridan' (to which the prompter added a pious 'Amen. W. Hopkins'), it was not so much because he had been dilatory, as because he would not let himself leave the work until he had made it as nearly perfect as possible; just as, later on, if he spent much of the day in bed, it was often because, as Greville said, he was preparing his speeches there.

The new comedy was given for the first time on 8th May. That evening a friend of Boaden's was passing through the passage of the Rose Tavern in front of Drury Lane when he was startled by 'a sudden roar or shout' which seemed far too great to have come from the audience in the theatre. It was the

---

[1] Sheridan, says Boaden (*Memoirs of Mrs. Siddons*), 'wrote with amazing difficulty.'

applause which greeted the falling of the screen in the fourth act. Boaden himself heard ·that applause later and it was still far beyond anything he had ever heard before in a theatre. As for Sheridan, he told Byron long afterwards that on the night of the grand success of *The School for Scandal* he was knocked down and put into the watchhouse for making a row in the street and being found intoxicated by the watchmen.

The triumph was complete: night after night the theatre was crowded. Mrs. Thrale was delighted to get an order from Garrick for seats at the new play, which, it appeared, was a *thing*. Besides its own excellence the piece· had the advantage of being extraordinarily well acted. Horace Walpole said that he could not remember any play in which there were more parts admirably performed, and he mentioned particularly Yates, Parsons, Miss Pope, Palmer, and, above all, Mrs. Abington—the most fascinating of all Lady Teazles, elegant, fashionable, and, according to Garrick, as silly as she was false. A similar tribute to the acting is paid by Genest: 'This comedy was so admirably acted, that though it has continued on the acting list at Drury Lane from that time to this [1832] and been several times represented at Covent Garden and the Haymarket, yet no new performer has ever appeared in any one of the principal characters that was not inferior to the person who acted it originally.' Lamb, likewise, thought that 'no piece was, perhaps, ever so completely cast in all its parts as this *manager's comedy*,' though by the time he first saw it, Miss Farren had succeeded Mrs. Abington as Lady Teazle. Since the time of Miss Farren, according to Hazlitt, that part was never well performed.

The season was nearly at its end when *The School for Scandal* appeared, and it closed, in the full tide of success, on 7th June, with the twentieth performance. Elizabeth's accounts show that the play drew, on average, more than £250 a night, the highest receipt being £272, when the king was present. Its attraction did not diminish in the following season; indeed, on one occasion it was played to a house worth £292. About the same time single performances of *Macbeth* and *Hamlet* were good for £212 and £160 respectively.

Sheridan would not allow the play to be printed, though he was offered the remarkably high price of £500 for it. It never was printed in any authorized edition during his life, though it was pirated in Dublin, and he gave permission for a translation into French which came out in London in 1789. In his later years he talked of publishing a collected edition of his plays, having, as Moore thought, a far too optimistic notion of the profits to be got by that means. At that time he was hard pressed for money. However, he did not carry out the intention. There were good reasons for not publishing the play while it was still new. As Alicia Lefanu pointed out, he chose to confine the performance of it, in London, to his own theatre, and once the piece was printed such a monopoly could no longer be enjoyed. 'Why,' she asked very reasonably, 'should Sheridan give Mr. Harris of Covent Garden an equal right to have it performed at his theatre?'

Nobody took a keener delight in Sheridan's success than Garrick, who attended the rehearsals and wrote the prologue to the play. After all, Sheridan was Garrick's choice and he had a warm interest in him, as well as a natural concern for the theatre which was still commonly referred to as his. 'He was proud of the new manager,' said Murphy, 'and boasted of the genius to whom he had consigned the conduct of the theatre.' *The School for Scandal* was the talk of the town and it was only to be expected that the voice of jealousy should make itself heard here and there in the chorus of admiration. It was hinted that the comedy was not original; and one fantastic report, to which allusion has already been made, declared that not a word of it was Sheridan's, the true author being a young lady, 'the daughter of a merchant in Thames Street,' just as a similar report accused him of stealing the plot of *The Duenna* from another defenceless young woman.

§

Not long before *The School for Scandal* came out, Sheridan was elected a member of the Literary Club, the proposal coming from Johnson himself, who was willing, perhaps, to make up old differences with Thomas Sheridan. 'He had,' says Boswell, 'the honour to be elected, for an honour it undoubtedly must be allowed to be, when it is considered of whom that society consists, and that a single black ball excludes a candidate.' Sheridan had a fair claim to mix in that august company, and to be regarded as a man of letters: it was by his pen that he had won distinction, and after such an achievement as *The School for Scandal* there could hardly be any doubt that he would go on in the same way for his own fame and fortune and the delight of the audiences at Drury Lane. 'He who has written the two best comedies of his age,' remarked Johnson, 'is surely a considerable man.' Between *The School for Scandal*, however, and his next (and last) original contribution to the theatre, there was an interval of nearly two and a half years.

In the meanwhile he turned his attention to the ownership of Drury Lane. He was full of confidence and felt all the attraction of dealing in property of such value, and in large sums of money. After all, it was he who managed the theatre and enriched the proprietors by his genius; and the importance of managing it was nothing compared to the importance of owning it. From every point of view the half-share in Lacy's hands would be better in his own. In the ordinary way, no doubt, even if Lacy were willing to sell and to ask no more than Garrick had done, Sheridan, still impecunious, could have had very little hope of buying it. As it happened, however, the possibility of doing so —without producing ready money—existed.

Garrick no longer owned any part of Drury Lane, but he still had a considerable financial interest in it, for Lacy's share was mortgaged to him for £31,500 on which he is said to have drawn £2,200 as interest. The transaction which suggested itself, therefore, and which Garrick himself appears to have proposed originally, was one after Sheridan's own heart. He might take over the mortgage; and this, essentially, was how the affair was arranged. The bargain proved not altogether an easy one, Lacy's price for his share being, not £35,000, but £45,000; and Sheridan, besides the mortgage, was obliged to bind himself to pay two annuities of £500 each. These heavy commitments he

contrived to lighten to some extent by inducing Ford and Linley
to take his original share at a price, according to his own statement, somewhere between Garrick's and Lacy's. Most of that
original share was, it will be remembered, provided by mortgage,
but £1,300 of it was his own money—the only money, indeed,
which he ever put into the undertaking. He now got it
back, and thus accomplished the considerable feat of buying
property to the value of £45,000 without spending a penny
of his own. This explanation of a matter which was long
found puzzling was first suggested by Brander Matthews
in 1885.

Sheridan now owned half the patent and the theatre might
henceforth be described, without much exaggeration, as his.
Ford and Linley had a quarter each, and all three shared the
responsibility for the payment of Garrick's interest, which showed
an unhappy tendency to fall into arrear. Two years later Sheridan
took over Ford's share, though it is unlikely that he parted with
any capital of his own for the purpose, and Ford ceased to have
any holding in the theatre at all. But he still had, as he was to
find to his cost, a troublesome obligation on the score of the
Garrick mortgage.

Sheridan's subsequent dealings with the property he had thus
acquired were so numerous and complicated that, under successive layers of borrowing, buying, and selling, the original
arrangement almost disappeared from view. The principle of it,
however, remained: the purchase was made with borrowed money,
and the interest on that money had to be paid. There was
nothing unusual or radically unsound in such a proceeding:
Garrick himself had borrowed money in similar circumstances,
and Kemble, when he bought his one-sixth interest in Covent
Garden for £22,000 after he left Drury Lane, could produce
only £10,000 in cash: the rest was to be paid off out of the
profits. But in Sheridan's case there were two significant features.
In the first place he borrowed, not part of the money, but the
whole of it; and in the second, instead of treating the transaction
as one to be cleared up by steadily setting aside part of the profits
for the repayment of the borrowed capital, he spent the profits

and relied on his ability and good fortune (which, to be sure, he had some reason to trust) for the rest. The theatre would increase in value, as it had done under Garrick, and make inconvenient economies unnecessary. The theatre did, in fact, increase greatly in value—but then the burdens he placed upon it did not fail to increase likewise. The truth is that he relied on ever-growing success, and found it so natural to count on this that he drove his fortune hard and strained his resources to the utmost. They had to serve his turn. The strain might often seem excessive; it might occasionally threaten collapse; but the future would pay for all and everything would be sure to come right in the end. He had an income now, and, what was more, a property which could, if necessary, provide money in other ways. In all this can be traced a considerable part of the pattern of the rest of his life.

Drury Lane Theatre, henceforth of such vital importance to him, was not altogether an ordinary property. It owed its value largely to the fact that it shared with Covent Garden what amounted to a monopoly of the theatrical business in the capital. These two, often called the 'patent' or 'winter' houses, were the only ones at which plays could be given during the profitable season from September to June—a privilege which they enjoyed by virtue of their patents. Would-be rivals were held in check by the Licensing Act of 1737. The patent, therefore, was extremely valuable, and any attempt to encroach on the exclusive rights it had come to confer was naturally resisted at once by the owners. Sheridan himself, though an interested party, did not hesitate to speak in the House of Commons in later years, in opposition to bills intended to procure licences for other theatres, and on each occasion the bill was rejected. In April 1794, against the motion 'that leave be given to bring in a bill to enable His Majesty to license as a playhouse during the summer season the theatre called the Royalty Theatre,' he said that 'the application was only a renewal of one made a few years ago and rejected on full consideration. The present petitioners had, contrary to law, rebuilt a theatre (near Wellclose Square in the neighbourhood of the Tower) which was shut up by judgment of a court of law.

Unless the House was prepared to abolish the monopoly of the winter theatres they could not grant such requests. The subject affected property of value. £100,000 had been given for the patent of one of the winter theatres, and £100,000 more had been laid out in fitting it up for the entertainment of the public.'

Here we have Sheridan speaking unashamedly of monopoly to the representatives of the country, and defending it on the familiar ground that so much money had been put into the business; though the licence in question was only to be for the summer season—that is, when Drury Lane and Covent Garden were closed. As he reminded the House, the Royalty Theatre had caused trouble before, when one of his own actors, the elder Palmer, tried to establish it at the eastern end of the town. Foiled by the patentees, Palmer went back to his acting with £3 a week added to his salary. The patentees could not afford to allow interlopers. Foote had actually succeeded (though in exceptional circumstances) in getting a patent for the little theatre in the Haymarket in 1766, but it gave him the right to produce plays there only between 14th May and 14th September, and was granted only for his life. He sold it eventually to Colman for an annuity of £1,600.

The dreaded possibility of a third theatre was one of the risks Sheridan had to face. As a matter of fact, a 'dormant' patent did exist at Covent Garden: he spoke of it as a *terror* to Drury Lane and ultimately bought it up at a heavy cost. It was not the only risk. The building itself lasted only until the end of the 1790–1 season, and then had to be pulled down. There was also the danger of fire—and how great this was may be judged by the fact that, in a period of twenty years, the Opera House in the Haymarket, the Pantheon, Covent Garden, and Drury Lane, were all burnt down. Very little protection could be got from insurance, for no theatre could stand the expense of being fully insured. When Sheridan built his new theatre he insured it for no more than £35,000, and this made no appreciable difference, as far as he was concerned, to the ruin the fire caused.

* C

§

The year was now 1778; the Americans had captured Burgoyne and his army, and signed a treaty with France; and Charles Fox was going about significantly dressed in a blue coat and buff waistcoat. Sheridan was not yet twenty-seven. In less than four years he had made such extraordinary progress that it seems natural to find him not only celebrated as a dramatist, but also controlling Drury Lane Theatre and dealing in very large sums of money. From this time onwards he was to deal constantly in large sums of money, and it is not always easy to remember that he began with nothing and was never out of debt. He had a real aptitude for finance, but there was also a distinct strain of the adventurer in him, and it remained visible to the end of his life. His charm, his persuasiveness, his optimism, his readiness to take risks and let to-morrow pay for yesterday, all contributed to it, and his ambition found it employment enough: he lived by his wits. Tradesmen might be unpaid; the tax collector, though answered *civilly*, might have to go away empty-handed; Peake, the treasurer of the theatre, might be exhorted by letter to send '£15 by to-morrow's coach,' but on another plane Richard Brinsley would be concerning himself, as a matter of course and without the least embarrassment, with thousands on his own account, and attacking Pitt's estimates 'with great financial ability' and abundant 'arithmetical demonstration' on behalf of the country.

It is easy to exaggerate his income, however, and important not to do so. To say, as one of his biographers has done, that he could count on an income of several thousands a year is highly misleading. A great deal of money certainly passed through his hands, and his own profits would have struck him, not long ago, as remarkably handsome; but he was not wealthy. Garrick's share of the profits in the 1775–6 season had been estimated at more than £2,500, and he drew £800 as actor and £500 as manager. But Sheridan had to carry the heavy burden of the two annuities and the interest on the mortgage; the success of *The School for Scandal* was not to be repeated, and it remained to be seen whether he would manage the theatre as diligently and successfully as Garrick.

The running of a theatre involved the taking and paying out of very large amounts, but the profits, besides fluctuating disconcertingly, were far smaller in proportion than most people thought. Some thirty years later, for instance, an independent committee (which had the governor of the Bank of England as one of its members) examined the accounts of Covent Garden for the purpose of justifying the increased prices which caused the O.P. riots.[1] It was found that the average annual profit for six years had been only £8,345, though the total receipts were nearly £366,000. This meant an income of no more than $6\frac{3}{8}$ per cent on the capital at a time when the theatre was prosperous, and had not only Kemble as actor and manager, and his sister, Mrs. Siddons, in the company, but also the extraordinary attraction of the celebrated Master Betty, the young Roscius. Moreover, if the theatre (which had recently been burnt down) were to be fully insured, the income, even with increased prices, would be only $3\frac{1}{2}$ per cent. The concern, in fact, as Boaden remarked, had been paying out £263 a night for a gain to the proprietors of a mere £42.

Nevertheless, Sheridan's position was a sufficiently enviable one, and he held in his own hands all the means of improving it. He had won fame and could 'sit attentive to his own applause' whenever he had a mind to it. As for money, he might have reflected that if he kept his shop his shop would keep him. But such prudent maxims were never much to his taste, and his ambition was soon to lead him in a very different direction from that of shopkeeping. In the meantime fortune smiled on him and seemed in the mood to give him anything. Drury Lane was his: it was larger than its rival, Covent Garden; its nightly expenses were higher, and it was held in greater esteem. It was the oldest theatre in London, a playhouse having stood on the site for well over a century. 'King Charles II,' says Colley Cibber, 'granted two patents, one to Sir William Davenant, and

[1] i.e. Old Prices. These riots were a protest against the arrangements (and in particular the increased prices) at the new Covent Garden Theatre, which was opened in the autumn of 1809. The previous building had been burnt down in 1808.

the other to Henry Killigrew, Esq.[1]; and their several heirs and assigns for ever, for the forming of two distinct companies of comedians: the first'—he means Killigrew's—'were called the King's Servants, and acted at the Theatre Royal in Drury Lane.' About ten of the company were on the royal household establishment, and had 'ten yards of scarlet cloth, with a proper quantity of lace, allowed them for liveries; and in their warrants from the Lord Chamberlain, were stiled Gentlemen of the Great Chamber.'

These were high traditions. From Betterton to Garrick, from Dryden and Congreve to the still youthful author of *The School for Scandal* — the succession should have been inspiring. But Richard Brinsley was to look elsewhere for his inspiration, and though he and Drury Lane were to keep company for more than thirty years to come, the union was to prove as uneasy as a bad marriage; and as for his dramatic career, so short and so brilliant, it was nearly at an end.

[1] A mistake for Thomas Killigrew.

CHAPTER SIX

Plays and Politics—Member for Stafford

AT THE END OF October 1779 the patrons of Drury Lane were able to enjoy a new play by Sheridan: they had had to wait more than two years for it, but were richly rewarded. It was *The Critic, or, a Tragedy Rehearsed*, described as a dramatic piece in three acts, and sometimes called a farce. It is not easy to describe, however, the first act being pure comedy—much of it as excellent as anything in *The School for Scandal*—and the other two burlesque. It holds an honourable place in English dramatic literature and would suffice by itself to keep its author's name from being entirely forgotten. It has the classic quality of being ageless, and just as *The School for Scandal* has no need to draw on the accidental charm of the period in which it was written, and owes nothing to fans, hoops, and feathers, so *The Critic* does not suffer from the fact that we have no longer any tragedies which bear even a distant resemblance to Mr. Puff's masterpiece, *The Spanish Armada*. Some of the allusions we may still find pleasant; for example, 'Writes himself!—I know he does,' and 'It will not be yet this hour, for they are always late at that theatre'; and though the 'new-invented stucco,' the question of getting the Indiamen out of the Shannon, and the fact that the original of Sir Fretful Plagiary was Richard Cumberland, are nothing to us now, such things do not hinder our enjoyment.

The Critic shows no sign of declining power, but it does contain a significant hint or two of want of fertility. To begin with, it is comparatively slight, and even so is made up of parts which have no necessary connection but appear to have been put together to suit the author's convenience. The best character in the play, Sir Fretful Plagiary, has very little concern with it and figures in one scene only. Then the idea of the burlesque as a satire on the exaggerations of tragedy is far from original, being well known in Sheridan's time from *The Rehearsal*, to say nothing of more recent examples.

The question is an important one, for if we conclude that
Sheridan, so ready in wit, was, after all, by no means so ready
in invention, it becomes much more easy to understand why he
should have written no more plays. There are several other
indications that this was at least partly the explanation: *The
School for Scandal,* for instance, was constructed by a joining process, and neither *A Trip to Scarborough* nor *Pizarro* was original.
A very early idea of Sheridan's was to dramatize *The Vicar of
Wakefield*—another unoriginal subject. Among the papers he left
were some notes for a comedy on the subject of *Affectation,* but
though several of the characters were worked out there was no
trace of a plot. 'Some of the characters in *The School for Scandal,*'
remarks Hazlitt, 'were contained in Murphy's comedy of *Know
Your Own Mind*'; the scene in *The Rivals* in which Captain
Absolute finds himself obliged to propose to Lydia Languish,
certainly bears a strong resemblance to that in *The Good Natured
Man* in which Leontine has to propose to Miss Richland; and
audiences had laughed at malapropisms time out of mind. It is
said that Sheridan got the idea of *The Rivals* from his mother's
unacted play *A Journey to Bath.* Altogether it seems reasonable
to suppose that he had very little of that faculty for turning
plots easily which is so often the enviable gift of otherwise
undistinguished writers.

This is not, of course, to deny that he could have written
more plays: no doubt he fully intended to do so. But then he
knew well enough how laborious the task was, and nobody could
have been more inclined than he to put it off from day to day,
especially if he had some new interest and some more absorbing
ambition to occupy his mind. Naturally, he would not admit
to himself, or to others, that he would never set to work seriously
again. Besides the comedy already mentioned, he had sketched
out part of a drama interspersed with songs, and when people
remarked how long it was since he had written a play, he would
reply: 'Wait till I bring out my *Foresters.*' But he never did
bring it out, and these unfinished attempts were found among his
papers after his death. It was Michael Kelly who told him that
the reason why he wrote no more plays was that he was afraid

of the author of *The School for Scandal*, but that was more than twenty years later, by which time the remark came painfully near the truth. Debauchery and other distractions — to say nothing of debts and disappointments—had produced their effects. It was not for nothing that he drank heavily all through dinner and as long afterwards as the company kept together, not sipping his wine but tossing it down his throat and immediately refilling his glass to the brim. His face became blotched and disfigured, and he had no appetite and was troubled with swellings in his legs; and he, the brilliant author of *The School for Scandal* and *The Critic*, could feel a pathetic concern on the opening night of *Pizarro*, continually running into Lady Holland's box to explain when anything went wrong, and otherwise sitting in his own in a state of 'unappeasable anxiety,' and could take a no less pathetic delight in the popular success of that worthless piece.

It is interesting and not uninstructive to speculate upon the fame Sheridan would have had if he had died at the end of this year, 1779. His fame would have rested, as it still does very largely, upon his plays, but in addition his career would have presented a remarkably brilliant and attractive appearance. There would have been no need to explain any failure; no need to dwell upon profligate habits; no need for Mr. Fraser Rae to attribute the redness of his face to *acne rosacea*; no threatened suit for crim. con. against him by Lord Duncannon. Elizabeth would have been spared many tears, though perhaps she had already shed some over his gallantries; and he would not have been advised by Lady Elizabeth Foster to speak the truth more often and not drink so much. It would have been pointed out by biographers, and historians of literature, that his death at the early age of barely twenty-eight had doubtless robbed posterity of many masterpieces, and his untimely fate would have excited something of the melancholy interest which we feel in those of Chatterton, Keats, and Shelley.

Perhaps he would not have found a grave in Westminster Abbey, but his achievement would have been fully recognized. It is not to be measured by the intrinsic merit of his plays, admirable as they are. The age, so rich in excellent actors, was unfavourable to the writing of good drama. In Restoration times the theatre had been smaller, and the taste of the audience courtly, lending itself to a kind of comedy which illuminated with remorseless brilliance the surface of a small section of life. In the following century the theatre became popular; sentiment was in demand, propriety had to be observed, and wit gave way to bustle, humour, and high spirits. Comedy might, for various reasons, be found entertaining, but it had no longer any merit as art. Tragedy, long since in decline, was to decline still further, and departing widely from reason and reality, was to be found hovering precariously on the extreme verge of absurdity.

The defects of the plays were concealed to some extent by the actors. Garrick could excel in bad plays as well as in good ones. Mrs. Siddons could not do justice to her powers unless she felt her part was 'in nature'—but then, such situations as a mother mourning for her child, or a wife torn between love and duty on the return of a husband long supposed dead, appealed to her as being very much in nature, and she was quite untroubled by the fact that they were brought about by means to which nature and common sense were only too often entire strangers. She could therefore perform in them as successfully as she performed the part of Lady Macbeth in the sleep-walking scene, and draw tears from the eyes of Charles Fox as he sat among the musicians in the orchestra in order not to miss a single stroke of her genius.

It was in such circumstances as these that Sheridan produced, in *The School for Scandal,* an almost perfect example of artificial comedy. He made use of none of the licence which the Restoration dramatists had allowed themselves, and without departing from the spirit of his own time, lost nothing in the way of wit and effect. 'Besides the wit and ingenuity of this play,' says Hazlitt, 'there is a genial spirit of frankness and generosity about it, that relieves the heart as well as clears the lungs. It professes a faith in the natural goodness, as well as habitual depravity, of human nature.' This could not have been said of any Restoration comedy. No doubt Lady Sneerwell and her friends would have indulged in a somewhat more downright kind of scandal if Congreve had written the play, just as Charles

Surface would have exhibited his profligacy in a much more decided fashion. As it is we are content to be told that, like Thackeray's Lord Kew, he was a *prodigious wild* young man, and to think him nevertheless a desirable match for the blameless Maria. Richard Brinsley himself, for that matter, was prodigious wild, and has often been treated by his biographers with a similar tenderness and delicacy.

Leigh Hunt accounted for the general feebleness of the dramatic productions of that age by 'its dearth of dramatic character.' He went on to observe that 'a great wit, by a laborious process and the help of his acquirements, might extract a play or two from it, as was Sheridan's own case; but there was a great deal of imitation even in Sheridan, and he was fain to help himself to a little originality out of the characters of his less formalized countrymen, his own included.' He also pointed out that the three most amusing dramatists of that time—Sheridan, Goldsmith, and O'Keefe—were all Irishmen.

O'Keefe's merits no longer concern anybody: Goldsmith, and Goldsmith alone, has a right to be named with Sheridan. This applies, not to their own generation merely, but to a barren stretch of not much less than two hundred years—a sobering reflection for lovers of British drama. Literature in dramatic form was written by Johnson, Coleridge, Wordsworth, Lamb, Shelley, Byron, Browning, and Tennyson—to mention no others; but none of it has, or ever had, any hold on the stage. On the other hand, the dramatists whose work was applauded at Covent Garden and Drury Lane did not write literature. Sheridan stands out 'like Hesperus among the lesser lights.' Three of his plays—*The Rivals*, *The School for Scandal*, and *The Critic*—have the miraculous principle of life in them. So has Goldsmith's *She Stoops to Conquer*, and, so, perhaps, has his other play, *The Good Natured Man*.

Something has been said already about Sheridan's originality, or rather, his want of it, which, however, was more apparent than real. No doubt he was an imitative writer, but he had all the essential originality of genius, and if he took anything he made it his own—which gave him a fair title to it. *The School for Scandal* may owe something to Murphy's *Know your own Mind*, but the fact remains that the former is alive and the latter dead. As to *The Rivals* and *The Good Natured Man*—

'Will not Miss Languish lend an ear to the mild accents of true love?' says the unwilling Captain Absolute in a hoarse voice. 'Will not——'

'What the devil ails the fellow?' exclaims the exasperated Sir Anthony. 'Why don't you speak out?—not stand croaking like a frog in a quinsy!'

This bears a family likeness to Leontine's 'Ask the brave if they desire glory, ask cowards if they covet safety——'

'Well, well, no more questions about it,' observes his impatient father.

'Ask the sick if they long for health, ask misers if they love money, ask——' continues the reluctant son.

'Ask a fool if he can talk nonsense!' interrupts his father. 'What's come over the boy? What signifies asking when there's not a soul to give you an answer? If you would ask to the purpose, ask this lady's consent to make you happy.' But there is no doubt which of the two scenes comes the more readily to the mind.

If Sheridan did not invent malapropisms it is the name of his Mrs. Malaprop which has stuck to them and added a word to the language. Lord Burleigh's shaking of his head; the admirable remonstrance of the Governor of Tilbury Fort to his daughter:

> The Spanish fleet thou *canst* not see—because
> —It is not yet in sight!

and Mr. Puff's explanation of his use of a line from *Othello*: 'all that can be said is that two people happened to hit on the same thought—and Shakespeare made use of it first, that's all,' are familiar to all sorts of people who never read a line of *The Rehearsal* or any other of the plays from which *The Critic* is supposed to have sprung.

Other pieces in which Sheridan had, or may have had, a hand were turned out mainly with an eye to the immediate needs of the theatre: they have no importance, and can add nothing to his

fame. *Robinson Crusoe, a Grand Pantomime in 2 Acts* was produced at Drury Lane òn 29th January 1781, and printed by
Thomas Becket in the same year. It was popular in the pro-
vinces, and an edition was published at Newcastle-on-Tyne ten
years later.[1] *The Glorious First of June* was a topical production
for the benefit of the dependants of those who fell in Lord
Howe's naval victory. Sheridan told Rogers that he had written
every word of *The Stranger*, which appeared in March 1798 and
was long popular, but probably all he did was to make alterations
to Benjamin Thompson's translation. *The Stranger* provided
Mrs. Siddons with one of her best parts, but, like *Pizarro*, it
was only an adaptation from Kotzebue's German, and had no
claim to originality, and very little to any other kind of merit.
The Camp,[2] which was attributed to Sheridan, was probably the
work of his brother-in-law, Richard Tickell, the author of
Anticipation, so much admired by the Prince of Wales.

When Garrick died, Sheridan wrote a set of verses to his
memory, which were 'spoken as a monody' on 2nd March 1779
by Mrs. Yates at Drury Lane. To the printed copy of these
verses he prefixed a dedication: 'To the Right Honourable
Countess Spencer, whose approbation and esteem were justly
considered by Mr. Garrick as the highest panegyric his talents
or conduct could acquire, this imperfect tribute to his memory
is, with great deference, inscribed by her ladyship's most obedient
humble servant Richard Brinsley Sheridan.'

The Right Honourable Countess Spencer was the mother of
the beautiful and celebrated Georgiana Duchess of Devonshire,
and the hardly less beautiful Lady Duncannon, afterwards
Countess of Bessborough. These ladies were both concerned in
Sheridan's life and career, the latter, indeed, so closely at one
time that her injured husband began a suit in Doctors' Commons
against the erring pair, and it was only with great difficulty that
he was persuaded to relinquish it. Lady Bessborough is well

---

[1] Articles by G. H. Nettleton on the text of *Robinson Crusoe* appeared in *The Times
Literary Supplement*, 23rd and 30th June 1945. Sheridan also had a hand in *The Forty
Thieves*; his outline of one of the scenes is reproduced by Moore.

[2] The scene was the camp at Coxheath. Mr. R. Crompton Rhodes thinks that Sheridan
wrote part, at any rate, of this piece.

remembered as the mother of Lady Caroline Lamb: she lived to be referred to by the resentful and irreverent Byron as old Lady Blarney—to such a pass can time bring beauty and gallantry.

It is Byron who relates that one day when he was in Sheridan's company the latter happened to pick up a copy of his Monody on Garrick, and read over the dedication—written thirty-four years ago. The Dowager Countess Spencer was still living. Sheridan, then not far from the end of his own life, flew into a rage at the sight of this dedication and went on for half an hour abusing the object of it, declaring that it must be a forgery, and that he had never in his life dedicated anything to such *a damned canting bitch.*

The Monody on Garrick is not great poetry, and, to tell the truth, Sheridan was not a poet, though he could turn verses smoothly enough and trim heroic couplets with neatness and wit. Songs like those in *The Duenna* serve their purpose and are all that the occasion requires. Hazlitt thought they were the best that ever were written, except those in *The Beggar's Opera*: 'They have a joyous spirit of intoxication in them, and a strain of the most melting tenderness.' But to others this praise seems excessive, and the melting tenderness appears as sentimentality— 'a touch of Irish sentiment,' as Michael Kelly put it.

Sheridan's adventures in the realm of literature had lasted ten years and were now at an end. What he achieved in that time has been recounted. His dramatic career, which must be reckoned to have begun with *The Rivals* and ended with *The Critic*, had a span of less than five years, and, brief as it was, was to earn him a grave in Poets' Corner and keep his memory alive. Thirty-six years lay before him—a long stretch of time. It remains to be seen what he did with it.

§

In the spring of 1779, while *The Critic* was still in preparation, and Sheridan's ownership of Drury Lane still a comparatively new thing, he began to turn his attention to politics, and wrote papers for the *Englishman*, a periodical which the Whigs set up

for the purpose of attacking the Government. Like such pub-
lications in general it had a circulation of hundreds rather than
thousands, and a short and somewhat irregular life: it was supposed to appear every Wednesday and Saturday, but was not
always punctual. It died a natural death on 2nd June. In this
periodical Sheridan wrote against those pillars of the Government,
Lord North and Lord George Germain, to whom one attack
more or less in the press or in Parliament can have made very
little difference.

It is not surprising to find Sheridan writing for the Whigs.
He already had a number of acquaintances in that party—among
them Fox, Burke, and Richard Fitzpatrick, whose sister had
married Stephen Fox and was thus the mother of the third Lord
Holland (born, as Charles Fox said, referring to his debts and
lost expectations, like another Messiah for the destruction of the
Jews), who was one day to attend Sheridan's funeral. Fitzpatrick,
a man of wit and the lifelong friend of Fox, wrote the prologue
to *The Critic*. Sheridan had also been for some time a welcome
guest at Devonshire House, and Devonshire House might be considered the centre, and the duke the head, of the Whig connection.

The Whigs, after enjoying political supremacy, and the honours
and emoluments that went with it, for nearly half a century, had
seen that state of affairs brought to an end in the present reign.
The days of Walpole, Pelham, and Newcastle were over. George I
and George II were foreigners, who cared more for Hanover than
for England. Neither of them was popular and each had been
reminded (if any reminder were needed) by a Jacobite rebellion
that a rival claimant to the throne existed. They were obliged
to leave the Government largely in the hands of their ministers
and to depend chiefly on the party which had established the
Hanoverian succession. The case of George III was very different.
He came to the throne as a young man born and bred in England,
and, unlike his grandfather and great-grandfather, could glory in
the name of Briton. He had nothing to fear from the Jacobites,
for Jacobitism was dead, though by no means forgotten, and even
such a staunch Tory as Dr. Johnson felt no scruple in accepting
a pension, observing with his usual good sense that £300 a year

was an ample compensation for the loss of the privilege of cursing the house of Hanover.

In 1780 Lord North had been minister for ten years, and the king had a party so amenable to his influence that the Government was his in fact, as well as in name: the Opposition, even when reinforced by Fox, had thundered against it in vain. However, there was the American war. It had been going on for nearly five years when the curtain first rose on *The Critic* at Drury Lane, and the items in Mr. Dangle's newspaper: 'Brutus to Lord North,' 'Letter the second on the State of the Army,' 'To the First L——d of the A——y,' 'Coxheath Intelligence,' and so forth, were topical. So was Mrs. Dangle's delightful remark: 'There are letters every day with Roman signatures, demonstrating the certainty of an invasion, and proving that the nation is utterly undone. But you never will read anything to entertain one.' The camp at Coxheath, near Maidstone, was formed in expectation of a French invasion, for by the summer of 1779 both France and Spain had declared war against Great Britain and their combined fleets had appeared in the Channel. The country, which, less than twenty years ago, had been at the pinnacle of glory, now had not a friend in Europe, and was, as Mrs. Dangle said, in danger of being 'undone.'

Whether the war in America was, as Lord North declared, 'founded in right and dictated by necessity,' or merely the result of high-handed oppression; whether the Americans were nobly asserting the principle of freedom, or merely rebels against their lawful sovereign—these were questions which it was no longer profitable to discuss. The time had gone by for debating the right of the Government to tax the colonists—a question, as Burke had said more than five years earlier, 'where reason is perplexed, and an appeal to authorities only thickens the confusion. For high and reverend authorities lift up their heads on both sides, and there is no sure footing in the middle. . . . The question with me,' he had added, 'is not whether you have a right to make your people miserable, but whether it is not your interest to make them happy.' The fact at present was that, after five years of war, the prospect of reducing the colonists to submission was more remote than ever. The struggle had to be carried on across three thousand miles of ocean and without the secure command of the sea.

With these difficulties and dangers the Government dealt as best it could. It had tried conciliation, but the Americans insisted on independence—the time for conciliation had gone by. It had tried to strengthen itself and weaken opposition by broadening the administration, but the Whigs considered that they could not join the present Government on honourable terms. They were in the fortunate position of being free of any responsibility for the war, and their sympathies were with the Americans, whose successes they were apt to regard as their own. The king held the sturdy conviction that the Americans were rebels, and Lord North, who lacked the single-minded obstinacy of his sovereign, had to carry the burden in Parliament. He tried several times to resign, but the king always persuaded him to stay at his post. Whenever Fox and his friends fell upon the administration, talking of impeachment, wicked ministers, ill-omened and inauspicious characters, secret influence, and the like, these shafts were directed in reality against the king, whose policy, as everybody knew, the ministers carried out. A victory for the Opposition would mean something more than a new set of ministers and a change of policy: it would mean a personal defeat for the king and the undoing of the work of twenty years. Lord North—'the noble lord in the blue riband'—might loll with good-humoured indolence on the Treasury bench, peering short-sightedly at the hon. member who was denouncing him, or closing his eyes altogether; but the king marked all the proceedings, stuck to his purpose, and was no more to be intimidated by the Whigs than by the Americans.

In April 1780 Dunning's motion 'That the influence of the Crown has increased, is increasing, and ought to be diminished,' was carried at midnight by eighteen votes, but the Gordon Riots, which broke out in June, had the unexpected effect of increasing the royal prestige, owing to the courage and firmness which the king, unlike his ministers, displayed on that trying occasion. On 1st September Parliament was dissolved and the Government hoped to recruit its strength at the elections. This was the state of affairs when Sheridan entered political life.

§

Fox, who stood for Westminster at the forthcoming election, signed, as chairman of the Westminster Committee, the resolutions passed by that enlightened body on the state of parliamentary representation—resolutions which went to the desperate length of demanding annual parliaments and universal suffrage. Sheridan signed the report of a sub-committee. His Whig views were not new, and not merely the result of the influence of his friends: they belonged to him naturally. He had been against the American war from the beginning and was necessarily opposed to the influence of the king, and a natural supporter of Fox. His great ambition now was to get into Parliament: the kind of distinction to be won there appealed to him strongly, and, no doubt, went hand in hand with a laudable desire to serve the country. Motives, in these cases, are necessarily mixed, but he was resolved to throw his weight on what he held to be the right side. In this respect, indeed, his conduct was, to the end, remarkably honourable, though he got little enough credit for it from his political friends. His thirst for distinction was accompanied by a disinterestedness which, in a worldly sense, he could very ill afford, and which many who could have afforded it never dreamed of practising. 'I have seen Sheridan weep two or three times,' noted Byron in 1813. 'It may be he was maudlin. . . . Once I saw him cry at Robins the auctioneer's after a splendid dinner full of great names and high spirits; I had the honour of sitting next to Sheridan. The occasion of his tears was some observation on the sturdiness of the Whigs in resisting office and keeping to their principles. Sheridan turned round: "Sir, it is easy for my Lord G., or Earl G., or Marquis of B., or Lord H"[1] —the initials were easily interpreted by the hearers—"with thousands upon thousands a year, some of it either presently derived or inherited, in sinecure or acquisitions from the public

---

[1] Grenville, Grey, Buckingham, Holland.

money, to boast of their patriotism and keep aloof from temptation, but they do not know from what temptation those have kept aloof who had equal pride, at least equal talents, and not unequal passions, and nevertheless knew not in the course of their lives what it was to have a shilling of their own." And in saying this he wept.'

'His parliamentary line of conduct,' says Wraxall, 'stands exempt from all reproach.' He goes on, it is true, to relate some less creditable circumstances of his private life, 'which would, of themselves, fill a volume'—his eluding the demands of his creditors and failing to pay the actors at Drury Lane (an accusation to which Mrs. Thrale was giving currency as early as 1781); his town house so beset with duns and bailiffs that the provisions requisite for his family were introduced over the iron railing down the area; his entertaining a number of opposition leaders in 1786, when his plate and books were in pawn, and his prevailing on the pawnbroker to release them for the occasion, two men, dressed in livery and waiting at table, being in attendance to see that they were duly returned—'Everything went off in the most joyous and festive manner, except that the spoons and forks were late in arriving.' Having related all this, and more—many of the details, no doubt, being artistically rather than literally true—he concludes: 'He was not above two years in office in the whole course of his political life. He would have done better to stick to his pen.'

This was an easy reflection when Sheridan's career was over; but the truth is, his political fortunes depended on others besides himself, and on circumstances beyond his control. If he spent most of his parliamentary life in opposition, so did the rest of the Whigs who did not change sides. How long was Fox himself in office? or Grey? How long would Windham have been in office if he had not gone over to Pitt? All this lay in the future and could not be foreseen. The accidents, the unexpected turns of fortune, the hopes, the expectations raised and dashed—these things, standing out against the background of history from 1780 to 1812, give Sheridan's political career its high dramatic interest.

He had some difficulty in finding a seat and seems to have

thought of Honiton and Wootton Bassett before standing for Stafford. Wootton Bassett reappears in his story, in curious circumstances, thirty-two years later. At Stafford he had the advantage of the influence of the Duchess of Devonshire and the Spencers, and the support of the Hon. Edward Monckton, who was also a candidate—Stafford returned two members. Sheridan took up his quarters at the 'Stafford Arms' and set himself to secure, by the usual methods, the interest of the free and independent voters; that is to say, he paid a substantial sum of money to each of some two hundred and fifty burgesses, issued ale and dinner tickets entitling the bearer to eat and drink at the expense of R. B. Sheridan, subscribed to the proper charities, and behaved in general in that open-handed manner which was expected of a candidate, and without which even the most enlightened political views would have had little chance of appealing to the electors. The result answered all his wishes: Monckton and Sheridan were returned. The most alluring prospects of distinction and fortune lay open before him, and he stole away by himself to contemplate his happiness. The new Parliament met on 1st November, and he took his place as a member of the Opposition (beginning as he was to end), with such men as Fox, Burke, Dunning, Barré— and young William Pitt, like himself a newcomer. His political career had begun.

§

It is reasonable to inquire, at this point, what it was that made parliamentary eminence seem such a desirable object to Sheridan. It was an expensive and uncertain pursuit, and to all appearance he was fully occupied with the management of Drury Lane and the writing of the best plays of his time. He was not born into politics, like Fox, who was a member of Parliament at the improperly early age of nineteen years and four months; he had not inherited a name famous in political history; he had no landed estate, and though he owned a large part of the Drury Lane patent and had recently acquired an interest in the Opera House (of which he got rid later) he could hardly be described as a wealthy merchant. The Whig party was aristocratic, and he was not an aristocrat: he had no family interest to draw upon. He was not a political philosopher, like Burke, whose genius the leaders of the party might do honour to themselves by employing and rewarding. The path was not made smooth for him: he certainly benefited to some extent by friendly influence, but nobody gave him a seat. Fox's original seat at Midhurst had been got for him; Burke came into Parliament as member for Wendover—one of Lord Verney's boroughs; and Pitt had just been brought in by Sir James Lowther, who had eleven seats to dispose of, and generally required the members returned for them to vote in strict accordance with his wishes. It is curious to observe how strongly Sheridan's case contrasted with these. He was not indebted to any patron, but fought his own election, and paid for it; and in this state of independence (and expense) he continued for the next twenty-six years.[1] It was conduct suitable enough to a man of property and independent means—but Sheridan's means had to come from Drury Lane and were heavily mortgaged.

Sichel thought his election expenses for 1780 were about £1,000, but the 'constitutional friend' who edited Sheridan's speeches put the bill at £2,000. In his Life of Sheridan Moore prints an account of the expenses at the 1784 election, and some curious and instructive facts can be learnt from it. The only item for the actual election is '248 burgesses paid £5 5s. 0d. each— £1,302 0s. 0d.,' but this is followed by a detailed account of the subsequent annual expenses, from which it appears that house rent and taxes, servant, coals, etc., cost £57 6s. 6d. a year; and ale tickets, members' plate, 'swearing young burgesses,' subscriptions, and 'ringers' came to £86 11s. 0d., making an annual amount of £143 17s. 6d. The total cost of six years in Parliament was therefore £2,165 5s. 0d.

A significant note at the end, however, points out that this was 'exclusive of expenses incurred during time of election, and your own annual expenses.' This is a highly necessary reminder that the £1,302 paid to the burgesses did not by any means cover the election costs. A candidate had to be prepared to spend lavishly

[1] In 1806, when he stood for Westminster, his expenses were met by a subscription.

at such times, particularly when the contest was a close one. Ale and dinner tickets were far from being the only favours supplied, and in addition there were voters to be brought up—a chargeable business which dismayed Elizabeth, who called it 'ruinous work.' In 1812, when Sheridan contested Stafford for the last time, he declared that he failed for want of £2,000, which, by his account, Whitbread owed him. In 1806, Lawrence, the painter, told Joseph Farington that Stafford cost Sheridan a great deal of money, and that every election lightened his purse by not less than £8,000. Lawrence had this information from Kemble, who, no doubt, had it from Sheridan himself. The figure is certainly exaggerated, but even so it gives a formidable idea of Sheridan's expenses, and when it is remembered that a reasonable price for a seat at that time was £3,000, it seems a fair conclusion that Stafford never cost him less than £2,000, and sometimes cost him a great deal more.

The whole question of expense is of such vital importance in Sheridan's career that it will repay a little further attention. The account considered above refers to the period of six years between the elections of 1784 and 1790, and a cost of £2,165 5s. spread over that time does not seem ruinous. But the calculation is deceptive, for, as we have seen, the real cost was much more; besides which, a parliament could not be relied on to enjoy a life of as much as six years. The election of 1780, for instance, was followed by another in 1784. Sheridan, therefore, had to be prepared, at irregular intervals (which might be brief), to find a sum of £2,000 and upwards, and to find it in cash. Writing to Sir Oswald Moseley in 1812 he said he had contested Stafford seven or eight times,[1] including two very 'tough and expensive' elections, and had not left a shilling of debt.

All this throws a good deal of light on his financial shifts and difficulties, but even so, it is not the end of the story, for if he took his political career seriously it was hardly likely that he would find time to attend very carefully to the affairs of Drury Lane. Parliament usually met in November or January and sat until June or July, and this covered the greater part of the

---

[1] This was a mistake. He stood six times in all, including the 1812 election.

theatrical season. Moreover, though he may have seen no reason why he should not continue to write plays, his heart (but not his treasure) was to be in politics, and he was henceforth to present himself to the notice of the Speaker instead of to that of the audience at the theatre.

He was not, of course, obliged to stay in Parliament if he found it did not answer or was too expensive; but his hopes and fortunes were soon committed to politics. Success beckoned him on, and success in that line meant more to him than literary fame. Political life had material rewards to offer, and he had good reason to expect his share of them. As the years went by that expectation rose and fell, and the need increased desperately. But though, by judiciously trimming his sails to the wind, he might, like others, have made his fortune, he remained incorruptible. His financial escapades became a byword, but he was never to be bought. He would do almost anything for his son Tom: he borrowed money from the Prince of Wales to further his career; he entreated the prince to transfer the gift of the receivership of the Duchy of Cornwall from him to his son, and shed tears when the prince refused; but he would not accept the Government's offer of a place for him, because it might have the *appearance* of a bribe.

His ambition to distinguish himself in Parliament sprang, no doubt, from more causes than one. Lady Holland attributed it to his desire to efface the meanness of his origin, and accounted in the same way for his displays of wit, gallantry, and fashion. Moore's explanation was of much the same kind, though more delicately put. He pointed out that Sheridan enjoyed 'the proud consciousness of having surmounted the disadvantages of birth and station, and placed himself on a level with the highest and noblest in the land. This footing in the society of the great he could only have attained by parliamentary eminence—as a mere writer, with all his genius, he never would have been thus admitted *ad eundem* among them.' He adds a general reflection which is very much to the point: 'Talents in literature may lead to association with the great, but rarely to equality.'

Nobody was better qualified to speak on this subject than

Thomas Moore. He himself was a writer, and was received as a favoured guest among 'the great,' in which situation he always behaved with perfect tact and a nice appreciation of his true position. He could be depended upon to make himself very agreeable with his small talk and his little songs, as he did, for instance, at Lady Harrington's in St. James's Gardens, where the young men about town used to come in after the opera to amuse the daughters of the house, and where he met the Prince of Wales, who helped to get him a *place*.

Up to the present Sheridan and his wife were received by the great on much the same terms, and the letter in which he thanked the Duchess of Devonshire for the help she had given him in the election shows that he was very well aware of the distance between them. It was his 'parliamentary eminence' which closed the gap, and it was the only thing which could have closed it. The spectacle of Sheridan mixing familiarly and as an equal with 'the highest and noblest in the land' is so well known that it is easy to forget that he had not by any means always enjoyed the privilege: there was a time when he must have coveted it greatly, and very likely the achievement of it seemed to him to set the crown on all his other successes. A remarkable achievement it certainly was, and it must be admitted that he carried it off admirably—as if the nobility of the ancient Sheridans (unaccompanied, however, by any of the large estates assigned to them by the 'ancient geographers') belonged naturally to him. His manner to the Prince of Wales, as Creevey noted, was perfect. One or two flaws might be detected—signs of the lowness of his extraction: he had a curious sense of honour which forbade him to accept any but the most trifling favours, and, oddly enough, he was sensitive about money. 'He was a proud man, sir,' said the prince. He would not have solicited a place or a pension for the world. Nobody would have dared to offer him a substantial sum of money as a gift; and he fully intended to pay off all his debts, not excluding the many claims wrongfully made against him—one day. These characteristics were rarely exhibited by the highest and noblest.

It was not enough for him to enjoy the barren honour of being

RICH.^D BRINSLEY SHERIDAN, ESQ.^R

Member for Stafford

'PARLIAMENTARY EMINENCE'

in the House of Commons merely as one of the 558 gentlemen who represented the country, and were, for the most part, content to give their silent votes as interest or conviction demanded. He had to distinguish himself, he had to gain eminence. Nothing less would satisfy his ambition, and nothing less would entitle him to expect a share in the rewards which the party would have to offer whenever it came into power. Without some such reward it was plain that his political life would entail a perpetual and perhaps a crippling expense. To distinguish himself he must speak, and what certainty could there be that he would shine in debate? His fame had been won in a very different direction: it would do him no service in the House. On the contrary, it was likely to be looked upon with disfavour, and, for that matter, Parliament has always viewed with some suspicion men who have displayed their talents successfully elsewhere. All this must have been in his mind when he first stood up to deliver his sentiments.

In the meanwhile Drury Lane had to be kept going. The manager was about to spread his conquests farther and seek glory in a different sort of campaign: the Theatre Royal would have to supply the sinews of war. Old Thomas Sheridan, who had given the establishment the 'benefit of his experience' as stage manager, threw up the position after three seasons and withdrew, denouncing his son's conduct as *base*. He himself had been too pedantic and overbearing to be popular with the company, and at one time he had treated with unpardonable rudeness Garrick's well-meant endeavours to help. The world had not done justice to his merits, his labours had been in vain, and his temper was soured. He complained that his salary was not regularly paid— and it is only too likely that the complaint was justified; but it is permissible to feel some sympathy with Richard Brinsley in this family quarrel. Tom King, the actor, who had played Sir Peter Teazle in *The School for Scandal* and Puff in *The Critic*, took over the post, which he soon found to be a remarkably thankless one. Here we leave the affairs of Drury Lane for a while in order to follow Sheridan's fortunes in Parliament.

CHAPTER SEVEN

A New Career

HAND IN HAND with Sheridan's eagerness for personal success in his new venture went hopes for the success of his party in their endeavours to turn out the Government, make peace with America, and enjoy the sweets of office. The cause —as usual in politics—was twice blessed.

The Opposition, in whose ranks he was to win his spurs, consisted chiefly of the followers of the Marquis of Rockingham, together with a small group of former adherents of Chatham— Pitt's father—who had died in 1778. The latter were led by Lord Shelburne. Sheridan's place was among the Rockingham Whigs, where Fox and Burke were the most distinguished figures. His fortunes actually depended on Fox more than on any one else. Rockingham himself, who, fifteen years ago, had been at the head of the short-lived administration which repealed that parent of many evils, the Stamp Act, was no orator and not a man of great ability. Sheridan was personally attached to Fox, whose talents made him the natural leader of the party, and who, as it turned out, was destined to decide its fate—and Sheridan's—for a quarter of a century to come. This makes it necessary to glance for a moment at his career.

He had come into Parliament as long ago as 1768, and two years later was one of the lords of the Admiralty in the Government of Lord North, whom he was now attacking with such unsparing energy and ability. This position he resigned in 1772 for no very good reason. At the end of that year he was made a junior lord of the Treasury, in which situation he embarrassed his leader by undisciplined conduct. Early in 1774 he was dismissed, His Majesty, as Lord North expressed it, having made out a new commission for the Treasury 'in which I do not see your name.' At the outbreak of the troubles in America he went into opposition: like Sheridan, he was to have a plentiful experience of it in the years to come. He was then twenty-five, and was described from the Government side as tender in years but tough in politics, and reminded that he had already been twice in place and twice out of it. He attacked the ministers and their policy with great energy and ability (but without producing much effect on their majority, which was not amenable to argument), urged Rocking-ham to support the Americans firmly, and by 1779 had thrown in his lot finally with that party. In 1780 Horace Walpole remarked that it was curious to see Fox, lately so unpopular a character, become the idol of the people: he added the charac-teristic comment that the family were still in possession of £200,000 of public money.

Not that any of the family fortune was to be found at this time in the pockets of Charles Fox, the gaming table having ruined him many years since. His father, the first Lord Holland, not long before his death had instructed his agent to pay the debts of his son, the Hon. Charles James Fox, not exceeding the sum of £100,000, but the debts far exceeded that amount. Fox's passion for play, which was shared by his brother Stephen and his friend Fitzpatrick, was extraordinary even in that age. According to Gibbon he once played hazard for twenty-two hours on end and lost £11,000; and in the early stages of his opposition to Lord North, when he was displaying the utmost vigour and ability night by night in the House of Commons, he was, says Horace Walpole, 'seldom in bed before 5.0 in the morning, or out of it before 2.0 at noon.' Nor could his life be described as exemplary in other respects. He was soon to take up with Mrs. Robinson, the *Perdita* to whom the Prince of Wales played the part of *Florizel* for a while, and to whom he gave his picture in miniature with a heart cut in paper inside the case. On one side of this emblem that least faithful of lovers had written *Je ne change qu'en mourant,* and on the other, *Unalterable to my Perdita through life.* It was under Sheridan's auspices that Mrs. Robinson made her appearance on the stage, and it is proper to observe that, of the many gentlemen who took an interest in her, he was almost the only one (if her own account may be believed) who did not make strenuous efforts to seduce her. She expressed her gratitude for his 'flattering

D

attentions,' and paid tribute to his 'delicate propriety.' Fox later developed a sincere love of quiet domestic life in rural surroundings, and found it in his retreat at St. Anne's Hill, where his companion was Mrs. Armistead, who was his mistress for many years and whom he eventually married. She suited his tastes exactly and made him happy. Joseph Farington noted in his diary that she was an agreeable woman and highly accomplished; and that Fox had a natural son about nineteen years old (this was in 1793), and a daughter, but not by Mrs. Armistead, who, however, was very fond of her.

Fox's endeavours to remedy the desperate state of his finances took forms at least as remarkable as anything Sheridan ever devised. The affair of the 'Honourable Mrs. Grieve' and Miss Phipps the heiress—already mentioned—belonged to 1772. In addition to this he contemplated at one time being called to the Bar, and at another making a certain fortune by the ingenious method of going round the country from one race-meeting to another, and thus obtaining a reliable knowledge of the capabilities of all the horses. In 1780—the year in which Sheridan entered Parliament—he set up a faro bank at Brooks's with Fitzpatrick as one of his partners, and was to be seen by the passers-by in the street actually winning money from the gamesters. His success, however, had the effect of stirring all his creditors into life, and in 1781 they seized his goods. Horace Walpole, passing his door in St. James's Street, saw coppers and old chests of drawers being loaded on to a cart, and observed that they did not seem worth removing. Fox himself came sauntering up to his coach window and talked coolly about the Marriage Bill, to all appearance completely indifferent to what was going on.

Through all his dissipations and trials Fox retained a deep love of classical literature and a natural sweetness of disposition which attached his friends to him far more closely than any purely political ties could have done. In their eyes he could do no wrong, and any divergence of opinion or independence of action was apt to be regarded as black disloyalty. To Creevey he was *the incomparable Charley*. Sheridan, though attached to

Fox, who admired his talents, enjoyed his wit, and 'worshipped' his wife, was not among his closest friends. He had an essential loyalty in him which was to operate often enough to his own disadvantage, but he was inclined to take his own course, which brought him under suspicion eventually, and accounts for many of the hard things said of him. Fox himself, perhaps, had a little of the weakness of being unwilling to bear a brother near the throne, and no doubt he did not consider that Sheridan's perpetual difficulties over money were at all of the same kind as his own, or reflect that Sheridan's habits of evasiveness and prevarication might be due to some extent to the precarious nature of his position. The two never actually quarrelled, but, according to Francis, Fox sometimes spoke bitterly to Sheridan, as if he were a Jew or a swindler, and Grey told Francis that Fox loathed Sheridan, and had done for several years before his death.

§

As soon as Parliament met the political struggle was resumed. To us, who look back on it across two World Wars, it seems immeasurably remote. Those heats have long since cooled, the dust has settled into History, and the antagonists have been quiet in their graves for more than a century. 'We are called on,' declared Fox on the address to the throne, 'to recognize the blessings of His Majesty's reign. I cannot concur in such a vote, for I am not acquainted with those blessings. The present reign offers one uninterrupted series of disgrace, misfortune, and calamity!'

Sheridan watched the proceedings in silence for three weeks, and then, on 20th November, rose to make his first speech. There was a general curiosity to see how the author of *The School for Scandal* would acquit himself in his new rôle, and no doubt he was keenly aware of the difference between his present audience and that of Drury Lane.

The speech was a short one, and the subject—a petition against his election, and a charge of bribery and corruption—was not particularly inspiring. It certainly did not call for high flights of oratory, but perhaps it was not the worse chosen on that account. He began by complaining of the ease with which petitions containing charges of bribery and corruption were presented—often vexatiously and for no other purpose than to harass returned members. He himself was a sufferer from a petition of this kind presented against his return and that of his colleague by Mr. Richard Wentworth. He went on to deplore the reflection thus unfortunately cast on the character of his constituents. Here we can hardly avoid remembering with a smile the various gratifications which those constituents had received.

He was answered by Rigby, who enjoyed the lucrative situation of Paymaster of the Forces. After a civil sentence or two Rigby proceeded to ridicule the extraordinary notion that the hon. gentleman could possibly be concerned for the character of the voters who had elected him. Fox got up to support his friend and the Speaker put an end to the exchanges. Sheridan remembered Rigby and in due course settled accounts with him.

The speech was heard, says Wraxall, 'with the greatest attention,' and the 'constitutional friend' who subsequently edited Sheridan's speeches, assures us likewise that it was 'heard with particular attention, the House being uncommonly still.' After all, the speaker was a celebrity. But Horace Walpole noted that the new member did not make the figure expected, and when Sheridan went up into the gallery to talk to Woodfall, the reporter, he was told, according to Moore, that politics was not his line and he would have done better to stick to his former pursuits. Boaden, also, says that Woodfall was discouraging, and that he went so far as to prophesy that Sheridan would never make an orator. Some of the members, observes Moore, complained of his 'thick and indistinct mode of delivery, which, although he afterwards corrected it greatly, was never entirely removed.' But Wraxall thought that, besides a countenance indicative of intellect, humour, and gaiety, he had a pleasant voice 'without any Irish accent such as marred Burke's.' After all, no less was to be expected in one who had had the benefit of Thomas Sheridan's precept and example.

Whatever disappointment he may have felt, Richard Brinsley refused to be discouraged. 'It is in me, however,' he is said to have replied to Woodfall, 'and by G—— it shall come out!' Very likely he recalled the failure of *The Rivals*, which he had faced in exactly the same way. A week later he spoke on the motion of thanks to Cornwallis and Clinton for successes in America. He had not forgotten Rigby, and found room in his few remarks for an observation on the Paymaster's way of ridiculing everything—except what related immediately to his own interest.

In the new year Pitt made his first speech, with a success very different from Sheridan's. Sheridan, looking at that youthful figure, so self-possessed and dignified, and listening to the clear, well-turned sentences, may have felt a touch of envy; but nothing told him that here was the adversary who would ruin so many of his hopes, and whom he was to attack so often—one day in such a style that Creevey would think it had never before fallen to his lot to hear such words used by one man to another in public or in private. When that day came Pitt was not far from his death, and Sheridan, his youth long since gone and his appearance so greatly altered as to suggest to Dr. Hayes that his liver was much inflamed, could look back on more than twenty years during which he and Pitt had sat on opposite sides of the House.

He himself spoke in this debate, solemnly rebuking Courtenay, the member for Tamworth, for his levity. This must have sounded a little oddly in the mouth of the greatest comic dramatist of the age, and Courtenay, well known for his rough tongue and ready wit, rejoined pointedly that the hon. member seemed to be an enemy to wit and mirth *in any house but his own*. Sheridan was not allowed to reply, but he soon learned to deal effectively with such allusions to his occupation as 'conductor of a public theatre.' He refused to be disconcerted by them, and, turning the weapons of his adversaries upon themselves, dealt out a suitable *chastisement*, as Wraxall puts it, without altering a muscle of his own countenance.

For his own part he had hardly ventured on any wit so far: he took the business too seriously for that. His progress was being watched with interest. Anthony Storer, writing to Lord Carlisle, noted that in the debate on Burke's Bill Mr. Sheridan did very well, saying a few words in answer to Mr. Courtenay, and placing each word exactly where it should be—as if he had studied them for a week past. This is a highly interesting and significant comment, and shows how extremely anxious Sheridan was to succeed. He always did take far more care over his speeches than was generally supposed, just as he had done over his plays.

During the rest of the session he spoke five times, once for more than half an hour, on which occasion he was complimented by Fox and Lord North. One somewhat unlikely subject to which he gave attention was the Solicitor-General's Bill for preventing abuses and profanations of the Sabbath Day. Before the House rose he had been noticed as one of the young men 'who made a considerable figure in opposition.'

§

The members dispersed for the summer, but the war went on. In October Cornwallis surrendered to the Americans at Yorktown, and the fatal news reached Lord North on 25th November. 'Oh, God!' he exclaimed, 'it is all over!' Two days later Parliament met. The king hoped that none of the ministers would suppose that the disaster made the smallest alteration in his principles or his conduct, but in less than four months the Government fell. On 20th March, after an interview with the king, Lord North informed a crowded House that His Majesty had resolved to change his ministers—after which he drove home in the bleak evening to Grosvenor Square.

The turn of the Opposition had come at last. Fortune was Sheridan's friend; but then, so it had been for years. Everything he touched succeeded. How long had Burke, for instance, had to wait for the present chance! During the past winter Sheridan's reputation and his importance to his party had increased remarkably. He spoke on the war and naval affairs; attacked Lord George Germain, Rigby, Lord North, and Lord Sandwich;

defended Fox 'with great judgment'; and dealt with Sir W. Dolben 'in a most admirable piece of satire.' He had gained experience and confidence, and the uncertain days when he had laboriously put together a few over-precise sentences were gone. One performance in particular was in the true Sheridan style and as bright and keen as anything in his comedies. It was against Rigby, who, while continuing to vote with the Government and enjoy his office of Paymaster, had taken care to let it be known that he was in favour of ending the American war. Sheridan 'believed the right honourable gentleman to have been sincere —he believed that, as a member of parliament, as a privy councillor, as a private gentleman, he had always detested the American war as much as any man; but then he had never been able to persuade the Paymaster that it was a bad war; and unfortunately, in whatever character he spoke, *it was the Paymaster who always voted in that House.*'

It was now the spring of 1782 and Sheridan had been in Parliament less than eighteen months. He was made an under-secretary of state in the new Government. He wrote to his brother Charles, in Ireland, that he had chosen this position because he wanted to get into habits of business and punctuality, and to acquire information. This, of course, was with an eye to greater things in the future. The idea of Richard Brinsley as a punctual and business-like public servant seems a little surprising, but there is no doubt that he was entirely in earnest, and it is not impossible that, if he had been regularly in office, he would have developed these unexciting but useful qualities. The appearance of easy carelessness which he liked to present to the world was a piece of vanity, harmless enough and even likeable, which he adopted as a defence against adverse circumstances.

His brother congratulated him on his appointment and was fully alive to the benefits he himself might get from it. He added a shrewd piece of advice: 'For God's sake improve the opportunity to the utmost, and don't let dreams of empty fame (of which you have had enough in all conscience) carry you away from your solid interests.' Charles understood the situation perfectly: Richard Brinsley was in a position to make his political fortune if he played his cards properly. Dreams of empty fame might lure him away from the road to success—so might far-fetched notions of personal loyalty and an over-delicate sense of honour. Charles did not mention these, but no doubt he had them in mind. A man must attend to his own interests first. He went on to speak of his own claims to preferment in Ireland and concluded by explaining why it was not convenient just then to repay £50 which he had borrowed from his brother.

Charles, who had been called to the Irish Bar and was, in his way, a man of ability, got his preferment: he was duly made Secretary of War in Ireland. In this situation he set an admirable example to Richard Brinsley (and nobody could have needed it more, or have been less apt to profit by it) along the lines of the advice given in his letter. Charles was never the man to neglect his 'solid interests': he got far more out of his politics than his brilliant brother, and never made the mistake of thinking empty fame a sufficient reward.

Sheridan, of course, could expect no consideration from any party except what he could earn by his talents. He had no interest to draw upon, and no other advantages of any kind. But however his career might be hindered by his 'disadvantages of birth and station'—to say nothing of other matters, such as character—it was certainly not want of ability which would keep him back. In particular, he had an importance as a speaker which could not be overlooked. Since 1771 the parliamentary debates had been reported freely in the newspapers and eagerly read; and in consequence the substance, at least, of what was said in the House might reach an audience which previously had had to be influenced mainly by political pamphlets. Sheridan possessed wit and eloquence, and in addition the peculiar gift of being personally interesting. These were counters which could be exchanged for solid, and even brilliant, gains. From his own point of view Charles Sheridan was perfectly right: on the assumption that Richard Brinsley's first business was to look after his material interests, it was folly and a mere flouting of providence to let anything stand in the way of it. The conclusion was as plain as daylight to Charles, and to more distinguished men than

THE PRINCE OF WALES IN 1779
From the Portrait by Sir Joshua Reynolds.

he, who did not fail to act on it. But Richard Brinsley was not one of them: what he did with his opportunities will appear in due course.

§

To be forced to take the Whigs was an unspeakable calamity in the eyes of the king. He talked of retiring to Hanover, and even (as George IV told Lord Holland) settled a great many of the details—particularly those relating to the vital matters of dresses and liveries. He approached Shelburne and Lord Gower —Fitzpatrick's uncle and at this time head of the Bedford party —but neither of them could undertake to form a government. At last he had to swallow the bitter pill and, with the worst possible grace, request Rockingham to form a ministry.

With Rockingham came Fox, and the king particularly detested Fox, who had long ago incurred his displeasure. Since then his offences had multiplied. Besides, his private life was scandalous. The king himself was a model of domestic virtue and notably faithful to his unprepossessing wife. His court was eminently respectable, though very dull. He was frugal, kept a plain table, and rarely drank anything stronger than a sort of lemonade which he called 'cup.' Returning wet through from hunting he would refresh himself with barley-water, and graciously offer the same uninspiring though wholesome beverage to his reluctant equerries. He was to be seen at early chapel even on the coldest mornings, and never failed to attend punctually to business. Fox's example he considered pernicious, and he particularly deplored the influence which he was beginning to gain over the Prince of Wales. He complained bitterly that his own brother, the Duke of Cumberland, was governed entirely by Fox and Fitzpatrick, and that the duke was leading the prince into all sorts of dissipation and vice. When he went hunting with his brother and the prince neither of them would talk to him, and once, when the chase ended at an out-of-the-way village, they took the only post-chaise available and left him to shift for himself. Furthermore, the prince, invited to dine at Windsor, arrived late, and the entire household beheld the monarch forced to wait an hour for his eldest son.

* D

So the king lamented his unhappy situation and laid it in large measure to Fox's account. The prince was being drawn into Fox's political views and would be found in opposition to his royal father.

Now Fox, standing out as the opponent of the king, carried his friends with him. He might, as Johnson put it, *divide the kingdom with Caesar*, and it might come to be a question whether the sceptre of George III or the tongue of Fox would prevail. Whatever the upshot proved to be, Fox's followers would find themselves vitally concerned in it. Sheridan was one of those followers.

The new administration was not altogether harmonious—a fact which the king thoroughly appreciated, and by which he counted on profiting. It contained adherents of Shelburne as well as of Rockingham, to say nothing of the fact that Thurlow remained as Chancellor. The two Secretaries of State were Shelburne and Fox—an arrangement exquisitely calculated, as things stood, to increase discord. The first business of the Government was to negotiate a peace, and peace had to be made with America—which was in Shelburne's department—and with France, Spain, and Holland—which were in Fox's. In such circumstances the negotiations were likely to prove difficult, even if the two secretaries had been of the same mind and thoroughly trusted each other, which was very far from being the case. Fox, who had now given up gaming and devoted himself entirely to business, sent Thomas Grenville to Paris to negotiate with Vergennes, and Shelburne sent a Mr. Oswald to Paris likewise, to deal with the hard-headed Benjamin Franklin. Lord Shelburne, observed Franklin shrewdly, thought the arrangements for the peace should be in his hands, and Mr. Fox considered that they were his affair.

The negotiations proceeded slowly and far from smoothly, and the Government meanwhile went on with its ordinary business. Sheridan enjoyed the dignity of his under-secretaryship and corresponded with Thomas Grenville at Paris and Fitzpatrick, who was Chief Secretary at Dublin. He spoke from the Treasury bench against Eden, who had come over from Ireland with the unseasonable question of the right of the English Parliament to legislate for that kingdom. He supported Pitt on the subject of the reform of parliamentary representation, and General Burgoyne told Fitzpatrick that on this occasion he surpassed all his former efforts, attacking Dundas with more wit than he—the general—had ever heard before.

So the affairs of the country, and of America, France, Spain, and Holland, were tossed back and forth in debate and discussion; the Cabinet wrangled; the king meditated on his painful position; the Prince of Wales grew heartily sick of his Perdita; and Sheridan's career was hammered into shape. At the beginning of July the curtain fell on the first act of a political drama: the Marquis of Rockingham died, and Fox, at odds with Shelburne, resigned. Sheridan, with a loyalty which left his 'solid interests' entirely out of account, resigned likewise. He had been in office just over three months.

CHAPTER EIGHT

Political Fortunes

THIS DRAMA—to keep so appropriate a figure—was played out in the next twenty months, and it is not too much to say that Sheridan felt the consequences of it to the last hour of his life.

When Rockingham died the king at once took the opportunity of inviting Shelburne to replace him. Fox protested that a friend of Lord Rockingham ought to be at the head of the Government—he meant the Duke of Portland, who had succeeded Rockingham as leader of the party. But the king had his way and Fox found himself in a position not much unlike that of Macbeth when he reflected that he had murdered the gracious Duncan merely in order to make the seed of Banquo kings.

Shelburne took Pitt into his government, and so it came about that Pitt, at the age of twenty-three and without having held any previous office whatever, became at one stride Chancellor of the Exchequer and virtual leader of the House of Commons. He also became, what he was to remain for twenty years to come, Fox's political enemy, though a little while ago he had been his 'hon. friend.' Here begins the long antagonism between Pitt and Sheridan.

Fox would not serve under Shelburne: instead he took a course so extraordinary as to verge on the incredible—he joined forces with Lord North. Fox and North in coalition! One indignant member called it a union between Herod and Pontius Pilate. For years Fox had been denouncing in unmeasured terms, not merely North's policy, but his personal conduct. He had threatened him with impeachment, and even spoken of the scaffold. Only a year ago he had declared in the House, with his usual wholehearted vigour and every appearance of conviction, that from the moment when he came to terms with the noble lord and his friends he would rest satisfied to be called *infamous*; and had gone on to say that he would not trust his own honour for a single moment in the hands of such men. These were bitter words: what was to be thought of them now?

Nevertheless, the thing was carried through. On the night of 16th February 1783 the agreement was concluded: Fox and North were to 'speak, act, and divide in concert.' It was put into force without delay and the Government was defeated. Shelburne resigned on the 24th, and the king saw himself betrayed by Lord North, of all men, into the hands of the hated Fox. He struggled hard against his fate, but there was no escaping it. He begged Pitt to form a government, but Pitt, after consenting for a few hours, had the wisdom to reconsider his decision. For five weeks there was no administration in office: the coalition became restless and Coke moved an address to the throne. Fox spoke of the delay as the most insolent domination that ever disgraced a free country, and the Prince of Wales was reported to have said in the queen's drawing-room that by G—— his father should be made to agree to the coalition. In the end the new ministers came into office, and the king, when he woke up of a morning, wished he was eighty or ninety or dead. He would ride out disconsolately (for he never failed to take his exercise) with an equerry and a footman, to neither of whom would he utter a word, and return in the same silent and dejected fashion.

An acute observer afterwards remarked that he had foreseen that the new administration could not last, because when Mr. Fox kissed hands at court the king turned back his ears like the horse at Astley's when he meant to throw the tailor who was getting on him. The inference was perfectly correct: before the end of the year Fox's India Bill was defeated in the House of Lords, the king having authorized Earl Temple to make it known among the peers that whoever voted for the Bill was not only not his friend, but would be considered by him as an enemy. He lost no time in requiring the two Secretaries of State to deliver up their seals of office—adding significantly that he did not desire a personal interview. The messenger, it is said, arrived so late at night that he found Lord North—but not

Fox—in bed. The play was over: the sceptre of George III had proved too much for the tongue of Fox.

There was an epilogue, however, which lasted until the spring. During those three months, Pitt, who now undertook the Government, maintained himself with admirable nerve and judgment against the majority of Fox and North—a majority which began to dwindle in January, sank to twenty or thirty in February, and was extinguished in March. The Opposition used 'harsh and indecent' language to Mr. Pitt, and Sheridan, confining himself to what he called proper and parliamentary terms, referred to him as 'one of the minions of the Crown.' But Fox's credit was gone: even at a Westminster meeting the shouts of 'No Coalition!' drowned those of 'No Backstairs Influence!' On 25th March Parliament was dissolved, and at the elections the Opposition were routed in such a style that 160 of them—'Fox's Martyrs'—lost their seats.

§

Sheridan was not (in this sense at any rate) one of the martyrs. He kept his seat at Stafford, and very likely felt he had good reason for satisfaction in spite of everything. His brother, writing to wish him success in his election, complimented him on the very considerable figure he had made in the House; and it was perfectly true that he had made a very considerable figure there. In the ill-starred coalition Government, moreover, he had been a secretary to the Treasury, a place which carried a handsome salary; and thus, in a parliamentary career of only three and a half years, he had been twice in office. He could reckon confidently on being in office again whenever his friends came into power, and nothing told him that more than twenty years would elapse before that time came. He had wanted distinction, and already he had had a very pleasant taste of it. Ten years ago he had been nothing but the obscure and awkward husband of a lovely and celebrated wife: times had changed since then. He was no longer the poor player's son; no longer even the brilliant young author of *The Rivals*, *The Duenna*, and *The*

School for Scandal. He was Mr. Sheridan, member for Stafford, a place which was annually beholden to him for forty pounds' worth of ale tickets, a subscription of five guineas to the infirmary, and another of two guineas to clergymen's widows. He had the ear of the House and was a man of consequence in his party; he was the friend of Fox, and of Fox's friends, whom he met constantly at Brooks's, where he had been a member ever since he came into Parliament. The doors of Devonshire House, Burlington House, and Carlton House were open to him, and he could bask in the smiles of Mrs. Crewe, the Duchess of Devonshire, and her sister—to carry the list no further. The Prince of Wales, now of age, was on his side in politics, and already enjoyed his company and his wit.

All this was undeniably gratifying, but there was another side to the picture. Sheridan's two periods of office together amounted to no more than a year: he had spent two and a half years in opposition, and was in opposition now—a member of a party which had been defeated, weakened to the point of impotence, and, above all, thoroughly discredited. Twice in less than four years he had been obliged to fight an election, and on the second occasion the contest had been, to use his own words, particularly tough and expensive. The money had been found somehow. If the present administration remained firmly in power, the best he had to expect was an annual expense of some £150 and another election bill within the next seven years. It was a high price to pay for distinction. What had become of the 'solid interests' of which his brother had once reminded him? Charles, it should be observed, contrived, like a man of prudence, to keep his place in spite of all the ins and outs of political parties. He kept it, in fact, for several years to come, and, when he parted with it, took care to get a pension of £1,000 a year—an edifying contrast to the £200 a year with which his father's talents and exertions had been rewarded.

The truth is, Richard Brinsley had got on the wrong side. Two events in particular had put him there in company with other friends of Fox. One of these was his resignation at the time of Rockingham's death. He resigned then because he was personally attached to Fox and entirely believed in his case against Shelburne. This was highly creditable conduct, but he would have done far better for himself if he had stuck to his office, as Keppel and the Duke of Richmond stuck to their places in the Cabinet. The wisdom of Fox's resignation was doubtful, whatever might be thought of it on the score of principle.

The other event was the coalition between Fox and North—that 'ill-omened and baneful alliance,' as Pitt called it. Ill-omened and baneful it certainly was to Sheridan. He himself said that he had opposed it warmly, but, according to Moore, Fox would not be dissuaded, declaring that the thing was 'as fixed as the Hanoverian succession.' Sheridan's word has been doubted. Long afterwards, Lord John Townshend told Lord Holland that he was actually one of the most eager and insistent supporters of the plan, and he poured scorn on the notion that Sheridan had nobly sacrificed his own judgment to the decisions of others. Sheridan's tales on this subject, said Lord John, were mere vapourings and nothing was heard of them until more than a twelvemonth after the thing had taken place. His motives for wanting the coalition were his hatred of Pitt and his eagerness to get into office, and if he had no part in the actual arrangements it was only because nobody had any sort of confidence in him.

Sheridan, however, spoke openly in the House of Commons on the subject in the course of debate on 3rd February 1784—less than a year after the coalition came into office, and less than three months after it went out. He must have been heard by many who knew the facts, and it is hard to believe that he would have ventured, without the slightest necessity, on a completely false assertion in such circumstances. What he said was that when Fox first mentioned the idea of the coalition to him, he advised him by no means to accede to it, as it 'would infallibly produce the loss of his popularity, character, and general estimation'—all which things, to be sure, it already had produced. He added that he now 'rejoiced at it even in contradiction to his own advice,' a piece of loyalty which, considering that the coalition had been driven out of office and was soon to suffer a crushing defeat at the elections, did him credit.

Altogether, it seems likely that he was speaking the truth, and that he really did sacrifice his own judgment to the decisions of others—in particular, of Fox. One thing is beyond dispute: the coalition was a disaster to his fortunes.

Lord John Townshend's account, it should be noted, was not written until 1830, by which time the Whigs had long since given up hearing or speaking any good of Sheridan. It betrays a strong determination to decry the unfortunate and discredited Richard Brinsley, who, by that time, had been fourteen years in his grave. It mentions his influence over Fox, and hints pretty plainly that it was undesirable, and that it was afterwards lost by disloyalty—though Sheridan's loyalty, like Lady Teazle's character, was 'like a person in a plethora,' absolutely dying from too much health. It suggests that he was so eager for office that he would do anything to get into it, though in that case he might have made his fortune in politics. If he liked the emoluments of office, so did others. It was not Sheridan, but Fox, who reminded the House (though the reminder was hardly necessary) that 'in point of fortune my condition is not by any means enviable.' And it was not Sheridan, but Burke, who said: 'I have a family and my means are small. I like my office: the house, the situation, the appendages, cannot be otherwise than pleasing to my taste. . . . Who can conceive that I would lightly sacrifice these objects and £4,000 a year?'

But then, there was no trusting Sheridan's word. He had been known to say, for instance, that Gibbon had first introduced him to Fox, though it was Lord John himself who had done so, soon after *The Rivals* came out. Here the writer was on safer ground. Others had observed that Sheridan did not adhere pedantically to the truth, and the fact is, as Lord Holland expressed it with some delicacy, he did occasionally show a regrettable indifference to it. The failing belonged to his character, and, like his vanity, was designed to meet an ever-present need to put a good face on things; for it must be remembered that he never knew the easy confidence which comes from security: from first to last he was in a false position. The inevitable discrepancy between appearance and reality had to be dealt with somehow, and he managed it with infinite resource, resolution, and courage. The consequence was that he found himself time and again in a situation where truth had become uncomfortable and difficult to the point of impossibility. He understood this himself, but could not, of course, explain it to anybody. What he said and did generally had a kind of artistic honesty, and if it sometimes appeared to have no honesty at all, that was only because the world was so badly ordered that it did not give him his due. He handled truth a little too freely, but not without gallantry and grace. No doubt his courage sometimes took the form of impudence, and his resource might be anything from charm to prevarication; but that could not be helped.

The incongruity appears in his actions, as well as in his words. Over and over again we find examples of it in his life: it is an ingredient in most of the stories about him, and nearly all the things that seem most characteristic of him are flavoured with it. Thus we recall Sheridan trying to cajole Hastings, long after the celebrated trial was over, with the bland assurance that the part he had taken against him was merely political; Sheridan being presented by his friends with numbers of handsome volumes designed to fill the empty shelves of his library—volumes which, like the silver cup given him by his constituents in token of their regard, eventually found their way into pawn; Sheridan, neatly dressed (as he always was) and with his hair carefully powdered, making his way rapidly down the staircase and vanishing out of the front door, leaving behind him two or three rooms full of creditors and others with inconvenient business, who had been waiting hours to see him; Sheridan arriving late for the funeral of his friend Richardson, prevailing on the clergyman to repeat the latter part of the service, dining comfortably at the inn with the funeral party, undertaking zealously to write an inscription for the tombstone—and not writing it[1]; Sheridan on the road from Barnes (where he was in debt to all the tradesmen) to London or Oatlands in a coach which he had hired, and on

[1] This story is related by Moore: the truth of it has been questioned.

which, nevertheless, he had insisted on having his arms painted; Sheridan, the friend of Fox, the generous sympathizer with the aims of the French Revolution, the committee member of the Society of the Friends of the People, writing an additional stanza (entirely worthy of the others) to the National Anthem on the evening when a shot was fired at the royal box at Drury Lane. . . . The list could be extended almost indefinitely out of the incidents of his political and his private life.

In this matter of untruthfulness he bore an odd resemblance to the Prince of Wales, whose favour he enjoyed and valued so much; and in both cases the reasons for the failing were, perhaps, much the same—even to perpetual difficulties about money. Lord Holland tells a delightful and characteristic story of Sheridan's informing him confidentially that a letter which the prince was to send to the king was almost entirely his—Sheridan's —composition, though the prince liked to fancy it was his own. The prince afterwards showed this letter to Lord Holland, observing that Sheridan had originally drawn it up, but that he —the prince—not thinking it satisfactory, had altered and improved it out of all recognition. He appealed to Sheridan, who was standing by, for the truth of this, and Sheridan solemnly nodded assent.

All this helps to explain why there was never much chance that Sheridan would gain the confidence of the body of gentlemen who made up an English political party: such a career as Pitt's was not possible for him. No doubt his birth and circumstances were against him, but far more important was the fact that his qualities, brilliant as they were, were not of the kind to inspire steady confidence. A certain solidity, which is essentially a matter of character, is required for that. Brilliance will not take its place, and dullness is by no means a fatal drawback. It was possible for the mediocre Addington to become Prime Minister, though he was only the son of a physician (to be sure, the great Earl of Chatham was his patient)—it was not possible for Sheridan, any more than it was for Burke. For all his gifts he was never recognized as Fox's second-in-command, and when Fox died it was not Sheridan who succeeded him.

As far as his material fortunes were concerned, it would plainly have been better for him if he had given up politics altogether; but this, of course, was not plain to him. Even if it had been, it is not at all likely that he would have given it up, or that when he reached the end of his career he ever regretted it. It is easy to think of Sheridan, dying miserably in debt, as an awful example of lost opportunity, imprudence, dissipation, and want of principle; but the picture is misleading. He had had too much out of life to see it in that way. He could be magnificently indifferent to his material fortunes—a characteristic which always annoys those who set much store by such things. Political life, in particular, gave him much that he would never have forgone willingly. His speeches won him admiration, and this flattered his vanity; but then, they also won him fame, and the treasury of British eloquence would be the poorer without them. They were quite independent of the success or failure of his party, indeed, they probably gained something by being delivered from the Opposition side of the House. Perhaps the fame was *empty*, as his brother said, but to the Charles Sheridans all fame unaccompanied by solid benefits is apt to seem empty. The truth is, Sheridan's speeches, like his comedies, were manifestations of his artistic powers and satisfied both his need for self-expression and his thirst for applause. They began, significantly enough, when the comedies ceased, and it is easy to find the same touch of genius in both.

§

However, he could no more guess at the interminable years of opposition which lay before him than he could guess at the French Revolution or Napoleon. The present was exciting enough. Having secured his seat at Stafford he came back to town to help Fox in the celebrated Westminster election. In that memorable contest he found himself in gallant and distinguished company. The Prince of Wales supported Fox, and the Duchess of Devonshire and her sister took the field on his behalf. Perdita and Mrs. Armistead likewise appeared in the cause of Fox and

Freedom. The Government brought out Lady Salisbury, but with less success. After a struggle of forty days Fox got the second seat. There was a procession with ostrich plumes, laurels, and banners—one of them bearing the inspiring inscription, *Sacred to Female Patriotism*. At Devonshire House the prince appeared with the leaders of the party—Sheridan among them—and Fox made a short speech. The mob departed to illuminate the town and break Earl Temple's windows. All this, with a magnificent fête on the lawn of Carlton House (which the king had the mortification of beholding as he passed in state on his way to open Parliament) and a banquet at Mrs. Crewe's, had the air of a triumph. It was a hollow one however. The party could think itself fortunate if it mustered sixty votes in a division; and even the election was unsatisfactory, for a scrutiny was demanded and the high bailiff refused to make a return. Fox was obliged meanwhile to appear in the House as member for Orkney, and Pitt congratulated him ironically on the extent to which his fame had spread.

But it was only the fickleness of fortune, and the wheel would surely turn again before long. Pitt had the numbers, but, apart from himself, the talent was all on the other side. Besides, he was young—a fact of which his opponents frequently reminded him, and if he had the support of the king (whom he had delivered from Fox), the Prince of Wales bestowed all his favour on the Opposition, who would have everything to hope for when he came to the throne. George III, it is true, was neither old nor ailing, though the present reign had already lasted twenty-four years. He kept the corpulency, which distinguished the family, at bay, not only by vigorous exercise (which his uncle, the Duke of Cumberland, had feelingly assured him would not produce the desired effect) but also by an abstemious life. Nearly twenty years ago he had had a somewhat mysterious illness, but since then his health had been excellent. The winter draughts at Windsor, where, as Colonel Goldsworthy observed to Fanny Burney, there was wind enough 'to carry a man-of-war,' were regularly too much for the queen and the princesses, to say nothing of their attendants. They dropped off, one after another, 'like so many snuffs of candles'; but these rigours never prevented the king from appearing at early chapel, where the luckless equerry was obliged to *freeze it out* with him. Still, he was not immortal, and in the meanwhile the favour of the heir to the throne was not without its importance.

§

Sheridan's hatred of Pitt, which Lord John Townshend alleged —rather surprisingly—as one of his motives for favouring the luckless union with North, had already produced some clashes. Wraxall thought there was a natural aversion between the pair: if so, it was certainly heightened by the circumstances in which they became political enemies. There was no real difference of principle between them at this time, or for several years to come —indeed, Pitt always called himself a Whig. But if Sheridan found himself constantly on the wrong side, Pitt, whose judgment in matters of political tactics was rarely at fault, was as constantly on the right one. He stood out as the enemy, and Sheridan never ceased to regard him in that light. This did not prevent him, however, from realizing Pitt's remarkable qualities, and from time to time he did full justice to them. He detested the dog, as he said later, but could not help admiring his talents. Just after Pitt's death General Phipps told Joseph Farington that he liked Sheridan because he always used to speak well of Mr. Pitt when the latter was alive. Others waited until he was dead. There is evidence that Pitt, on his side, had a high opinion of Sheridan's abilities, whatever he may have thought of his character. But no quarter was given in debate. At first Pitt imagined he could overbear Sheridan by taking a lofty and superior tone—as he did, for instance, in the debate on the treaty with Holland, only to be answered by Sheridan that 'he wished he would use as high a tone to our enemies.'

Three days later he made a more elaborate attempt in a similar style: 'No man admired more than he did the abilities of that hon. gentleman, the elegant sallies of his thought, the gay effusions of his fancy, his *dramatic turns*, and his epigrammatic points; and if they were reserved for a proper *stage*, they would, no doubt, receive what the hon. gentleman's abilities always did receive, the plaudits of the *audience*; and it would be his fortune *sui plausu gaudere theatri*. But this was not the proper *scene* for the exhibition of these elegancies, and he must therefore call the attention of the House to more serious considerations of public importance.'

This was taking an unfair advantage, and Pitt, young as he was, had an air well calculated to give his irony the most chilling effect. But Sheridan was not the man to be dashed by such methods. Besides, if he had his theatre and his plays, Pitt had his youth: it was tit for tat. He proceeded with the utmost coolness to deal with the freedom which his opponent had allowed himself. 'The propriety, the taste, the gentlemanly point of it, must have been obvious to the House. But let me assure the person who has had recourse to it that whenever he may think proper to repeat such allusions I will meet them with perfect good humour. Nay, more, encouraged by the encomiums bestowed on my talents, should I ever again engage in the occupations to which he alludes, I may, by an act of presumption, attempt to improve on one of Ben Jonson's best characters, the "Angry Boy" in the *Alchymist*.' [1]

The name was long remembered, and Pitt never again ventured on such tactics against Sheridan. 'Both,' declares the admiring Wraxall, 'were the prodigies of the age!'

Here, for the time being, we leave Sheridan's politics in order to see how he fared in his life outside the House. It was the summer of 1784, and he was thirty-two years old.

---

[1] i.e. the (would-be) roistering blade—Kastril, brother of Dame Pliant.

CHAPTER NINE

Richard Brinsley and Elizabeth—Drury Lane Affairs

THERE IS SOMETHING peculiarly attractive in the story of Sheridan's marriage to Elizabeth Linley. It has all the most approved and engaging features of romance—the unhappy heroine, ethereally lovely, delivered by the desperate means of an elopement; the duels, the stolen meetings, the verses exchanged, the secret letters, the sternly forbidding parents, the gallant, high-spirited, and penniless hero. . . . Nothing is wanting. The pair were, as was only proper, extremely young, and their life together was an adventure, crowned, after not too long an interval, with fortune. A brightness seems to lie on it all, delightful to contemplate; and in later years Sheridan sometimes did contemplate it and regret its lost raptures—for this bright thing, like others, came in the course of time to confusion.

Elizabeth, brought so early into public notice and made the object of so much flattering attention and admiration, had no love of these things. There was no vanity in her: success left her unspoiled, and what she longed for above all were the affections and quiet satisfactions of domestic life. She was admirably fitted by her natural refinement and grace—to say nothing of her beauty and talent—to shine in the highest circles, and in fact she did shine there; but it was for a simple life that she had been born, as she told her husband after many years of marriage, and of a life neither simple nor quiet. That was her natural element, and she would be happy in it—if only she could see him contented in it, too. The story that Lady Cork, calling on her one morning in the early days of the marriage, found her cooking a pudding for her as yet undistinguished Horatio, has a pleasant sound.

But she was fated never to have the kind of life she wanted: celebrity—first her own and afterwards her husband's—was her enemy. Richard Brinsley's career was so complicated and uncertain, and, in spite of its brilliance, so unaccountably richer in

MRS. R. B. SHERIDAN AND HER SISTER, MISS LINLEY
From the Painting by Gainsborough.

fame than in fortune, that it was impossible to feel settled. Even when she saw only too clearly that the world and its seductions were ruining both her and her husband, she could not escape, and he, of course, had no wish to do so, the world and its seductions being much to his taste. So she visited the great houses and was admired and courted; and she played whist and even faro and lost her fifteen or twenty guineas with an uneasy feeling that it was all wrong and not in the least what she had expected when she insisted on marrying her dear, obscure Sheridan, whose delicacy and chivalry had won her heart. Extravagance was foreign to her nature, for she had been brought up in a family where thrift was the rule and the value of money was well understood. Her mother would sit in the dark to save a candle, and be vexed a whole day if she lost a few pence at cards.

Yet nobody could have shared more passionately in Richard Brinsley's hopes and successes. Her delight in the triumph of his speech at the trial of Warren Hastings was so keen that she could hardly find words to express it and it actually made her ill. She would take notes for him and copy papers. The reply of the Prince of Wales to Pitt's letter at the time of the regency question was written out carefully by her and signed by His Royal Highness. She watched anxiously over the finances of the theatre and worried over the ruinous charges—particularly the annuities—which her husband's share of that undertaking had to carry. The election expenses of 1790 alarmed her, and she wisely concluded that Sheridan must look elsewhere than to politics for fortune. She brought up her son carefully, and after the death of her sister, Mrs. Tickell, in 1787, took care of her children. She wrote verses, smooth, sweet, sad, irreproachable, and undistinguished, and the sentiments they expressed so unoriginally were really her own.

For a portrait of her and Sheridan as they appeared to a clearsighted observer in 1779, we may turn to Fanny Burney, who, calling on Mrs. Cholmondeley in Hertford Street, found the family at home, 'but who else, think you?—why, Mrs. Sheridan! I was absolutely charmed at the sight of her. I think her quite as beautiful as ever, and even more captivating; for she has now a look of ease and happiness that animates her whole face. Miss Linley was with her; she is very handsome, but nothing near her sister: the elegance of Mrs. Sheridan's beauty is unequalled by any I ever saw, except Mrs. Crewe. I was pleased with her in all respects. She is much more lively and agreeable than I had any idea of finding her; she was very gay and very unaffected, and totally free from airs of any kind.'

They talked about the opera, and Mrs. Sheridan declared she could not hear Pacchierotti without tears. Other callers arrived and eventually 'the door opened and Mr. Sheridan entered.' Miss Burney considered herself in luck, for she had 'more wished to meet him and his wife than any people I know not. . . . Mr. Sheridan has a very fine figure, and a good, though I don't think a handsome face. He is tall and very upright, and his appearance and address are at once manly and fashionable, without the smallest tincture of foppery or modish graces. In short, I like him vastly, and think him every way worthy his beautiful companion.'

It must be confessed that Sheridan took some pains to captivate the authoress of *Evelina*. He praised that novel unsparingly; urged her warmly not to 'suffer her pen to lie idle'; suggested that she should write for the stage, and undertook to accept anything of hers and 'make her a bow and his best thanks into the bargain.' Fanny was not altogether proof against such delightful flattery, but it probably did not seriously affect her judgment. 'And let me tell you,' she adds (the account was written for the benefit of her sister, Susan), 'what I know will give you as much pleasure as it gave me—that by all I could observe in the course of the evening, and we stayed very late, they are extremely happy in each other: he evidently adores her, and she no less evidently idolizes him. The world has by no means done him justice.'

These were comparatively early days: *The School for Scandal* was getting on for two years old, but Sheridan had not yet entered Parliament. He had been married nearly six years. The world, it appears, had already taken occasion to say something, and that something was, as usual, ill-natured; but whether it had done

Richard Brinsley much injustice in reflecting on his constancy to his wife is another matter. That same Mrs. Crewe, the elegance of whose beauty surpassed, in Miss Burney's opinion, even that of Elizabeth, already counted Sheridan among her admirers. He had addressed to her 'with the comedy of *The School for Scandal*,' a highly flattering piece of verse running to 122 lines, which is called *A Portrait*, and on which it is evident that he had bestowed a great deal of care. In this effusion Mrs. Crewe appears as *Amoret*:

> But praising Amoret we cannot err,
> No tongue o'ervalues Heaven, or flatters her!

Amoret is modest, simple, discreet,

> in deportment mild,
> Not stiff with prudence, nor uncouthly wild:
> No state has Amoret, no studied mien;
> She frowns no *goddess*, and she moves no *queen*.
> The softer charm that in her manner lies
> Is framed to captivate, yet not surprise.

Her lips are taught to move by 'Love himself,' and an 'ambush'd Cupid' in her eyes carefully

> Veils and unveils those beams of heavenly light,
> Too full, too fatal else, for mortal sight.

She is 'in mind supreme as well as charm,' and, moreover, 'Read in all knowledge that her sex should reach.' In short, this Amoret, the subject of such hyperbolical praises, is the true image of 'Thee, my inspirer, and my model—CREWE!'

Horace Walpole, to whom these verses were repeated by his nephew, George Cholmondeley, thought them very good. 'Has your ladyship seen them?' he wrote to the Countess of Ossory. 'I trust they will not long retain their MS.-hood.' Mrs. Crewe, no doubt, liked them vastly, and so did her mother, whom the flattering author had ventured to couple in his poem with the *Muse*. He also found room for a graceful allusion to 'Devon's eyes,' which, as every one knew, were remarkably bright, though not more so than Mrs. Sheridan's.

Mrs. Crewe, the daughter of Fulke Greville, who had been

Dr. Burney's patron, was a celebrated beauty, and it was to her, and to 'buff and blue,' that the guests drank at her party after the Westminster election. In the course of time Elizabeth was to write that Mr. Crewe and herself were in the country, and Mrs. Crewe and Sheridan in town, and to inquire of her correspondent, with a half pathetic touch of irony, whether that was not a convenient arrangement. In 1788, Sheridan's younger sister, writing to the elder, remarked that Richard Brinsley had formerly been numbered among Mrs. Crewe's favoured lovers. It is likely, however, that the discreet *Amoret* set reasonable bounds to her favours: at all events, Elizabeth and her husband continued to be visitors at Crewe Hall. Moreover, Sheridan's fame and importance increased greatly as the years passed, whereas Mrs. Crewe merely grew older; for which reason Miss Sheridan concluded that the bond between them was no longer passion.

If Sheridan's marriage, on which fortune had seemed to smile so kindly, came to grief, it was not because of debts, or incompatible tastes, or even the seductions of the world, but simply because he could not be faithful. He was generous by nature, and in many respects had an extreme and inconvenient sense of honour, which, as the Prince of Wales observed, operated persistently to his own disadvantage. In politics he showed a chivalrous inclination to support the cause of the weak and the oppressed, and generally spoke, as Hazlitt thought, on the right side. To his relatives he was unfailingly kind. In 1788 old Thomas Sheridan died at Margate, without having induced the world to set a proper value on his abilities and his labours. Dr. Parr, it is true, composed a handsome, not to say pompous, inscription for a memorial, but the memorial was not erected. The learned doctor described him as 'husband to the ingenious and amiable author of *Sidney Biddulph*,' 'father of the celebrated orator and dramatist, Richard Brinsley Sheridan,' and 'friend of the well-known Dr. Parr'; and concluded that 'in his manners there was dignified ease, in his spirit invincible firmness, and in his habits and principles unsullied integrity.' It was not the favoured Charles, but the reprobate Richard

Brinsley, who came and stood by their father's death-bed and saw to it that 'nothing was omitted that could have prolonged his life or eased his latter hours'; and it was Richard Brinsley who paid the bills. But in love the case was otherwise: there he was as concave as a worm-eaten nut, and incapable of constancy to any woman—even to such a woman as Elizabeth, whose devotion he finally wore out by his infidelities.

And yet, all the while, his affection for her remained, after a fashion, but it was never strong enough to keep him from running after other women. Women, in fact, had an irresistible attraction for him, as if the excitement of pursuing them, and the reassurance of their favours, were necessary to him. He was one of those men, who, like Byron, can never see a woman come into the room without feeling their spirits grow lighter. Sir Gilbert Elliot thought that his gallantries and intrigues were the result of vanity rather than of vice; and Lady Holland remarked shrewdly that they were attempts to compensate for the obscurity of his birth—an interpretation of 'vanity,' which, as far as it goes, is almost certainly correct. Vanity, for that matter, has more to do with love affairs than is generally supposed, and Sheridan's vanity appears in more than one guise; but it always betrays a sense of insecurity, and, perhaps, of injustice.

However, it would be a mistake to conclude from all this that his affairs with women were essentially innocent. Vanity, as well as passion, demands sacrifices from which there is no escaping in honour with the safety of a pure blush; and Sheridan was a man of flesh and blood, and the frailty that goes with them. By 1790, his vagaries, as Elizabeth charitably called them had produced their inevitable effect. She wrote from Crewe Hall to her friend Mrs. Canning that she and her husband would probably arrange a separation on their return to town, and that they had already been separated for some while in the sense that they did not live together as man and wife. Sheridan and herself, she said, were both victims of the snares of the world, and matters had been brought to a crisis by his becoming involved in a love affair with Lady Duncannon. What hurt her, even more than the thing itself, was the deception he had practised—but then, infidelity and deception commonly go hand in hand. This had destroyed all her affection for him, and her happiness as well.

Matters between Sheridan and Lady Duncannon had, in fact, gone so far that the injured husband actually began a suit in Doctors' Commons, and was only induced to withdraw it by the intervention of the Duke of Devonshire. Many a miserable hour did poor Elizabeth spend at Crewe Hall while all this was going on. Sheridan, brought to book, was deeply penitent: he implored her to forgive him, and swore fervently that if ever he gave her the least cause for uneasiness again, he would be ready to endure the most fearful retribution a just heaven could rain on his head—and in the very midst of these prayers and asseverations he was discovered, to the confusion of the entire household, locked in a bedroom in a remote part of the house with the governess.

There is something so preposterous in this episode that morality is all but disarmed, and finds difficulty in keeping its stern features from relaxing into a smile. Even Elizabeth, outraged as she was, could hardly write of it to the virtuous Mrs. Canning with all the solemn denunciations it demanded. It was as if her sense of right and wrong had been bewildered, and she could only speak helplessly of her incorrigible husband's *awkwardness* in being discovered. His entreaties and professions were loudly renewed; the persuasions of Charles Fox and Mrs. Bouverie were added to them, and at last Elizabeth, in spite of everything, consented to forget the past and take him once more into favour, though, as she explained to her correspondent, without feeling the least confidence in anything he said. In consequence they were now going on comfortably together again.

It was a bad world, she observed sadly, and it is true that its morality was lax and its influence entirely opposed to the kind of happiness she needed. She herself did not altogether escape the ill effects of it.[1] Many men admired her. The Duke of

[1] Long afterwards Lady Duncannon (then Bessborough) told Lord Broughton that both Sheridan and Elizabeth were extremely jealous, and when staying at Chatsworth used to cause much amusement by their attempts to get hold of the letter-bag. She added that each of them had fifty lovers—but her ladyship cannot be accepted as a witness against Elizabeth.

Clarence paid her his most gallant attentions, but she had no vanity to be flattered by the addresses of a royal duke who was ten years younger than herself, and he was unable to win her affection. At the time of the unhappy business with Lady Duncannon, when she was exasperated beyond endurance by the complicated faithlessness of her husband, she told Mrs. Canning that if the duke had been thirty-six instead of twenty-six she might perhaps have run away with him; but she added that, if she had done so, she would certainly have hanged herself afterwards. It is impossible to feel anything but relief that she did not succumb to the seductions of His Royal Highness, who, though genial and hearty, was not distinguished, even in his youth, for delicacy of feeling or brilliance of intellect. Forty years later he came to the throne as William IV, and in the meanwhile the place which Elizabeth declined to fill was competently occupied by Mrs. Jordan.

The tragic figure of Lord Edward Fitzgerald came into Elizabeth's life, and perhaps he alone succeeded in touching her heart. After her death he married Madame de Genlis's Pamela, who, it was remarked, bore a strange resemblance in the style of her beauty to Elizabeth. Sheridan likewise, whether for this reason or a less exalted one, was attracted by her. Elizabeth, not long before her death, gave birth to a daughter whom she confided to the care of Mrs. Canning. Whether Lord Edward was the father of this child is impossible to say, but whatever Elizabeth's guilt may have been as the world measures such things, she was guilty in her own eyes and in those of the rigidly correct Mrs. Canning. When the latter touched on this subject to Sheridan, however, he would not hear a word against his wife, declaring that she was an angel, if ever there was one, and that it was all his fault. His heart was tender enough and his contrition was real, but if the dying Elizabeth could have been miraculously restored to health, nothing is more certain than that he would have gone on deceiving her. During her last illness he took her to the Hot Wells at Bristol and stayed devotedly at her side through all the poignant fluctuations characteristic of consumption. She died on 29th June 1792, and was buried in Wells Cathedral. To all appearance Sheridan was heartbroken, but that disease is rarely fatal.

§

When Elizabeth died Sheridan was past forty: his youth had gone and in some respects he had begun to degenerate. In losing her he lost, not only a devoted wife, but also a wise friend whose influence was entirely for his good. It may be doubted, however, whether even she had much effect on the general course of his life, for he was never very amenable to influence, and his career was determined by his own character, and by circumstances which neither he nor she could control.

As yet his affairs were not hopelessly involved, and his debts were not overwhelming, though, no doubt, like the influence of the Crown, they had increased and were increasing. The turn of fortune on which, consciously or unconsciously, he always counted to put everything right, had not yet arrived—but then, it was always going to arrive. In the meanwhile he did not practise the strict economy which might have set his affairs in order. Not that he had any very marked extravagances. He was a member of Brooks's, but he had none of the mania of Fox, Fitzpatrick, and others for gaming, nor did he concern himself with horse-racing. He certainly had a weakness for making bets, and these occasionally involved such sums as £200 and £250. When he lost, they became, of course, debts of honour, to be paid without delay at the expense of more deserving creditors. But Moore's extracts from the betting book at Brooks's belong to 1793, and it is possible that this form of dissipation did not begin until after Elizabeth's death. One road to ruin he did not follow: his love affairs never drained his purse. Nor were his houses (though at one time he had as many as three on his hands) a very important expense. He rented a country house at Isleworth in addition to his town house in Grosvenor Street, but he did not purchase Polesden until after his second marriage, and he was never encumbered with such a burden as the estate which Burke acquired at Beaconsfield, and which cost him £20,000.

Sheridan had, in fact, no obviously ruinous tastes, but there are ways in which large sums of money can disappear without leaving much sign of the manner of their going. An unsettled way of life, a want of due attention to small expenses, an indifference to the unexciting business of keeping accounts, are quite capable of swallowing up even a considerable income. The case of Pitt (whose income was far larger than Sheridan's and had the additional advantage of being fixed and regular) is a good example of this. If Pitt was robbed by his butcher and his tailor, so was Sheridan, and for the same reason. He paid, says Moore in his Journal, 150 per cent on everything he owed. He had more than one temptation to wastefulness and want of order: his income was variable, he had a property which could serve as security, and as long as audiences paid for admission to Drury Lane he could always lay his hands on ready money.

During the years between his entering Parliament and the death of Elizabeth, Sheridan's fondness for wine increased to the point where he habitually drank too much. Public men of all sorts drank heavily at that time, and Wraxall remarks that the Duke of Montrose, who entertained Pitt's Cabinet in 1784 and twenty years later, said that any one of the former drank more than the whole of the latter. In 1788, Sir Gilbert Elliot, referring to the principal men of his own party, told his wife that Fox drank a great deal, though he was considered to be comparatively moderate; Sheridan drank excessively, and the worst of them all was Grey—this, somewhat surprisingly, was the 'high and mighty' Grey (at that time still young) whose airs the Prince Regent was afterwards to find so uncongenial, and who, long surviving Fox and Sheridan, lived to achieve the passing of the Reform Bill.

A year later Sir Gilbert noted that Sheridan's face had become extremely red, and that he had a very ill look. By the time of his second marriage he had, as William Smyth observed, 'entirely destroyed his looks by his intemperance.' His second wife at first thought him a *fright*, but later—such is the power of love—was convinced that he was not only the best but the handsomest of men. Sheridan's habits in the matter of drinking did not

E

mend, but, as might have been expected, grew worse. Lord
Holland thought that, in the later years of his political life, his
habitual drunkenness would, of itself, almost have sufficed to
incapacitate him for high office; and Byron remarked that his
way in society was to get drunk very early and very thoroughly.
'At this time,' says Wraxall in 1784, 'excesses of wine had not
yet eclipsed the fine expression of his face, covered him with
disgusting eruptions, and obtained for him the dramatic nick-
name of Bardolph. The change in him between thirty-three and
sixty was enormous.' At the latter age, indeed, he seemed to
Wraxall like one of Ulysses' companions after drinking Circe's
cup. 'His conduct enfeebled his intellect, produced premature
old age accompanied with diseases and terminating in death.'
But all lives terminate in death and Sheridan was well past sixty
when he died: moreover his intellect was not so enfeebled in
his later years as to prevent Byron from admiring him and
relishing his company.

§

In the absence of political fortune, Sheridan still had to rely
on Drury Lane for his support. No new play was forthcoming
from the manager's pen, for the *Grand Pantomime of Robinson
Crusoe* could hardly be so described, but at times he was heard
to allude confidently to his opera, *The Caravan*, as being shortly
to appear, and to speak of a new comedy on the subject of
Affectation, which, according to him, was 'in great forwardness.'
Nothing was seen of either of these productions, but in other
respects the affairs of the theatre went on favourably enough.
At the beginning of the 1782–3 season Mrs. Siddons returned
to the London stage, and for many a year to come enthralled the
audience at Drury Lane. Even more important was the fact that
her brother, John Philip Kemble, joined the company a year
later. He was engaged at a salary of five guineas a week, which
was five shillings more than he had been getting from Daly at
the Smock Alley Theatre in Dublin—formerly the scene of old
Thomas Sheridan's ill-rewarded labours. In his first season he

appeared fifty-five times, and in the following year his salary was doubled.

Kemble was a conscientious actor with an imposing appearance. He lacked Garrick's wonderful versatility—his style was too stiff and formal to lend itself easily to comedy—but in tragedy he was, in his own way, remarkably effective. His delivery was carefully considered and deliberate—the slowness being partly due to the fact that he was troubled with asthma. It was Sheridan who suggested that the orchestra should play during the pauses. Before long the town accepted his style and he was considered to have outdistanced all rivals except Henderson of Covent Garden.

Boaden, calling on Sheridan one morning, found Kemble waiting in the library. The actor pointed to a pile of manuscripts heaped up on the table and observed that, in these morning attendances, he had read more of those hopeful productions than the proprietor himself—for Sheridan would not allow King, the manager, to accept or reject plays, and had neither leisure nor inclination to attend to that business himself. Sheridan's habit, adds Boaden, referring to the waiting Kemble, 'was to keep his visitors distributed variously, according to their rank or intimacy. Some penetrated into the library; others tired the chairs in the parlours, and the tradesmen lost their time in the hall, the butler's room, and other scenical divisions of the premises. A door opening above stairs moved all the hopes below, but when he came down his hair was dressed for the day and his countenance for the occasion; and so cordial were his manners, his glance so masterly, and his address so captivating, that the people, for the most part, seemed to forget what they actually wanted and went away as if they had come only to look at him.'

Kemble was a man of character, and though he began as a strolling player, had some pretensions to culture. He had been educated at Douay, and had written a tragedy (*Belisarius, or, Injur'd Innocence*) which, though almost entirely devoid of merit, had been acted. He and Sheridan got on well together. They were both given to drinking, and on one occasion the actor, generally remarkable both on and off the stage for extreme dignity, appeared at Lady Cork's in a half-tipsy condition. On another he threw a decanter at Sheridan's head, but this did not impair the cordiality of their relations. Kemble, says Boaden, had a *veneration* for Sheridan.

In 1788 King, the actor-manager, resigned his position, describing it, with some justice, as intolerable. He had no power, though he was expected to shoulder the responsibility. He could not venture to command so much as the cleaning of a coat, or buy a yard of copper lace. He was not allowed to consider new plays which were submitted to the theatre, or to treat with the actors about their salaries. 'If any one asked him, "If he was not the manager, who was?" he would have to reply, "I can't tell."'

Kemble succeeded him and was given more authority, but Sheridan still kept the reins in his own hands. In all matters of money he had the last word, and nothing could be done without him. He depended on the theatre: it was his only source of income and his only means of raising money. The control of it meant everything to him and he dared not part with it. This would have mattered less if he had made the prosperity of the theatre his chief concern, but in fact it was only too often treated as the means of supplying his immediate and pressing needs. The results were unpaid bills, salaries in arrear, and desperate parsimony over expenses—things which were bound to cause endless vexation to the unlucky manager, and which did not improve as time went on. By 1792 Kemble had become bitterly dissatisfied with this state of affairs, and Boaden describes him as waiting one night for Sheridan to come in when the House rose, and meanwhile 'fortifying his wrath and resolution with claret.' At last Sheridan made his appearance, and sitting down next to Mrs. Crouch, regarded Kemble with kindness 'which was neither returned nor acknowledged. The great actor looked unutterable things and occasionally emitted a humming sound like that of a bee, and groaned in the spirit inwardly.' When this had gone on some while, 'at last slowly uprose Kemble, and in these words addressed the astonished proprietor, "I am an EAGLE whose wings have been bound down by frosts and snows; but now I shake my pinions and cleave into the general air unto which I was born!" He then deliberately resumed his seat and looked as if he had relieved himself from insupportable thraldom. Sheridan,' concludes Boaden, 'won him over in two minutes.'

Kemble was an excellent manager, strict, thorough, and regarded by the company with respect. His own preference was for well-established plays, particularly Shakespeare's—Hamlet was his favourite part—and this suited Sheridan, who, though he had no such extreme devotion to Shakespeare, greatly disliked the labour of reading manuscripts. The public showed a commendable readiness to fall in with Kemble's taste, and since they could, for instance, see him as Macbeth and Mrs. Siddons as Lady Macbeth, it is plain that they had no reason to be dissatisfied. The increasing receipts showed the success of Kemble's management: in 1788 they were £29,644; in 1789, £32,750; and in 1790, £39,264, and Kemble himself took careful note of them.[1] About a quarter of the receipts usually remained as clear income after expenses had been paid, but Sheridan, it will be remembered, had only his own share, and that share was burdened with heavy liabilities.

Altogether the theatre was in a prosperous state. It was fortunate in having an extraordinarily strong company, such as Covent Garden—especially since the death of Henderson—could not hope to rival. In 1785 Mrs. Jordan made her first appearance at Drury Lane, and Boaden, recording the fact, adds with remembered delight, 'I seem to hear again the magic of her laugh.' Hazlitt likewise remembered it, and dwelt fondly on the memory. Her attraction was unique, and owed little or nothing to beauty. She was 'neither beautiful, nor handsome, nor even pretty, nor accomplished, nor "a lady," nor anything conventional or *comme il faut* whatsoever,' wrote Leigh Hunt in his Autobiography, 'yet so pleasant, so cordial, so full of spirits, so healthily constituted in mind and body, had such a shapely leg withal, so charming a voice, and such a happy and happy-making expression of

[1] The figures are actually his, as given by Herschel Baker. (*John Philip Kemble*, Harvard University Press, 1942.)

countenance, that she appeared something superior to all those requirements of acceptability, and to hold a patent from nature herself for our delight and good opinion.'

She first appeared as Hoyden—a part which exactly suited her —in 1786. In such characters she would wear 'a bib and tucker and pinafore with a bouncing propriety,' and 'to see her when thus attired shed blubbering tears for some disappointment and eat all the while a great thick slice of bread and butter, weeping and moaning and munching, and eyeing at every bite the part she meant to bite next'—was an experience never to be forgotten. In gentler and more confiding characters she had equally delightful but more winsome ways, and in her cajoling of a refractory husband was 'a whole concentrated world of the power of loving.' All this did not prevent her from being very well able to look after herself. Whenever she thought her salary inadequate she demanded more in such peremptory terms that Sheridan did not venture to refuse her. It is recorded, indeed, that he actually went in fear of her.

Besides Kemble, Mrs. Siddons, and Mrs. Jordan—three stars of extraordinary brilliance—the company included such excellent performers as Wroughton, the two Palmers, Suett, Bannister, Parsons, and Dodd, among the men; and Miss Pope, Miss Decamp, Miss Farren, and Mrs. Crouch, among the women.

In 1791, however, Sheridan's career as a theatre manager (already a tolerably lengthy one) came to a turning-point: the building—Garrick's Drury; the scene of the triumphant first night of *The School for Scandal*; the property of which Sheridan had so adventurously gained control, and which paid the expenses of his parliamentary fame—was condemned, and the last performance in that historic house was given on 4th June. The walls which had echoed to the applause of Garrick were pulled down; the boxes, the chandeliers, the stage which he had trod (except one plank, which Sheridan piously caused to be preserved) were dismantled. To Sheridan, never daunted and invincibly optimistic, it was not disaster but opportunity. A new theatre should arise on the site, a theatre far larger, far more magnificent, than the old one, which, to tell the truth, had very little claim to be described as magnificent: indeed, it struck a foreign visitor as mean and shabby, and very well suited to its unruly and ill-mannered audience. A larger theatre would mean a larger income: there was fortune in it. True, the manager was in no position to finance such an undertaking himself; but the money would be found.

In the meanwhile he had to lease the Opera House in the Haymarket for the next season, and thither the company (destined to exile for nearly three years) duly migrated, not without some damage to the scenery and properties by the way.

CHAPTER TEN

In Opposition—Oratory and Warren Hastings

THE PARLIAMENT WHICH assembled in 1784 with Pitt at its head furnished the world, according to the Whig wits, with the remarkable sight of 'a kingdom trusted to a schoolboy's care.' The Whigs, indeed, tired their ingenuity in satirizing their victorious opponent for his youth, writing of him as 'the infant Atlas' and 'the new Octavius'; and for his stiff and haughty manner ('solemn dignity and sullen state'). They even reflected on his seeming indifference to the charms of the fair sex, attributing it uncharitably to impotence; and Sheridan, who was not open to any reproach on this score, was once heard to remark when Pitt entered the House: '*Jam redit et virgo!*'

The earliest of their political satires was *The Rolliad*, so named in ridicule of Mr. John Rolle ('Great Rollo's heir') one of the members for Devonshire. Rolle, an awkward character with whom Sheridan had more than one encounter, had made himself obnoxious to the Whigs, and was well armoured against their shafts by a certain respectable and prickly dullness. He was subsequently raised to the peerage. *The Rolliad* dealt with several members of the Government—Grenville, Dundas, and Thurlow, for instance—besides Pitt. Fitzpatrick was among the contributors, but Sheridan, by his own account, was not. The Opposition, in fact, had all the wit on their side, and nearly all the talent. Their attack was headed by Fox, Burke, Sheridan, Windham, and Grey—a remarkably brilliant company, in comparison with whom the ranks behind Pitt looked drab and commonplace. 'Of Mr. Fox's adherents,' wrote Brougham long afterwards, '. . . the most remarkable certainly was Mr. Sheridan, and with all his faults and all his failings and all his defects, the first in genius and the greatest in power.'

Pitt's own reputation stood very high, and the period between 1784 and the outbreak of the war with France nearly ten years later was the most splendid and successful part of his career.

He inspired confidence, and confidence was what the nation, now at peace after an exhausting and humiliating war, needed above all. He had the support of the king, as well as of the country, and virtuous denunciations of secret and backstairs influence had lost their old effect. As to Fox, he was so thoroughly discredited by the coalition and the prejudice stirred up against his unlucky India Bill, that Pitt was in no more danger of being turned out to make way for him and his friends than Charles II had been, a century earlier, of being murdered for the purpose of putting his brother on the throne.

Fox and his supporters attacked the Government with admirable spirit and persistence. They were the Opposition: it was their duty to oppose, and they discharged that duty faithfully and with zeal. Sooner or later they would be in office themselves. Nobody showed more zeal and devotion than Sheridan. 'He was a first-rate speaker,' said Brougham, 'and as great a debater as a want of readiness and need for preparation would permit.' But if he lacked Fox's extraordinary readiness in debate, his attacks were highly effective and Pitt did not venture to leave them unanswered. Indeed, in Wraxall's opinion, Pitt feared Sheridan a great deal more than he did Fox; and in one respect, at least, he had good reason to do so, for Sheridan's armoury included the terribly destructive weapon of ridicule.

Pitt's financial genius was generally regarded with a respect which did not fall far short of reverence, but Sheridan never hesitated to attack him on this ground. Indeed, he went out of his way to engage him there. If the spectacle of the impecunious manager of Drury Lane Theatre challenging the estimates of William Pitt in the matter of the national income and expenditure seems to approach the comic, it is only fair to recollect that neither the one nor the other was conspicuously successful in balancing his private budget. Between 1785 and 1789 Sheridan spoke at least seventeen times on financial subjects, attacking Pitt's figures and his policy, and not even sparing the sacred and celebrated Sinking Fund, which, like the scheme of Hogarth's bankrupt enthusiast in the debtor's prison, was to pay off the debts of the nation. In one speech he 'dissected every

* E

proposition' of the minister 'with great financial ability,' basing his arguments carefully on statistics. In another, concerning a tax on cottons, he declared that he had been in Lancashire and had seen for himself the distress there. The egregious Mr. Rolle here intervened to say darkly that a person had been in Lancashire stirring up tumult and distributing seditious handbills, and that 'if he could bring the proof home to the party whom he suspected, he would take proper steps to have his head stuck on Temple Bar.'

Sheridan modestly replied that 'he knew nothing of handbills, and thought that possibly the gentleman had been irritated not so much by prose compositions, *as by some in verse*—in which, however, he (Sheridan) had had no hand whatever.' At this allusion to *The Rolliad* there was a general laugh. Rolle repeated his threat, and this time Sheridan, changing his tone, replied that 'if the gentleman charged him with having any concern in circulating seditious handbills, he should reply to him, both there and elsewhere, in very plain and coarse terms.' On this Rolle retired from the encounter.

Sheridan, assiduous in his attention to his duties in Parliament (though less so in attending to those concerned with his theatre), figured prominently in nearly all the important debates. He spoke on the Westminster Scrutiny, which Pitt was eventually obliged to give up; and on Pitt's India Bill, to which twenty-three new clauses were to be added, designated by the letters, A, B, C, . . . Sheridan *hoped some gentleman would come forward with three more clauses, to make up the minister's horn-book.* 'The old clauses, now left out, are known by being in black-letter, where, to be sure, they stand in mourning for the folly of their parents.' He concluded by declaring that he 'relied on the candour of the minister to re-commit the bill, that it might be divested of its slovenly dress and made conformable to common-sense—even if its principles were to be divested of common justice.'

A long speech of his on the Irish Propositions led to a sharp brush with Pitt ('the debates this session were conducted with a great deal of acrimony'); and, dealing with the question of the fortification of the dockyards at Portsmouth and Plymouth, he ridiculed the Duke of Richmond—once a colleague, but now Master-General of the Ordnance—unmercifully, and handled the minister himself without ceremony. Wraxall thought that this speech was one of the most splendid exhibitions of genius which he had witnessed since he sat in Parliament.

The exertions of the Opposition, however, did not bring them appreciably nearer the desired haven of office. Pitt had his reverses, but his position remained unshaken. The question of India now came uppermost. In June 1785 a middle-aged man, bald, thin, and not very tall, landed at Plymouth after a voyage from Calcutta so favourable that it lasted only four months. He was Warren Hastings, the late governor-general.

§

Hastings's great services in India, which served indirectly to enhance the fame of Sheridan, were performed in difficult circumstances. His own council thwarted him, and one member of it—Philip Francis, chiefly remembered as the supposed author of the *Letters of Junius*—was his bitter and dangerous enemy. The quarrel culminated, as is well known, in a duel, and Calcutta was given the unedifying example of the governor-general and a member of the council meeting with pistols, as they might have done at home at Chalk Farm or on Wimbledon Common. Francis was wounded, and when he came back to England he brought his hatred with him undiminished, together with a fortune of £80,000 accumulated in the short space of six years.

Two committees of inquiry investigated the affairs of India, and the governor-general was severely censured. A resolution to recall him was carried in the House of Commons, but the proprietors of the company refused to act on it. He resigned of his own accord in 1785 and returned to England, where he was well received in Leadenhall Street and likewise at court. His wife, too—his 'elegant Marian'—who had come home before him, had been shown marked favour by the queen, though she had been set free from her former husband by a divorce. Her Majesty, indeed, had been graciously pleased to accept the gift of an ivory bed from her, which caused Burke to observe that the queen had only one virtue—decorum, and only one vice—avarice, but that the vice had proved too strong for the virtue. Mrs. Hastings, however, was not looked on with so much favour in society, the ladies disliking her fashion of wearing her hair unpowdered.

Four days after Hastings returned to England, Burke, who had studied the question of India with his usual thoroughness, and whose ear had been gained by the rancorous Francis, rose in the House to give notice that he would bring forward a motion on the late governor-general's administration. It was not until the middle of the following February, however, that he opened the attack, for justice, throughout this case, moved with majestic deliberation.

The details of the proceedings do not concern us, but one assertion made by Scott, Hastings's agent, whose activities commonly showed more zeal than discretion, is of interest. Scott declared that, in 1783, an offer had been made to give up all intention of proceeding against the governor-general if he would support the Government—which was then the Fox-North Coalition. Fox denied this flatly, but Scott persisted, and it transpired that Sheridan had made some such advance and had sent an agent to Scott. Sheridan admitted the fact but denied that he had had the least idea of 'bartering impunity for support.' He said he had questioned his agent on this point and had been assured that no such suggestion had been made. The agent, he added, had now given a similar assurance to Scott, who was obliged to admit that this was the case, though he observed that he had had a different impression at the time. The assurance, of course, proved nothing, but Scott seems to have been bewildered by Sheridan's plausible explanation. Fox rose and expressed his satisfaction (though he could hardly have felt any) that the misunderstanding had been cleared up, 'but,' remarks Wraxall, 'some very natural incredulity was felt by others.'

It is impossible to avoid sharing this incredulity, for Sheridan's explanation, though ingenious, is not convincing. The significance of the incident lies in the fact that it shows him taking a line of his own before he had been three years in Parliament. This tendency brought him under suspicion in the years to come. As the Duchess of Devonshire noted in the diary which Sichel printed in his *Sheridan*, he never could resist the temptation to play a sly game: she acquitted him handsomely, however, of anything like treachery. His real motive, in fact, was nothing worse than vanity, which, as we have already seen, was apt to bring him into awkward situations and lead to a regrettable sacrifice of the truth.

To return to Hastings—in April Burke produced charges whose mere bulk made it appear that a man accused of so much could not possibly be entirely innocent. At the beginning of May, Hastings was heard in his own defence, but the House found his speech dull. It was read, now by himself, and now (when his voice failed) by a clerk. It was long—but not so long as the charges. A month later Burke moved the first charge, which was defeated, Pitt voting against it. The second, however, brought forward by Fox, was carried by a majority of forty. On this occasion, Pitt, though he attacked part of Fox's argument, concluded that Hastings had acted 'in an arbitrary and tyrannical manner,' and, to the astonishment of his supporters, he voted in favour of the motion. The impeachment might now be considered a foregone conclusion.

The House rose, and it was not until the new year that the third charge came forward. It concerned the Begums of Oude, and was moved by Sheridan on 7th February 1787. This was the occasion of his famous speech which began about half-past six and ended at midnight; and the subject was the same as that on which, nearly eighteen months later, he gave to a brilliant and crowded assembly in Westminster Hall, 'that display of genius,' to use the words of Gibbon, 'which blazed four successive days.'

§

Every one knows that Hastings was acquitted in the end, and there is a natural tendency, therefore, to suppose that the charges against him were unfounded—which was not altogether the case. The eloquence of Sheridan cannot induce any one now to shed tears over the woes of the Begums, though, to be sure, the sufferers were not only women, but princesses—two powerful incentives to sympathy. Even if they had been fortunate enough to possess the further qualifications of youth and beauty, it is doubtful if we should much care whether Hastings had grievously oppressed them or not. Probably few people know what, precisely, the case against the governor-general was, for it is as true now as it was in Macaulay's time that the English feel only the most languid interest in the affairs of India, and that 'even gentlemen of highly cultivated minds' cannot be relied on to know 'who won the battle of Buxar, who perpetrated the massacre of Patna, whether Sujah Dowlah ruled in Oude or in Travancore, or whether Holkar was a Hindoo or a Mussulman.'

The facts of the case, which moved Sheridan to apostrophize the Great God of Justice in the House of Commons, and to dwell upon the subject of Filial Piety in Westminster Hall, were, in brief, these:

The Begums were the mother and the grandmother of the Vizier of Oude. In 1781 the vizier was heavily in debt to the company, his payments being in arrear. The situation in India was critical: Hyder Ali had overrun the Carnatic, and Hastings was in desperate need of money. He himself had recently been in grave danger in Benares, where he had gone to call the rajah, Chait Singh, to account for failing to comply with his demands. An insurrection had broken out and the rajah, whom Hastings had imprisoned in his palace, had contrived to escape. These matters, it should be observed, formed the subject of the second charge—which Fox moved, and for which Pitt voted.

The vizier, unfortunately, could not supply the money required: he declared he was unable, not only to pay what he owed, but even to continue to maintain the company's troops which were stationed in his dominions. These were the circumstances in which Hastings turned his mind to the treasure of the Begums, which had been amassed by the late vizier and had come into the possession of his widow and his mother after his death. The present vizier, in return for £500,000, had granted the ladies the unquestioned right to keep the remainder —an agreement which received the due approval of the company.

In September 1781 the governor-general concluded a treaty with the vizier, providing, among other things, that the latter was to take the rest of the treasure—which would enable him to pay the company. Hastings justified this by accusing the Begums of having been concerned in the insurrection at Benares.

It is doubtful if there was any truth in this accusation: no reliable proof of it exists, and the Begums themselves naturally protested their entire innocence. On the other hand the officer commanding the company's troops in Oude declared he believed it to be true, and so did Middleton, the resident—described later by Sheridan as *prevarication personified*. Very likely, in such a case, nothing like complete proof was to be expected. Hastings apparently felt that his proceedings might be called in question. He took the unusual course of sending for the chief justice, Sir Elijah Impey, to collect affidavits—a move which added nothing to the weight of the evidence, and gave rise to suspicion.

The vizier showed considerable reluctance to seize the treasure, but did so at last under pressure from Hastings, who threatened to come in person. The palace of the Begums was occupied, the household was put under arrest, and the ladies were confined to their quarters. The eunuchs in charge of the treasure were imprisoned, but before they could be made to give the required information they had to be put in fetters and tortured.

Such, in barest outline, were the facts on which Sheridan built his case, and it is plain that, at the very least, they justified strict inquiry. In many of its essentials the story he unfolded was true. A son had, at the governor-general's instigation, outraged 'filial love, the morality of instinct, the sacrament of nature and duty'; a chief justice had condescended 'to execute the functions of a pettifogging attorney, running up and down the country ferreting out affidavits and carrying them upon his shoulders in a bundle like a pedlar with his pack'; an agreement had been broken; and the eunuchs, whose chief crime was fidelity to their mistresses, had been fettered and put to the torture.[1] Hastings, it is true, might have pleaded necessity. He might also have

---

[1] It is said that one of them was still alive, and in prosperous circumstances, twenty years later—from which it has been inferred that the torture was not very severe.

claimed that his extraordinary services should be set off against any harsh measures he had felt obliged to use, and that he had done nothing for his own gain. Actually, he believed in and asserted his entire innocence: what he had done was right. Sheridan's view of the matter was that of Burke, Fox—and Francis, and there is no reason to doubt that he fully believed in the case he presented. He was sincere, but it was no business of his to be impartial: he was an advocate, not a judge. To some extent he imitated Burke in the extravagant violence of his denunciations, but nobody could deny that there had been oppression in India, and, as he saw it, he was speaking on the right side.

§

His speech in the House lasted upwards of five hours, and was delivered with such fluency that one hearer reckoned that, if it had been read, it would have lasted twice as long. The report of it is meagre,[1] occupying only nineteen octavo pages, but it is not likely that the world has thereby lost anything which it would have prized very highly. The effect of oratory is immediate, and depends on the occasion, the voice, and the audience. If the best speeches of Burke seem to be exceptions to this rule, it is because, in reading them, we do not think of the voice (which was unpleasant) or the audience (which was only too often bored) but of the splendour of the prose, the force of the intellect, and the flashes of universal truth. Sheridan had no deep truths to utter and his sublime passages hardly bear warming up. They had their appeal at the time, and it is certain that he was heard with emotion when he exclaimed, 'Great God of Justice! canst thou, from thy eternal throne, look down upon such premeditated outrages and not affix on the perpetrators some signal mark of divine displeasure!' But the words will never make the *bone rise* in any one's throat again.

Nevertheless, Sheridan's achievement was brilliant: it was

---

[1] 'Mr. Sheridan now rose and, during the space of five hours and forty minutes, commanded the attention and admiration of the House by an oration of almost unexampled excellence. . . .' It was impossible to attempt more than an outline of the speech— 'a miniature of an unequalled original.' (*Parliamentary History*, xxvi. 275.)

oratory in the grand manner—a kind of performance not particularly well suited to his special talents. Nor was the subject one which lent itself to the strokes of satire and the play of fancy which delighted his hearers so often on less momentous occasions. Here and there he introduced something of the sort (he described Hastings, for instance, as 'a man holding in one hand a bloody sceptre, while with the other he was employed in picking pockets'), but in the main his appeal was to the emotions and the keynote of his speech was righteous indignation. Five hours is a long time, and his audience, never notable for patience, had an easy remedy against dullness: the subject was complicated and unfamiliar, but he was heard with rapt attention from first to last, and concluded with an overwhelming climax.[1]

A good deal has been said already of the tributes paid to this speech. In some ways the most notable was Pitt's (for Pitt was not by any means given to enthusiasm, and had no reason to love Sheridan)—'A more able speech has, perhaps, never been pronounced.'[2] Able it must have been, and not merely brilliant. Like nearly all Sheridan's best work it was the result, not of effortless talent, but of careful labour joined to a quality, which, at its highest, deserves the name of genius.

The House having adjourned so that the debate should not be continued in so heated an atmosphere, the motion was carried on the following day by 175 to 68. Sheridan later had the task of opening the seventh charge, which concerned bribery, but on this occasion he did not feel called upon to rival his previous flight of eloquence.

A committee was appointed to prepare articles of impeachment: it consisted of twenty members, Burke, Fox, Sheridan, Grey, and Windham being among them. Burke tried to get Francis chosen, but the House rejected him: it was not easy to decide whether 'his own impudence in offering to serve, or Burke's perverse want of decency in putting his name forward,

[1] '. . . the whole House, the members, peers, and strangers, involuntarily joined in a tumult of applause.' (*Parliamentary History*, conclusion of report.)

[2] 'As we have not, for want of room, entered into a detail of this business, we shall only observe here, that Mr. Sheridan's speech was acknowledged on all sides of the House to be the most astonishing effort of eloquence, argument, and wit united, of which there is any record or tradition.' (*Gentleman's Magazine*, March 1787.)

was the greater.' In May Burke moved 'that Warren Hastings, Esquire, be impeached of high crimes and misdemeanours,' and Frederick Montagu followed with the motion that Mr. Burke, 'in the name of the Commons, do go to the bar of the House of Lords and impeach Warren Hastings.' The stage was thus set for the great trial in Westminster Hall, in one scene of which Sheridan enjoyed the most spectacular triumph of his life.

§

The trial began in the following year (1788) on 13th February. The hall, hung with scarlet and 'pervaded by a damp, cold vapour,' was crowded by ten o'clock in the morning, and just before midday the managers of the prosecution entered, headed by Burke, who walked alone, carrying a scroll in his hand. 'His brow,' observed Miss Burney, 'was knit with corroding care and deep labouring thoughts.' After him came Fox, then Sheridan, relishing keenly, no doubt, the solemn pageantry and the conspicuous part he was playing in it, and very likely recalling the days long ago at Harrow when he had to stand close by the master's desk so that his grammar might receive much-needed attention. Even now, his satisfaction was not entirely unalloyed, for, as Lord Holland told Moore (who recorded the information in his Journal), 'it went to Sheridan's heart to see Burke in the place set apart for Privy Councillors, himself excluded.' But Sheridan, in Lord Holland's opinion, was always jealous of Burke.

The preliminaries (which the audience found tiresome) lasted two days, and then Burke opened the charges in general. He spoke for four days, his passionate eloquence producing a great effect and proving too much for the acute sensibility of Elizabeth. 'I impeach Warren Hastings,' he concluded, 'of high crimes and misdemeanours.' He impeached him in the name of the Commons of Great Britain in Parliament assembled, whose trust he had betrayed; in the name of the entire nation, whose ancient honour he had sullied; in the name of the people of India, whose rights he had trodden under foot, whose property he had destroyed, and whose country he had turned into a desert; in the name of the eternal laws of justice which he had broken. . . .

And lastly, rising to an impassioned and overwhelming climax, he impeached him in the name of human nature itself, of which he declared the late governor-general to have been the enemy and oppressor without respect of sex, age, rank, or condition in life.

§

On 3rd June, the thirty-second day of the trial, Sheridan's turn came. For months past expectation had run high: the eagerness to hear him was so great that tickets were sought for by all possible means and as much as £50 was paid for a seat. The fame of his earlier speech had spread, and he was faced with the exacting task of making another on the same subject. Fox's opinion was that, there being no possibility of surpassing the former, Sheridan's best course was to repeat it, but this advice did not commend itself to Richard Brinsley. He determined to deliver an entirely new speech—one, moreover, which should not be on a less imposing scale than Burke's.

On the night of 2nd June, many people, including ladies, slept at coffee-houses in the neighbourhood so as to be sure of reaching the door of the Hall in time—a precaution which proved not unreasonable, for before half-past six next morning Palace Yard was crowded. As soon as the door was opened there was a lively struggle for admission, in the course of which several ladies lost portions of their attire. Shoes were the articles most frequently separated from their owners, and a number of fair enthusiasts went in barefoot. Others wore odd shoes which they had managed to pick up in the crush. The lady whom Sir Gilbert Elliot was escorting saved her shoes but lost her cap. Having secured their seats the audience had three hours to wait.

In this atmosphere of excited anticipation, more appropriate, perhaps, to Drury Lane than to Westminster Hall, Sheridan rose to begin his speech. He spoke from the manager's box, with Burke on his left and Hastings, in a separate box, on his right. Before him, in the middle of the hall, was a long table, at which sat the judges, with the Lord Chancellor at the head. Beyond were the peers, and behind them rose the throne flanked by the boxes of the queen and the Prince of Wales. The green benches to the left were occupied by the Commons, irreverently described by Lady Charlemont as 'creatures looking so little like gentlemen and so much like hairdressers.' From all these places, and from the crowded galleries, eyes were turned expectantly upon Richard Brinsley, and it is not likely that any one ever lived who was better fitted to appreciate the position.

He was nervous at the beginning, and at times he was heard with difficulty. Elizabeth, watching with anxious devotion and trembling sympathy, suffered with him, and once, when his memory failed him entirely for a few moments, was overcome with terror. He recovered himself and spoke on, and the audience listened with growing emotion and admiration, as they had listened to Burke. Altogether he spoke four and a half hours on the first day. On 6th June he continued, and again on the 10th, but in the course of his remarks on that day 'Mr. Sheridan was taken ill' and the court adjourned until the 13th, when he brought the speech to a triumphant conclusion in the style which seems to have been thought appropriate to the impeachment, using hyperbole and climax in the manner of Burke. The peers, he exclaimed, were exhorted to give due weight to the evidence brought before them, 'by everything that calls sublimely upon the heart of man, by the majesty of that justice which this bold man has libelled, by the wide fame of your own tribunal, by the sacred pledge by which you swear in the solemn hour of decision; knowing that the decision will then bring you the highest reward that ever blessed the heart of man, the consciousness of having done the greatest deed of mercy for the world that the earth has ever yet received from any hand but Heaven.—My lords, I have done.' And the orator sank back into the arms of Burke, who assisted him to his chair. The sceptical Gibbon remarked that he called upon the invalid next day and found him *perfectly well*. 'What an actor!' he added. But Gibbon (to whom Sheridan paid a handsome compliment in the course of his speech) confessed that 'Mr. Sheridan's eloquence commanded my applause,' and spoke of it as a 'display of genius.'

Sir Gilbert Elliot likewise described the speech as admirable, and a 'wonderful effort of genius.' He considered that Sheridan was at his best on the fourth day, causing the future governor-general of India to cry more heartily than he had ever done before on a public occasion—but for that matter he believed there were very few dry eyes to be found in the assembly. Burke delivered a panegyric in his own magnificent manner to the House of Commons, declaring that 'of all the various species of oratory, of every kind of eloquence that had been heard in ancient or modern times; whatever the acuteness of the Bar, the dignity of the Senate, or the morality of the Pulpit could furnish, had not been equal to what the House had that day heard in Westminster Hall.'

But the most human tribute, and the most moving, came from Elizabeth, who, within two years, was to come near to separating completely from her adored Horatio. 'It is impossible, my dear woman,' she wrote to her sister-in-law, 'to convey to you the delight, the astonishment, the adoration, he has excited in the breasts of every class of people!' She went on to dwell rapturously on his 'genius, eloquence, and *goodness.*' 'But pleasure too exquisite,' she concluded, 'becomes pain, and I am at this moment suffering for the delightful anxieties of last week.'

In short, it was a public triumph of the most complete kind. Sheridan had longed for distinction—he had it now, and of the kind which brings immediate gratification, delightfully strong and not too delicate. He was entitled to be described as 'the celebrated orator and dramatist.' His fame and importance, which had been increasing steadily, had reached, in Moore's opinion, their highest point. To be sure, his solid interests had not been advanced correspondingly: he had to feel himself sufficiently rewarded with fame and the consciousness of having done his duty. Not a penny the richer was he for setting forth with such generous eloquence the woes of the Begums and the iniquity of Hastings, Impey, and Middleton. He might have made a very handsome sum by preparing the speech for the press, but he did nothing of the kind. The speech, however, was reported fully, if not with perfect accuracy. By some it was considered to be inferior to his previous one, and Sir Gilbert Elliot, who

heard and admired both, thought that Sheridan was a little
hampered by his resolve not to repeat the earlier performance.
He also thought that the fine passages were a little too obvious
and laboured, and that, unlike Burke's, they did not seem to
belong naturally where they occurred. Nobody who reads the
speech is likely to quarrel with this criticism, but the fine
passages are, after all, only a small proportion of the whole.
For the rest, the eager ladies who struggled in shoeless were an
unimportant part of the assembly: Sheridan's facts and arguments were submitted to lords, judges, lawyers, and commons,
who were not likely to be much impressed by empty rhetoric,
or even to put up with it patiently for twelve hours and more.

The trial does not much concern us beyond this point. Public
interest came to a climax with Sheridan's speech, after which it
waned rapidly. The trial itself dragged on year after year, to
the affliction of the accused and the weariness of every one else
except Burke, to whom the prosecution was a sacred duty, like a
crusade. The procedure was cumbrous, and the court necessarily
unable to meet regularly. The actual time taken was 142 days,
but these were spread over seven years. Sheridan's interest
slackened and had to be stimulated by Burke, who appealed to
Elizabeth for that purpose. Richard Brinsley was heard, indeed,
to wish that Hastings would fly the realm with Burke yelping
at his heels. In 1794 Joseph Farington looked in at the trial
and found very few of the Commons present, and only a score
or so of the Lords. The formality of dress, so strictly observed
at first, was no longer regarded: he saw Grey in the manager's
box, wearing boots and spurs.

On 14th May 1794 Sheridan was called on to reply on the
Begums charge. As he had to deal with the evidence given at
the trial, the minutes of that evidence should have been carried
into court in a bag for his use. Sheridan, however, preferred to
rely on his memory. He allowed the bag to be called for several
times, as if he fully expected it to be there, and Mr. Michael
Angelo Taylor (who should have had charge of it) had to whisper
to Fox, who was becoming agitated: 'The man has no bag!'

But Sheridan had prepared his reply thoroughly, and made a

most able speech. He dealt very severely with Law, a counsel for Hastings, who had accused him of conducting the examination of Middleton unfairly. He also quoted from the Psalms and from *The Faerie Queene.* Burke delivered a final oration which lasted nine days in all and the verdict was given nearly a year later—April 1795. Hastings was acquitted on every charge, the minority never exceeding six, and only reaching that number on the charges concerning Benares and the Begums.

The trial was over at last and much had happened while it was going on. When it began Thurlow was Chancellor: when it ended, Loughborough (who, long ago, when he was plain Alexander Wedderburn, had had the benefit of lessons in elocution from old Thomas Sheridan) had taken his place. Of the peers who were present at the beginning, about a third had died before the end. Elizabeth, whom the eloquence of Burke and Richard Brinsley had affected so much, had been three years in her grave when the trial closed; there was now another Mrs. Sheridan, whose name was Esther Jane. In the course of the impeachment the Theatre Royal, Drury Lane, was pulled down and rebuilt; the king went mad and recovered; the Prince of Wales very nearly became Regent and Sheridan very nearly became Treasurer of the Navy with an official residence in Somerset House; the French Revolution began; Louis XVI and his queen were executed; war broke out between Great Britain and France; and Burke publicly separated himself in politics from Sheridan and Fox.

In one respect, however, there had been no change. When the trial began, Sheridan was in opposition: he was still in opposition when it ended.

CHAPTER ELEVEN

Sheridan and the Prince of Wales—Regency Crisis: Hope deferred

THE CHARACTER OF the Prince of Wales, afterwards Prince Regent and finally George IV, has not found many admirers. Sheridan was acquainted with him, more or less closely, for thirty years, and the connection has often been regarded unfavourably, as one which did very little good to him and no particular credit to His Royal Highness.

At the outset, Sheridan, then beginning to make a considerable figure in the Whig party, had wit and charm of manner to recommend him. The prince, though not distinguished for wisdom, was a man of intelligence, and there was an artistic strain in him together with a good deal of sensibility—and even generosity, though it usually got no farther than his feelings. He admired Sheridan and found him congenial: he could be easy in his company as he could not be in that of such men as Fox and Grey. It must be admitted that some of Richard Brinsley's failings bore a distinct resemblance to those of the heir to the throne, and this, no doubt, made a bond of sympathy between them.

'He was a great man,' the prince told Peter Moore, but too ready to place confidence in others. He was very willing to grant favours, but not to accept any, in case it should be imagined that he had parted with his independence. Altogether, he was a *proud man*, with certain 'conscientious scruples' which perpetually made against his own interests. This is a shrewd judgment as far as it goes, and there is no reason to doubt the accuracy, or for that matter the sincerity, of the prince's description of Sheridan as 'a firm friend and a sound adviser.'

Sheridan was always fiercely jealous of his independence: it was a point of honour with him to cherish it at all costs, even though his general reputation might be in tatters. It had to be above suspicion, and nobody must be allowed to suppose for a moment that he had been, or could possibly be, bought by any person or any party. An example of this occurred in 1795, when, speaking on the subject of the prince's debts, he felt called upon to declare 'in the face of the House and of the country, that he had never received from the Prince of Wales so much as the present of a horse or of a picture'—an assurance in which the House and the country perhaps took no great interest.

He did, however, take money from the prince later, for the benefit of his son Tom, and in 1804 the prince gave him the receivership of the Duchy of Cornwall (which, as it turned out, had already been promised elsewhere, so that Sheridan did not get the profit of it for some time to come) 'as a trifling proof of that sincere friendship which His Royal Highness has always professed and felt for him through a long series of years.' To this the prince added an informal sentence which did honour to his feelings, 'I wish to God it was better worth your acceptance' —its value varied between some £800 and £1,200 a year. Sheridan, informing Addington of the gift, was careful to point out that it was not 'the result of a mean and subservient devotion to the prince's every wish and object.'

Long after Sheridan's death the prince told Croker (though, as he said, he felt a natural delicacy in mentioning the matter) that Sheridan had had, at one time and another, as much as £20,000 from him. The prince's word (like that of Richard Brinsley himself) is not to be invariably relied on, but taking everything into consideration, the figure is probably not much exaggerated.

However, there was nothing of the sycophant about Sheridan. He could disarm an importunate creditor and wheedle money out of an attorney, but he could not be suspected of playing the part of a flatterer, even to the heir apparent. His attachment to the prince was genuine and essentially disinterested, and he was far too proud to presume on the intimacy. Nevertheless, the connection, though it was described by both parties as 'friendship,' was bound to require a certain deference on his side, and neither he nor any one else was the prince's friend in the full sense of the word. No delicacy and no independence could altogether do away with a sort of obligation, any more than it could do away with the difference of rank or the value which Sheridan undeniably set upon the prince's confidence.

On one occasion, at least, he was driven to express this in a letter. 'It is a matter of surprise to myself,' he wrote, 'as well as of deep regret, that I should have incurred the appearance of ungrateful neglect and disrespect towards the person to whom I am most obliged on earth, to whom I feel the most ardent, dutiful, and affectionate attachment, and in whose service I would readily sacrifice my life.' He went on to give a long and somewhat involved explanation of a misunderstanding caused by some words which he had been told—untruthfully—the prince had used about him; the consequence of which was that he (Sheridan) had kept away. He concluded by referring warmly to the 'attachment I feel, and to my death shall feel, to you, my gracious Prince and master.' This belongs to Sheridan's later years, and perhaps the writing of it caused him some pain—it is hard to avoid feeling some in reading it.

The truth is, the prince's favour was important to Sheridan, who needed, above all, support and consequence. Between him and such men as Fox, Grey, Windham, and Fitzpatrick there was an essential difference: they were privileged and he was not. He might have been accepted by them as a sort of poor relation, but from first to last the place he claimed and took was that of an equal. This accounts in part for his 'conscientious scruples' about receiving favours, which Lord Holland, like the prince, noticed. Indeed, Sheridan was apt to regard as an enemy any one who did him a considerable favour. But no amount of independence could do away with the disadvantages against which he had to struggle. They arose not only from his birth (though it was undesirable to have a poor player for a father) but also from the fact that he depended for his livelihood on his management of Drury Lane. Even as an ordinary member of Parliament he was, as we have seen, exposed to rebuffs on this account.

In political life, therefore, and particularly among the leaders of his own party, he needed any support he could get. He carried himself bravely, and with such apparent assurance that it is easy to overlook the astonishing nature of the feat; but the ground beneath him was never quite solid. His influence with the prince gave him something to lean on: after all, the prince was not merely the heir to the throne, but also a main hope of the Whigs. Unhappily the Whigs never got much good from him, but it might easily have turned out otherwise—indeed, it very nearly did turn out otherwise. Sheridan's influence, therefore, gave him a certain power, which, towards the end of his career, he exerted in a very odd manner: as Creevey says with no more exaggeration than is pardonable, he twice kept the Whigs out of office. It is characteristic of him that this feat was not attended with the smallest benefit to himself.

§

In the spring of 1787—that is, about three months after his first speech on the Begums—Sheridan was able to do the prince some service in the House. The prince's allowance was much less than he, or his Whig friends, could have wished, and his debts having become unmanageable, Alderman Newnham gave notice of a motion for his relief. Pitt observed grimly that he was anxious to avoid the unpleasant task of an investigation, but if it became necessary he would not shrink from carrying out his duty to the public. This hint sounded uncommonly like a threat, and there was worse to come. Rolle, with the solemn satisfaction of conscious virtue, declared that if the motion were ever brought forward he would move the previous question upon it—it involved matter which ought not to be discussed within those walls, and which affected the Constitution essentially, *both in Church and State.*

This horribly ominous remark brought Sheridan to the defence of his gracious prince and master, who, he assured the House, 'wished every part of his conduct to be laid open without ambiguity or concealment'; but Rolle remained unmoved and the alderman was urged to withdraw his motion. Sheridan would not hear of this: he appealed to Pitt to acknowledge that such a step would make it appear that the prince feared inquiry; whereupon Pitt, throwing oil on the troubled waters, deprecated the raising of a question 'big with public mischief,' and condescended to explain that his own allusion to an investigation concerned nothing but the prince's debts and had no reference to any *extraneous matter*. Nobody had said what this extraneous matter was, but everybody knew, and had had it in mind all the while—it was the prince's marriage to Mrs. Fitzherbert.

The ceremony had, in fact, taken place as long ago as 21st December 1785. It had been kept as secret as such a thing could be, but it was widely suspected. Fox had previously written to the prince warning him against it and pointing out its many dangers—which, to be sure, were obvious enough. Even the lady's own friends, he considered, must, in the circumstances, think any other sort of connection preferable. The prince's reply amounted to an assurance that he would not marry Mrs. Fitzherbert. A fortnight later her married her.

Fox was not in the House when Rolle made his allusions to the mysterious danger threatening the Constitution in Church and State—Mrs. Fitzherbert was a Roman Catholic—but three days later he went out of his way to condemn the report as a vile calumny. He denied it *in toto*: the thing never could have happened legally—as, of course, every one knew—and never did happen in any way whatsoever. He spoke from direct authority. '"Villain," murmured Pitt, "be sure you prove my love a whore."'

Sheridan hereupon challenged Rolle to admit that he was satisfied, but Rolle was not the man to give any such satisfaction. He had 'certainly received an answer, but the House must form their own opinion of its propriety.' Sheridan indignantly denounced this conduct as 'neither candid nor manly,' and went so far as to say that the House ought to resolve it seditious and disloyal to spread reports injurious to the prince's character. Rolle, awkward as ever, merely replied that he did not invent the reports—'he had heard them and they made an impression on his mind.' Pitt rebuked Sheridan for his warmth and tactfully suggested that the House should be grateful to Rolle for raising a question which had been answered so satisfactorily. Sheridan, however, insisted that Rolle ought to admit he was satisfied or take steps to discover the truth. 'The honourable gentleman,' replied the immovable Rolle, 'has not heard me say I am unsatisfied,' and beyond this ambiguous statement neither Sheridan nor Grey could induce him to go.

Fox's downright and well-meant declaration cruelly embarrassed the prince, who found himself in a situation not unlike some of those which Sheridan occasionally occupied, and by the same means—that is to say, prevarication. Mrs. Fitzherbert did not at all consider that the divine sanction granted by a marriage ceremony (secret, moreover) ought to make her indifferent to her reputation. She was greatly afflicted, and furious against Fox; and the prince, accordingly, was 'dreadfully agitated.' At midnight he scribbled a note to Fox saying that he felt 'more comfortable' after hearing the accounts of Grey and Sheridan, but Grey afterwards denied flatly that he had said anything which could give him the least comfort. He also declared that the prince urged him to say something in Parliament to soothe Mrs. Fitzherbert's wounded feelings, and that he positively declined to do so, because it would be against the prince's interests. He might have added that, since the required statement would, presumably, have to save Mrs. Fitzherbert's character without admitting the marriage, the task approached the impossible. 'Well,' said the prince, 'if nobody else will, Sheridan must.' And Sheridan (who, no doubt, had more aptitude than Grey for a performance on the tight-rope) did.

Long afterwards, when the affair was nearly forty years old, the prince, who by that time had become George IV, gave his own version of it to Croker. By this account Sheridan's remarks in the House were made entirely on his own initiative—having called on Mrs. Fitzherbert on the morning following Fox's unlucky declaration, he found her in an 'agony of tears,' and chivalrously resolved to comfort her. But the prince's memory was not always reliable, and he had a way of glossing over uncomfortable facts: he referred, for example, in this statement, to 'my supposed marriage.'

However it may have been, Sheridan certainly did throw a veil over Mrs. Fitzherbert's nakedness, taking an opportunity to observe with great solemnity in the House that, though the feelings of His Royal Highness had received very proper consideration, there was 'another person entitled, in every delicate and honourable mind, to the same attention—one whom he would not otherwise venture to describe or allude to but by saying it was a name which malice or ignorance alone could attempt to injure, and whose conduct and character claimed, and were entitled to, the truest respect.'

This highly ingenious eulogy may have served its purpose in soothing Mrs. Fitzherbert and the prince, who referred to it as 'that celebrated eulogium.' What the House understood by it is another matter, but Daniel Pulteney, mentioning it in a letter to the Duke of Rutland, said that every one smiled.

§

In the following summer the king went to Cheltenham, where he lived as quietly and with as little ceremony as any of his subjects, drinking the waters regularly and taking his evening stroll on the public walk. He also made an excursion to Worcester, but he did not get as much benefit from these innocent diversions as might have been expected. In the autumn he was not at all well, and there was 'an uncertainty as to his complaint not very satisfactory,' as Fanny Burney observed. He was feverish and agitated, and at times his behaviour was disconcertingly eccentric. He talked rapidly and incessantly, and his voice became painfully hoarse, but still he went on talking to any one who was by. He could not sleep and had a pathetic fear that his faculties were breaking down: he told Lady Effingham that he felt 'all at once an old man.' By November he had become so weak from his nervous and feverish exertions, and want of rest, that he walked 'like a gouty man' and could not get on without a stick.

The postponement of levees and drawing-rooms, which in the ordinary way he attended with unfailing regularity, was an unmistakable sign that something was wrong, but no precise news was to be had. Sir Gilbert Elliot noted towards the end of October that a great mystery was being made of the affair, but though he was convinced that the king was ill, he did not think it was anything serious.

On 5th November, Fanny Burney, as she sat in her room at Windsor, was oppressed by a mysterious stillness which descended on the entire household. There was no coming and going, and no sound of voices anywhere; the musicians had been ordered away and there was to be no concert. At last Colonel Digby came in, looking very grave, and told her dreadful news. At dinner the king had broken out into 'positive delirium'; the queen had been 'so overpowered as to fall into violent hysterics'; the princesses had been reduced to a state of misery; and the Prince of Wales had burst into tears.

The physicians were summoned in all haste: the king had no love of doctors, and hitherto the only one in attendance had been Sir George Baker, subsequently described by the royal but delirious patient as 'an old woman.' The gates of the lodge were shut and no answers were given to any inquiries, but though the details might be kept from public knowledge, there was no concealing the main fact—the king was mad. Parliament was to meet on the 20th and members of both parties hurried to town —the Whigs with high expectations. Since His Majesty was unable to discharge his royal functions there would have to be a regency, and the regent would, of course, be the Prince of Wales. The prince would dismiss Pitt and place the Government in the hands of Fox and his friends. The wheel had turned at last.

Fox was travelling on the Continent with Mrs. Armistead, but a messenger, sent after him in haste, ran him to earth at Bologna, and he returned with such speed that he made himself ill. Meanwhile Sheridan was not idle: he and Lord Loughborough were reckoned to be the prince's chief advisers and he enjoyed a position of great importance. He was concerned in an intrigue to induce Thurlow to come into the new Government on the understanding that he should keep his place as Chancellor. This move was very much in Richard Brinsley's style, and on general grounds it had a good deal to recommend it. It was not liked by Loughborough, however, who wanted to be Chancellor himself; and it did not please Fox when he heard of it. George Selwyn suggested to Lady Carlisle that Fox might have quoted to Sheridan the lines of Hecate:

> Saucy and overbold! How did you dare
> To trade and traffic with Macbeth
> In riddles and affairs of death . . .?

The business, in fact, caused Sheridan to be looked on with a jealous suspicion which was never forgotten; and it was at this time that the Duchess of Devonshire took note of his love of playing a sly game—she was attached to him, but felt a whole-hearted devotion to the interests of Fox. Moreover, she had, as Lady Holland says, an exacting lover in Grey.

However, these things could not alter the main fact, which was that the Whigs had good reason to expect that they would soon be in power. As early as the beginning of December a correspondent in town told the Earl of Charlemont that the arrangements for the new Government would probably be made within the next ten days, and all the members of the present administration — except the Chancellor — dismissed. Fox and North were to be secretaries of State: *Sheridan was to be Chancellor of the Exchequer.*

Chancellor of the Exchequer . . . the mere rumour carried an intoxicating suggestion of fortune with it, as if the clouds were opening and showing riches. However, it was corrected later—Sheridan was to be Treasurer of the Navy.

The post was a considerable one, but his hopes went beyond it. Sir Gilbert Elliot thought that he counted on being Chancellor of the Exchequer at some future time, or on holding some other Cabinet office, but was willing to wait for the present, in case he should be regarded with envy as an *upstart*—a significant suggestion. In short, Sheridan was to have his share of the profits, but no excessive share of importance; and he allowed himself modestly to be put off with promises. However, all these arrangements had a certain resemblance to the disposing of the bear's skin while the animal was still alive.

Pitt, in the meantime, could only hope that the king would

soon recover, and his only resource, therefore, was to gain time. He was helped by the mistakes of his opponents: Fox rashly asserted that the prince had as clear a right to exercise the sovereignty as he would have had if the king were dead; Burke supported him, and Sheridan was ill-advised enough to warn Pitt of the danger of provoking the prince to assert his right. By all this the Whigs lost valuable time and were made to appear indecently eager to get into office. Indeed, Fox's behaviour was compared—not without a certain aptness—to that of Falstaff on hearing of the death of King Henry IV.

Before the end of the year Pitt wrote to the prince informing him of the restrictions which he proposed to lay on the regency —restrictions which Fox and his friends warmly denounced. The prince's reply was drafted by Burke, but in its final form it was partly, at least, the work of Sheridan. It was copied fairly by Elizabeth and the prince added his signature. He could not approve of the restrictions, but 'accepted the painful trust imposed on him.'

Meanwhile the king, whose unhappy case excited deep public sympathy, was no better. He was visited officially at Windsor by Thurlow and Pitt, and the former was so affected that, though not much used to the melting mood, he shed tears; while the latter was 'more composed' but expressed his grief with the greatest possible respect and attachment. The royal sufferer was then moved to Kew, and Dr. Francis Willis, who had devoted himself to the treatment of lunatics, was called in.

The doctors' opinions did not agree. Warren, the chief physician, maintained that the king's case was hopeless, but Willis declared that he would recover before very long. The former was suspected, on the Government side, of being under the influence of Carlton House: the latter was described by Sheridan as a quack and Burke said His Majesty's life was not safe in such hands.

Pitt brought forward his restrictions and did not hesitate to warn the House that another 'conspiracy and cabal' might be formed, such as (according to him) had tried to overthrow the Constitution in 1783. The proposals were bitterly—but vainly

F

—attacked by the Whigs, and Sheridan, charging Pitt with duplicity, arrogance, and calumny, 'repelled with scorn' the imputation cast on the unfortunate Coalition Government. Among the proposals was one to place the royal household under the authority of the queen. Sheridan, with a reminiscence of his Begum style, accused Pitt of a want of delicacy in taking the queen out of 'that domestic station in which she had acted so irreproachably.'

At the end of January the king had still not recovered, and a deputation of the Houses waited on the prince to present their address. The prince's reply was confidently ascribed by Wraxall and others to Sheridan, but Sir Gilbert Elliot claimed to have written the whole of it himself.

The prize was now almost in the hands of the Whigs and Pitt contemplated returning to the law. Early in February the king's condition showed signs of improvement, but Burke insisted that his madness was 'total eclipse'; 'the Almighty had hurled him from his throne'; he was 'a monarch smitten by the hand of Omnipotence.' Sheridan having observed that Pitt had often signified his departure from office and 'taken leave of the House over and over again,' Pitt replied that he had never yet heard the least circumstance which authorized Sheridan to declare that he was about to quit his place. 'When he did hear anything like it he should have much to say to that House, to express his acknowledgments, etc., and declare his hope that he should not quit his situation avowing principles less worthy of their regard and esteem than he brought with him into office'—to which Sheridan drily rejoined that 'the right hon. gentleman, he did not doubt, would make a fine speech at his exit from office, or, according to the vulgar expression, an excellent delivery of his last dying words and confession.'

The king's health continued to vary, but on the whole it tended to improve. He ran after the horrified Fanny Burney in Kew Gardens, put his hands on her shoulders, and kissed her on the cheek. Pitt, however, went to Kew and had an interview of a quarter of an hour with him. From Bath, where he had gone to recuperate, Fox wrote to Fitzpatrick that he should be

A Peep behind the Curtain at Drury Lane.

'A PEEP BEHIND THE CURTAIN AT DRURY LANE'
(The occasion is the regency crisis, and the suggestion is
that Sheridan does not wish the King to recover.)
Caricature by Sayers.

much obliged to be told by return of post on what day the regency was likely to commence. Two days later, Thurlow (whose negotiations with the Whigs had been long since broken off) informed the Lords that the king was in a state of convalescence; the doctors signed a report that His Majesty 'appeared to be free from complaint,' the bulletins were discontinued, the regency crisis—that three months' drama—was over. The prince was not to be regent—yet, and as for Sheridan, he was never to be Chancellor of the Exchequer, never to have a place in a Cabinet. Nobody was to have any reason to look on him with envy as an upstart.

§

The king's recovery was hailed with joy by his loyal subjects: he went to Weymouth, where he bathed to the strains of *God Save the King*.

It was 1789—the year of the outbreak of the French Revolution. A future (as yet unguessed at) of upheaval, war, distress, and danger was soon to be opened. By the time it closed, Sheridan's long parliamentary career was over, and he himself was very near the end of his life. On hearing the news of the fall of the Bastille, Fox wrote to Fitzpatrick, 'How much the greatest event it is that has ever happened in the world, and how much the best!' Sheridan was no less enthusiastic: he saw with warm sympathy the unprivileged and oppressed rising against their privileged oppressors. Bliss was it in that dawn to be alive. The time came when he narrowly escaped the honour of being offered French citizenship.

In 1790 Parliament was dissolved and he was faced with a bitter contest at Stafford, though it was reported that the ladies were all on his side. He was returned, but the expense frightened Elizabeth, who had drawn her own conclusions from the disappointments of the past ten years. 'I am more than ever convinced,' she wrote, 'that we must look to other resources for wealth and independence, and consider politics merely as an amusement.' By other resources she meant Richard Brinsley's theatre—and, perhaps, his pen, so long idle; but the theatre above all. She was right. She did not suggest that he should give up Parliament altogether: she knew how much it meant to him, and she shared his delight in the distinction he won there. But nobody can live on distinction alone: wealth and independence are very desirable things, and however loftily Sheridan might soar, he was really tied by the leg all the while to the plain matter of pounds, shillings, and pence.

The theatre meant the new theatre. While strange and terrible events were happening in France, and the political situation at home grew steadily worse; while Elizabeth drooped under the fatal shadow of consumption, the Drury Lane company left the Opera House in the Haymarket and crossed over to the little theatre, once Foote's, now Colman's. It was a troublesome and expensive business, but to the accompaniment of contractors' estimates, architects' designs, ground-rent agreements, loans, interest, and the raising of capital; and in spite of the delays and disputes incidental to such undertakings, the new theatre was coming into existence—Sheridan's Drury, with a plank from Garrick's old stage inserted in the new one, a dome, tier upon tier of boxes, and chandeliers of cut glass; not to mention such further sources of wealth as a Chinese hall and a tavern.

CHAPTER TWELVE

The New Theatre—View of Mr. Sheridan—Second Marriage

WEALTH AND INDEPENDENCE—Sheridan, now past forty, had not yet achieved either of them. He was a public figure; his comedies were still favourite pieces in the theatre; and when he spoke in the House the reporters did not fail, if necessary, to add point to what he was supposed to have said, and even, occasionally, to lend him some abuse of their own—because he was Mr. Sheridan, the manager and dramatist. But as to his livelihood, he still had to look to the theatre for it, and wealth (if it ever came) must be looked for from the same quarter. It was Drury Lane that paid—all too tardily—the landlord, the butcher, the wine-merchant, and the tailor; and it was Drury Lane that supplied the guineas he gave to the servants in great houses, postilions, and so forth, and maintained the loyalty of the burgesses of Stafford.

An illusion of wealth, however, was always there. Ready money might not be forthcoming very freely, but Sheridan was sure to be found dealing in impressively large sums. The new theatre, for instance, cost about £130,000 to build, and the capital was raised by 300 debentures of £500. It was a financial operation on the grand scale. David Barclay had paid a similar amount—£135,000—for Thrale's brewery, which Dr. Johnson described as no mere parcel of boilers and vats, but the potentiality of growing rich beyond the dreams of avarice. So, perhaps, Sheridan may have regarded the new Theatre Royal—and not without reason, for it was nearly twice as large as the old one. It was 320 feet long and 155 feet wide; the four tiers of boxes could hold 1,800 people; the pit, 800; the two-shilling gallery, 675; and the shilling gallery, 308. The increased size was not in the best interests of the drama, but Sheridan, like managers in general, was not concerned with the best interests of the drama: his business was to make money. A full house, if every one paid, was worth more than £800, and since the theatre was generally open for 200 nights in the year, the possible annual income should have been something like £160,000.

This has an extremely satisfying sound: it was potential wealth which raised extravagant expectations in the manager. But theatres are not so dependable as breweries, and wherever Sheridan is concerned ordinary calculations of profit are curiously misleading. There was no possibility of filling the theatre night after night: the stock attractions would not do it, and a new play which would hit the popular taste was hard to come by. On rare occasions, such as that of the performance of Ireland's celebrated forgery, *Vortigern*, the house might bring in £800, but in the ordinary way it was worth far less. Sheridan himself, a few years after the theatre was opened, put the annual income at £60,000, and added that, with careful management, this could be increased to £75,000. These figures are reliable enough: they compare fairly with those of Covent Garden, allowing for the fact that the latter theatre was not quite so large. They were intended for Kemble, who, as Sheridan probably knew, kept careful accounts of his own. In the 1803–4 season the income, according to Boaden, fell below £50,000, averaging only £242 a night.

The expenses, on the other hand, were heavy. It cost £200 to send up the curtain at Drury Lane, and there were many 'encumbrances,' as Sheridan called them, quite apart from the ordinary costs. The interest on the debentures was five per cent; the old theatre had been heavily in debt; the sojourn at the Opera House and the little theatre in the Haymarket had been expensive, the receipts having fallen off in spite of increased prices; damage had been done to scenery and properties; and the building costs of the new theatre had enormously exceeded the estimate. In these and many other ways were the profits diminished, and less than two years after the opening Kemble threw up the management in disgust. The house was already overwhelmed with debt and the salaries often went unpaid. A leading actor or actress, complained Kemble, would refuse to go on unless arrears of salary were forthcoming. Stage furnishers would not supply goods needed for a forthcoming performance 'unless Mr. Kemble would pass his word for the payment,' as he sometimes did. On such occasions the bill was generally paid sooner or later, but once he was actually arrested for the debt 'to his extreme indignation,' as Boaden remarks.

Thus the new theatre did not, unhappily, bring the sanguine manager wealth or independence: on the contrary, it greatly increased his difficulties, which, in the course of its brief existence, became notorious. After all, it was a public institution, secured by its patent and by act of Parliament against competition, and its affairs were matters of common interest. If Miss Farren did not appear in a new play, the management might attribute her absence to indisposition, but the disappointed audience would decline to believe it. Joseph Farington would write in his diary that the true reason was that her salary was unpaid, adding that Kemble and Mrs. Jordan stayed away for the same reason, and that Mrs. Siddons would probably do likewise if she did not receive her salary regularly. He would conclude, naturally enough, that Sheridan's conduct was *unprincipled*. At the same time Sheridan would be denouncing Pitt's new taxes: 'We are told that the people must now submit to great burdens. With what face can the ministers and their converts tell them this, when they themselves care only for their individual jobs? The new taxes make against *economy*. To the sacred principle of saving I cannot but profess myself a friend, though the habits of my own life have been little regulated on it.'

§

The new theatre began its chequered career with due solemnity on the first Friday in Lent, 12th March 1794, with a sacred oratorio; and on 21st March opened 'for the representation of dramas.' The play was *Macbeth* in Davenant's version, with some additional lines by Garrick, including what Sheridan might have called Macbeth's last dying words and confession. The scenery and costumes were new. 'A prologue,' says Michael Kelly, 'by the Right Honourable Major-General Fitzpatrick'—Fox's friend —'was spoken by Kemble with great applause.' The epilogue, written by Colman, was delivered by Miss Farren. It explained to the audience 'the utility of an iron curtain and a reservoir of water in case of fire.'

In the eighty or so nights which remained of the season, the receipts were upwards of £30,000; but Malton, an architect, told Farington that he had not yet been paid for the work he had done. Farington himself went to the new theatre to see a performance of *The Glorious First of June* (a spectacle contrived with remarkable speed before the general enthusiasm had time to cool) and considered that the proportions of the building were bad and the decorations tawdry. Altogether it was in very poor taste, and the only good he could find to say of it was that the seats in the boxes were convenient. Well or ill proportioned, however, it was Sheridan's only resource.

He himself was of interest to the public in many ways: he was the theatre manager, the orator, the dramatist, the friend of reform. He drank, it was well known, to excess; indeed, his face now showed it all too plainly.[1] But the thing which struck the general imagination most strongly was his everlasting indebtedness and want of money. Nothing else seemed quite so characteristic. It was not that his debts were spectacular in their mere amount, though, as nobody knew what the amount was, report naturally exaggerated it; it was that they were never cleared up—he seemed to be surrounded by them and to spend his life among them, as if they were an essential condition of his existence. And this raised a problem which puzzled many people: what became of all the money that passed through his hands? If he paid anybody it was only after delay and repeated applications. Prince Hoare wrote to him once a week to get paid for a theatrical production—after the twenty-sixth week he succeeded. It was useless, he said, to argue with Sheridan: the only way was to keep repeating doggedly the original demand.

Charles Fox, going home to the calm enjoyment of an eclogue of Virgil after losing a small fortune at the gaming-table, or lying peacefully in bed till noon while his creditors flocked into the ante-room which he facetiously called his Jerusalem Chamber,

[1] Caricaturists did not miss this point; they usually shaded his nose.

is a pleasant sight to those who admire a superiority to misfortune or a magnificent carelessness about money. But what
are such things to Sheridan's experiences? The money with
which he took such aristocratic freedoms represented the daily
bread of himself and his family. No friends would ever make
him easy with a subscription, and even if such a thing had been
proposed he would not have accepted it. Indeed, it would have
looked uncomfortably like charity in his case. There was no
need for Fox to have any scruples. When someone did express
a doubt as to how he would take it, the answer came pat—he
would take it *quarterly*, of course.

It would be absurd to suppose that Sheridan had any love of
being harassed by duns and bailiffs. If he showed a remarkable
gift for raising money and no great alacrity in repaying it, that
was the result of circumstances and not inclination. It would
have been better, no doubt, if the tradesmen had been paid
punctually and poor stage-hands had not sometimes gone home
at the end of the week without their wages. He would have
preferred it so himself, but what was to be done? Things would
improve and every one would be paid in the end.[1]

Then what did become of all the money that passed through
his hands? The truth is, very little of it belonged to him.
Sichel thought his income from the theatre was about £5,000,
and this agrees with Sheridan's own estimate of what Kemble
would get if he bought a share of the patent. But Sheridan was
reckoning that the theatre would be properly managed and bring
in £75,000 a year; whereas it was badly managed and brought
in between £50,000 and £60,000 a year. Besides, the estimate
leaves out of account the charges incurred in raising the capital
to make the purchase. Kemble, in fact, had a capital of £10,000
to invest, but Sheridan, as we know, had bought his share without
any money of his own, and since he never accumulated any he
merely shifted the burden from one shoulder to the other without
getting rid of it. If he raised money it had to be at the expense
of the theatre, for he had no other security; and if salaries and

---

[1] Lady Bessborough assured Lord Broughton that Sheridan was not shabby about money
and never meant to swindle people.

* F

wages went unpaid he was only anticipating his own income and incurring a debt which would have to be cleared off sooner or later.

Unfortunately things did not improve as time went on. Kemble, it is true, thought that 'the theatre, fairly treated, was a profitable concern,' and Linley, according to Ozias Humphry, died worth £25,000—but then, Linley managed his business in a very different style from that of his son-in-law. By the time the theatre was burnt down, it was, says Boaden, £300,000 in debt.

There is not much mystery about what Sheridan did with his money: he never squandered vast amounts in some inexplicable fashion, for though he occasionally contrived to raise considerable sums, he never had vast amounts to squander. It was not that he had a great deal of money and wasted it, but that he did not have enough. Joseph Richardson was right: if he had had a fortune he would have been a most moral man—at all events, as far as money was concerned. If he did not attend carefully to his accounts it was because the most careful attention would have made no particular difference. His affairs were never straightened out. His friends did not altogether neglect him when, towards the end of his life, he was almost overwhelmed with debt, but that undertaking they regarded as hopeless.

The astonishing thing is that he should have gone on so long in this way. Such a feat required something more than resourcefulness and an irreverent attitude towards the sacred principles of economy. It needed courage of the enduring sort—a gallant and invincible superiority to adverse circumstances. Hazlitt, writing with feeling on the subject of the want of money—'that uncertain, casual, precarious mode of existence in which the temptation to spend remains after the means are exhausted, the want of money joined with the hope and possibility of getting it, the intermediate state of difficulty and suspense between the last guinea or shilling and the next we may have the good luck to encounter'—points out that 'this gap, this unwelcome interval constantly recurring, however shabbily got over, is really full of many anxieties, misgivings, mortifications, meannesses, and deplorable embarrassments of every description.'

Such reflections naturally led him to speak of Sheridan. 'It
required a man to be the author of *The School for Scandal*.' he
observed very justly, 'to run the gauntlet of such disagreeable
occurrences every hour of the day.' He went on to relate a
number of anecdotes illustrative of Richard Brinsley's behaviour
in these circumstances. 'Taylor, of the Opera House, used to
say of Sheridan that he could not pull off his hat to him in the
street without its costing him fifty pounds; and if he stopped to
speak to him it was a hundred.' And again: 'Once when a
creditor brought him a bill for payment, which had often been
presented before, and the man complained of its soiled and
tattered state, "I'll tell you what I'd advise you to do with it,
my friend," said Sheridan, "take it home and write it upon *parch-
ment*."' And so on—for there are numbers of such stories, all part
of the Sheridan legend. They may not be true, but their mere existence is significant, and fair evidence of Sheridan's extraordinary
power of rising above the anxieties, misgivings, mortifications, etc.,
referred to above.

In some ways, however, they are certainly misleading. Sheridan's character was by no means so easily understood as they
seem to imply: on the contrary, it was made up of curiously
contradictory elements. Whatever Taylor, of the Opera House,
might say, Sheridan was not given to sponging on his friends;[1]
indeed, he was almost morbidly unwilling to accept favours.
Nor, in spite of his unpaid bills, did he intend to defraud his
creditors. It is to be feared, in fact, that his creditors only too
often defrauded him. When some of his friends undertook to
sort out his debts in 1808, they found genuine claims to the
amount of £10,000, and others, many of which they considered
should have been contested, amounting to five or six times as
much. Sheridan insisted that they must all be paid. Even when
he was near the end of his life, and had lost both his seat in
Parliament and his theatre, he still talked cheerfully of paying
off his debts.

It must be remembered that he was not without the solid

---

[1] He said it was his rule never to borrow from private friends—but, as will be seen,
he was obliged to break the rule in the closing years of his life.

backing of property. The theatre gave him an income and the means of raising money, and the gap between his income and his expenditure was filled in by various expedients. Fortune, which he could hardly be blamed for expecting, and which, if he had looked after his own interests, he might have had, did not come his way, and thus the debts accumulated. But even here it is easy to be deceived. Creditors are not, for the most part, so simple-minded as to allow debts to be incurred by people who are not likely to pay. And Sheridan did pay—in all probability, as Moore says, far more, in many cases, than he owed. He never got free of his debts, but, on the other hand, they never entirely defeated him. As long as he was in Parliament he was safe from arrest for debt; and even when this precious immunity was lost he found himself only once in a sponging-house, and then for no more than a day or two. The indignity filled him with bitter resentment. He was detained in a large room in a house in Fetter Lane, says Wraxall (the actual locality was Tooke's Court, Cursitor Street), together with one of the latter's friends and Sir Watkin Lewes, who had once been Lord Mayor. He was 'morose, taciturn, and gloomy before dinner . . . but when he had drunk nearly two bottles of wine he became comparatively cheerful and communicative.' His release was arranged by Whitbread, and Sheridan maintained that the withholding of money due to him for his share of the Drury Lane patent was the cause of the unfortunate experience. He was so far from seeing himself in the character of an insolvent debtor that he was convinced he should never have been arrested.

The idea that for upwards of a quarter of a century he went on accumulating debts and paying nobody, so that in the end he was ruined, thus providing the thriftless with an awful example, is a mere caricature of the truth. Not even he could have accomplished such a feat. He was not driven to seek safety in exile, and though it is true that, during his last illness, he was in danger of being carried off for debt, he may be said to have died as he had lived, with his face to the enemy. He brought up his two sons handsomely enough, and left his wife well provided for. Two years after his death his debts were only about £5,500.

§

When Elizabeth died, Sheridan, much occupied with politics and the building of the new theatre, thought it would be advisable to provide his son Tom with a tutor, for Tom was now growing up, and, deprived of a mother's care, was 'running wild.' In the hope of getting this desirable post young William Smyth came to town. He was to be introduced by a friend of his—a Mr. Morris 'who had been guilty of writing a farce'—and Joseph Richardson; and an appointment was arranged with Sheridan for seven o'clock. The hopeful tutor[1] arrived punctually and passed an hour in conversation with Richardson and Morris, but no Sheridan appeared. Another hour went by and it was decided that the party had better dine. At last a note arrived from Sheridan—it had been sent from the House of Commons, where, it appeared, he was detained. He lamented extremely his inability to meet them at dinner, but should be most happy to receive them all at the St. Alban's Tavern at twelve o'clock to eat a little supper with him. This left the party with another two hours on their hands, but in due course they went off expectantly to the tavern, which was conveniently close to the House. No Sheridan was to be seen there and no news of him was to be had. What was more, no supper had been ordered. They waited a considerable time in some embarrassment and then went for a stroll in Pall Mall. Returning to the tavern they found matters in exactly the same state as before, and at two o'clock in the morning the prospective tutor was forced to give it up and retire for the night with some odd thoughts of Mr. Sheridan's way of doing business.

On the following day matters improved. He was to call at Grosvenor Street to take a chaise down to Isleworth. He found the Grosvenor Street house 'forlorn and dirty'—Mr. Sheridan could not bear to live in it since his wife's death, but slept at Nerot's Hotel. Tom was at Isleworth, and Sheridan, both that evening and the following day (he 'appeared about noon'), was

---

[1] He subsequently became Professor of Modern History at Cambridge. He was a great-uncle of Dame Ethel Smyth, as we learn from *Impressions that Remained.*

'very kind.' Smyth was fortunate enough to be engaged. Long afterwards, when Sheridan had been twenty-four years in his grave, and the world he had known had changed beyond recognition, Smyth, then getting on in years and entirely respectable, wrote a short Memoir—a modest book of seventy-four pages— in which he set forth what he remembered of his celebrated employer.

To some extent the Memoir bears out the traditional idea of Sheridan, with all his preposterous unpunctuality, his way of forgetting or ignoring his engagements, his tendency to vanish beyond the ken of those most anxious to get in touch with him, his complete neglect of his correspondence, and his 'habitual and extreme' procrastination. On his table were piled 'heaps of unopened letters, MSS. of plays, pamphlets, and papers of every description.' He breakfasted in bed, and lay there 'making his speeches.' When he had finished dressing he would go rapidly through his ante-room, down the stairs, and out of the street door, and 'happy was the man who, if he had business with him, could catch him in the transit, for if he once made the door, there was an end of him for that day—no one ever knew where to find him afterwards.'

These touches are all in the accepted style, but there are others which suggest that the real Sheridan had qualities unseen by the world in general, and not much noted by posterity. The spectacle of someone pursuing a carefree and irresponsible course through life and exercising remarkable talents without effort or seriousness is undeniably engaging, but a thoughtful observer will probably suspect that this can hardly be the whole of the picture.

Sheridan's charm, for example, was felt by nearly every one with whom he came in contact. It was felt by Smyth, but it did not deprive him of his critical faculty. It was felt by Lord Holland, who found it impossible to be angry with him though he had just used in a speech the very information his lordship meant to use himself and had imparted to Sheridan under a promise that he would not divulge it. This charm was not due to vivacity, or to a flow of brilliant conversation. Sheridan's good things were said only at intervals and where they came in naturally. 'Sheridan,' remarked Michael Kelly, 'though a delightful companion, was by no means inclined to loquacity.' Prince Hoare, who had a good deal to do with him in theatrical matters, told Joseph Farington that he was not ill-natured where those trying affairs were concerned, but could be ill-humoured, and when drunk—which was not infrequently the case—quarrelsome and even savage. Byron, who always found him 'very convivial and delightful,' observed that he had seen him 'cut up Whitbread, quiz Madame de Staël, annihilate Colman, and do little less by some others (whose names, as friends, I set not down) of good fame and ability.' But beneath all this there was a certain fundamental kindness and generosity of mind, and in spite of all his errors he was on the side of the angels. He was kind to Smyth; after the tragic death of Tickell he was kind to the widow and her children; indeed, though he caused both his wives much unhappiness, he had strong family affections and was very good to his relations. His love for Tom Sheridan was extreme and unfailing, and he could be anxious about him to the point of morbidity. There was, in fact, an anxious strain in Sheridan, though he rarely showed it to the world, as if he knew in his heart that fortune, whatever its appearance might be, was not his friend, and his riches were only fairy gold.

We have already observed his love of giving an impression of careless mastery. He talked flippantly about his reply on the Begum charge, and spoke brilliantly, without the help of the minutes of evidence, when the time came. But he had worked hard in preparation for the speech. He arrived at Wanstead (where Smyth and his pupil were) 'in a chaise containing as many bundles of papers and red boxes as would have loaded a handcart,' and 'never stirred out of his room for three or four days and evenings, and much of three nights.'

Smyth's experiences of Sheridan were of a mixed kind—like those of most people who had to do with him. But without being at all blind to his defects, he could not help liking him, and he had an enthusiastic admiration for his talents. 'He would,' he concluded (almost, one could fancy, with a sigh), 'have been the best Cabinet minister among them.'

§

While Smyth and his pupil were staying at Bognor, a letter came from Sheridan, instructing his dear Tom to meet him at dinner at six o'clock on Wednesday at Guildford—'I forget the inn.' He wanted particularly to speak to him. Tom went off accordingly, 'horse and groom,' leaving his tutor marooned at Bognor. About a week later a letter arrived from him. He was still at Guildford and had seen nothing of his father. All he could hear of him was that he had passed through Guildford on the Wednesday about midnight on his way to town 'with four horses and lamps.' As for Tom, he had only a few shillings left, and had written 'letter after letter' without getting a word in reply. Considering Sheridan's way with letters, this is not very surprising.

However, the meeting took place at last, and the important business turned out to be Sheridan's intended marriage to Miss Ogle. 'My father talked to me two hours last night,' wrote the unsympathetic Tom, 'and made out to me it was the most sensible thing he could do. Was not this very clever of him? Well, my dear Mr. Smyth, you should have been tutor to him, you see. I am incomparably the most rational of the two.'

Esther Jane Ogle was the daughter of the Dean of Winchester, and it must be admitted that Sheridan's second marriage was of a highly respectable kind and showed how far he had progressed in the world. This time the bride was of good social standing, and the bridegroom was very far from being merely the obscure son of a not very successful actor and teacher of elocution. The lady was only twenty, which might have seemed a drawback in Tom's eyes, though doubtless it did not appear so to his father. Esther Jane was lively and affectionate, though not distinguished by any particular talents; and attractive enough, if not regularly beautiful. She was bound to suffer to some extent in the general estimation, by comparison with the peerless Elizabeth, but Sheridan did not see things in this way: his 'sweet Hecca' had all the advantage of her twenty years and her high spirits. He himself was forty-three and somewhat battered by time and experience. Nothing remained of his pleasant looks except his 'dark hazel eyes, uncommonly brilliant and expressive.' However, he was in the full flush of his powers: he had his celebrity and his new theatre—he even had the outward appearance of wealth. He was in love with Esther Jane as a middle-aged man will be with a girl of twenty. She was dark and had green eyes, which seemed to him very delightful indeed. She was his 'own gypsey,' his 'dear bit of brown Holland'; she was the prettiest of all that his eyes ever thought pretty. These things come nearer to the heart than all the Amorets and Delias in the world. He was in love—really in love, perhaps for the first time in his life. He had loved Elizabeth after a fashion, but not after this fashion. She had inspired him with high and chivalrous thoughts, and though she felt love like any mortal, she had her angelic quality. He was not equal to the task of loving an angel as an angel should be loved.

There was nothing ethereal about Hecca: her attractions were of a more ordinary kind. Perhaps, after all, his affection for her was only infatuation, but for a while it was strong. Such flames are apt to burn out quickly, and, where women were concerned, he was inconstant by nature. The time came when poor Hecca thought very seriously of a separation—just as Elizabeth had done; and, like Elizabeth, she was persuaded out of it by her repentant but incorrigible husband. She herself was faithful and devoted. It was not to be expected that she should bring Richard Brinsley into the ways of order and economy, and from that point of view the second marriage was not a success for it led to various kinds of extravagance. But she was good to Tom, with whom her relations might easily have been difficult, and there is a pleasant story of her being seen, dressed in a man's frock-coat and trousers, and escorted by Lord Lauderdale, under the gallery of the House of Commons, where she could hear her admired husband make one of his brilliant speeches.

Sheridan's position in the world, never very easy to fix, depended largely on the point of view of the beholder: his second marriage is an excellent illustration of this. It could hardly be supposed that Miss Ogle would be allowed to marry Sheridan unless he could satisfy her family that he was a suitable partner for her, and, in particular, that he was able to keep her in the style to which she was accustomed. And, in fact, he did satisfy the dean in these respects, and what was more, he made a marriage settlement so generous as to verge on extravagance and even ostentation, as if he meant to show the world that he could afford to deny his young bride nothing, and would bestow upon her, not only heart, but fortune. These were the early and palmy days of the new theatre, when expectation ran high and money could be raised. Joseph Farington, who picked up a good deal of gossip about Sheridan—not all of it accurate—noted that the settlement he made on Miss Ogle was £15,000 in the three per cents. Moore likewise said that he added £15,000 to Miss Ogle's £5,000. The true figures were £12,000 from Sheridan and £8,000 on the lady's side. The total of £20,000 was placed in the hands of Grey and Whitbread (and certainly no more solid and respectable trustees could have been found) and Sheridan undertook not to touch the money until the sum should have doubled itself.

This business was highly characteristic of him. The provisions were so handsome and unselfish as to seem unreasonable. The sum involved was considerable—and, of course, he was in no position to afford it. But this did not at all lessen the satisfaction he took in the arrangement: there was a sort of magnificence in it which appealed to his imagination. Besides, it was a tribute to his Hecca, as well as a generous recognition of the fact that she was less than half his age. The money was raised by the sale of Drury Lane shares, which means, in effect, that it was raised partly at the expense of the income on which he and his wife would have to depend; and partly at the expense of the shareholders, who, like most people who invested their money in that theatre, had no reason to congratulate themselves on their bargain. But to consider in that way was to consider too curiously.

Meanwhile there was the money carefully tied up and out of Sheridan's reach. In 1798 the trustees advanced £8,000 from it for the purchase of the estate of Polesden in Surrey from Sir

William Geary. There were rumours that Sir William found some difficulty in getting his money, and it was even said that Sheridan contrived to borrow £80 from his attorney in the course of the transaction. Farington saw the house in 1803 and observed that it had a fine terrace but otherwise gave evidence of complete neglect and disorder. There it stood, however, no bad symbol of Sheridan's marriage settlement and of his own life. At his death it passed into Hecca's possession, and when she died, into that of her son Charles.

CHAPTER THIRTEEN

The Friend of the People

'THE FRENCH ARE a vain and childish people,' wrote William Cowper to his dearest coz, Lady Hesketh, 'and conduct themselves on this grand occasion with a levity and extravagance nearly akin to madness.' It was not to be expected that, as it developed, the French Revolution should find favour in the eyes of Englishmen in general. Even those who hailed it at the outset and felt the breath of freedom and the hope of a new and better world, were hard put to it as time went on to sustain their enthusiasm. Disorder, violence, attacks on religion, aristocracy, royalty, and property—such things were to be deplored rather than defended. Émigrés, escaped to speak of horrors, appeared in quiet English towns and villages. The times were calamitous: how long would England itself be spared? Sedition, it seemed, was rife. What was to be thought, for instance, of the London Corresponding Society, whose members paid a penny a week and doubtless contemplated nothing less than the violent overthrow of the constitution?

Even the Society of the Friends of the People, where the subscription was two and a half guineas and the committee included Grey, Sheridan, and Whitbread, thought it necessary to point out that their reforms were not innovations, and their object was not to change, but to restore. The case of England was totally different from that of France, and they 'utterly disclaimed the necessity of resorting to similar remedies.' But in spite of these reassuring words they were regarded with the deepest suspicion. Sheridan, on the eve of war with France, 'hoped it was not understood that those who rejoiced at the revolution likewise approved of all the subsequent excesses.' 'God keep us all safe and quiet!' exclaimed Fanny Burney, and she wished fervently that the French king and his family might be saved. 'If the Jacobins hear that Fox has called him an "unfortunate monarch," that Sheridan has said that "his execution would be an act of injustice," and Grey that "we ought to have spared that one *blast to their glories* by earlier negotiation," surely the worst of those wretches will not risk losing their only abettors and palliators in this kingdom.'

Sheridan's sympathy with the revolution was obviously not calculated to further his interests: it was undesirable to be classed as one of the abettors and palliators of the Jacobins. If, keeping an eye on his political fortunes, he had refrained from committing himself to extreme opinions, he might easily have profited, as others did, by the course of events. But there was nothing of the political adventurer in the manager of Drury Lane. His principles were so strong that they constantly stood in the way of his own advancement, and so odd that he was commonly suspected of having none. His enthusiasm for the revolution was too wholehearted to be discreet. At a meeting held to celebrate the anniversary of the fall of the Bastille his zeal embarrassed his friends to such an extent that, on the next occasion, Fox agreed with his nephew, Lord Holland, that Sheridan had better not attend if he could avoid it.[1] Burke, alarming the House with an account of seditious speeches made at a dinner at White's in Paris, 'aggravated the horror,' as Sheridan said, 'by assuring the members that the healths of Mr. Fox and Mr. Sheridan were drunk.' He was, as we have seen, a member of the Society of the Friends of the People (to which Fox never belonged) and though the objects of that society seem blameless enough now, restoring 'freedom of election and more equal representation,' and securing to the people 'a more frequent exercise of their right of electing their representatives' had a very different sound in 1792. When Chauvelin, the French ambassador, got in touch with the Opposition in the hope of preventing war, it was Sheridan who visited him secretly. At the time of the Treason and Sedition Bills the Whig Club called a meeting of the inhabitants of Westminster, and Fox, with his hair unpowdered and cropped short (it was, observed Farington,

---

[1] He did not attend, but this, as he stated in his evidence at the trial of Horne Tooke, was not owing to any change in his opinions. On the previous occasion he had been responsible for a motion beginning, 'That this meeting does most cordially rejoice in the establishment and confirmation of liberty in France. . . .'

who witnessed the scene, 'grisly grey'), [1] appeared on the hustings in front of the King's Arms Tavern, with Sheridan on one side of him and Tierney on the other, and harangued the crowd. Afterwards, still supported by Sheridan and Tierney, he made his way along the street amid a cheering mob, and looked, in the opinion of the same unenthusiastic observer, very much like a drunken fellow being helped home by his friends.

It did not seem at first that the French Revolution would seriously affect English politics, but as early as February 1790, Fox, having taken occasion to praise French soldiers for refusing to obey the 'dictates of the court,' or, in other words, for refusing to obey orders, was warmly opposed by Burke. Between these two lay a friendship of twenty-five years, and their difference of opinion was soothed on this occasion by sincere expressions of regard. But between Burke and Sheridan there was no such friendship, and whether Sheridan was jealous of Burke or not, he saw no reason for sparing his feelings. He was seen to redden while Burke was speaking, and may have thought some parts of the speech were levelled at him. Burke having argued that the French could have had a good constitution from their king, 'What,' said Sheridan, 'was it preparing for them in the camp of Marshal Broglie, or were they to search for it in the ruins of the Bastille?' In the end, Burke, complaining bitterly that his words had been misrepresented, declared that henceforth he and his honourable friend were separated in politics. In spite of every effort the two could not be reconciled. Burke would meet Sheridan, and indeed, could hardly avoid meeting him, seeing that the trial of Hastings still had upwards of four years to run, but political friendship was at an end—an omen of what was destined to happen to the party. Sheridan was blamed for provoking this break, which was the talk of London; but as the event showed, it must have happened sooner or later. Nothing could reconcile Burke's ideas on the revolution with those of Sheridan and Fox, and little more than a year later the separation from Fox came likewise. In the meanwhile Burke published his

---

[1] Hickel's portrait of him, which may be seen in the National Portrait Gallery, was painted in 1793.

Reflections on the Revolution in France, which, far unlike his previous writings, was highly approved of by the king, who declared that every gentleman should read it.

The revolution was too profound a disturbance to be isolated, and by 1793 England was at war and the Whig party was hopelessly split. There had been some talk of a coalition: it was thought that Pitt would favour such an arrangement, and that the king, for all his hatred of Fox, might agree. But there was no real possibility of such a solution—'Mr. Fox's coach,' said Burke bluntly, 'stops the way.' The two sides of the party could not be kept together, and, as Fox said, he had friends whom he *must* attend to. He meant the more extreme section, in which Sheridan was to be found. The more conservative members of the party had come to dislike Sheridan, partly because they regarded him as an outsider who had acquired too much influence, and partly because they could not stomach his opinions. Two years earlier he had complained in the House of attacks made on him—'charges of a singular nature,' endeavouring to rob him of the esteem and friendship of those whom he valued most in society. In particular it was whispered that 'a noble duke'—this was Portland—had opposed some views or expectations which he (Sheridan) was said to have entertained. There was, he declared, no truth in these charges: 'if he had it in his power to make the man whose good opinion he should most dearly prize think flatteringly of him, he would have that man think of him precisely as the noble duke did, and then his wish on that subject would be most amply gratified.' The noble duke certainly had, on one occasion, expressed approval of Sheridan's conduct—it was when the prince contemplated contracting a highly imprudent loan. But there is very little doubt that his esteem had declined since then.

At the present juncture, Fitzwilliam (Rockingham's heir) suggested that Sheridan might be given a lucrative place if the coalition came about, 'but never could be admitted to one of trust and confidence.' The idea that Sheridan could be kept quiet by a lucrative place is significant, but the case did not arise. Burke was right: there was nothing for it but to split the party.

Accordingly Portland, Fitzwilliam, Windham, and all those whose principles were of the same cast, went over to Pitt. It was not easy to leave Fox, in whose extraordinary personality was something that naturally commanded attachment and loyalty. They went for the most part reluctantly, and even with distress of mind; but they went, and were suitably received by Pitt.

This was something that Sheridan could never forgive. That men should fail in loyalty was bad enough, but that they should be willing to accept places, to profit by desertion, and make their political fortunes by it seemed to him to touch the lowest depth of dishonour. He would listen to no excuse. It was useless to argue that their talents might be valued by the minister; that they were serving the country; that the emoluments and gratifications of office were merely accidental matters. A man's business was to avoid even the appearance of corruption; his political honour ought to be above suspicion; like a woman's reputation it should be so jealously guarded that not the faintest breath of slander could touch it. Pitt and his friends were no better: in times of national distress they thought only of places, pensions, and honours, and never proposed to give up a single farthing of their swollen incomes.

These remarkable notions rankled in Sheridan's mind. Again and again, in season and out, he gave utterance to them in his speeches. One would have thought that political jobbery was a new thing—a sin which had never before outraged the innocence of Parliament. He denounced it bitterly, not merely in general terms, but bringing forth the culprits one by one for castigation. He was accused of personal ill will and of appealing to popular prejudice. Mr. Rose, whose places he read out from a list ('clerk of the parliament, master of the pleas office, surveyor of the green wax, secretary to the treasury,' and two others which he said he was unable to make out, the list being in pencil), replied acidly that he did not see why placemen and pensioners should be more taxed than the hon. gentleman as manager of his theatre, or than a man who travelled the country with his puppet-show at his back.

The extraordinary thing is that Sheridan was perfectly sincere, though it was too much to expect that any one should believe it.

He meant what he said, and the principles which sounded so preposterous were the ones he practised himself. He got no credit for this delicate purity, which from time to time we find him displaying anxiously to the House, so that there should be no possibility of mistake on the subject. Every one knew he was in debt, and that actors, actresses, stage-hands, and musicians at Drury Lane frequently went unpaid because Mr. Sheridan had swept off the contents of the treasury.

§

When Portland, Fitzwilliam, and the rest left Fox, Sheridan had been twelve years in Parliament, Elizabeth had been dead a few months, the Drury Lane company was performing at the little theatre in the Haymarket, the new theatre was being built, and the trial of Warren Hastings was still going on. Richard Brinsley, apparently so careless and easy-going, really led a full and distracting life. When, neatly dressed and powdered, he came down to the House, he left behind him a remarkable variety of vital interests and businesses, and if he often failed to keep his appointments it is not altogether surprising. If he had had time and attention to spare he might have looked more carefully into the builder's contract for the theatre. He might have spent his mornings attending to his correspondence instead of composing his speeches. Behind his political life how many concerns, expectations, affections, shifts, and anxieties must have swarmed. Now it would be Elizabeth with her wasted arms and flushed cheeks; now the house at Isleworth, for which he paid (or owed) £400 a year; now Tom and his tutor, Hammersley's and their interest, the Duke of Bedford and his ground-rent, Devonshire House and the ladies, Carlton House and the prince, Brooks's and the betting book, Miss Ogle and her green eyes— a tangled skein in which the incongruous strands of the theatre and politics never failed to appear most prominently.

Politics. . . . Sheridan was one of the small band of the faithful to which the Opposition was now reduced. They were few in numbers, but, it was said, every man of them would have died for Fox. For the most part their devotion was complete and uncritical. Coke of Norfolk (whose grandfather had once taken him on his knee and solemnly warned him never to trust a Tory as long as he lived) took a friend with him to Burlington House as a witness, and there expressed to the Duke of Portland in the plainest language his sense of the latter's proceedings, and concluded by declaring he would never again set foot within those doors. He might have had a peerage, but, said Sheridan, 'Mr. Coke disdained to hide his head in a coronet.'

As to Fox, at this trying time, he was—Sheridan told the House—'a man in whose mind, however its generous nature might be wounded by a separation from long-formed and deeply cherished connections, he was confident there would ever be found a paramount attachment to the safety, the prosperity, and independence of his country, and to the liberty and happiness of man in general; a man who, at that very moment, he believed, did not appear less to the public eye for being more alone. . . . To him, in the stormy hour, the nation would turn, and they would find him

> Like a great sea-mark, standing every flow,[1]
> And saving those that eye him.'

These were generous words, but unhappily there was no prospect whatever that the nation would turn to Fox in any hour, stormy or otherwise. The Opposition could do nothing but lift up their voices against war and oppression, and on behalf of liberty, justice, and reform. It was an essential service—all the more valuable because the Government had an overwhelming majority. But it had to be its own reward. There were places and pensions for the supporters of Pitt; there were also peerages in unprecedented numbers. Sheridan indignantly denounced them as bribery—'there have been no less than 160 peers created since the commencement of the present administration.' He added a characteristic touch: 'I have heard a member of this House say that some persons were made peers who were not fitter for that office than his groom; but *unfortunately I cannot call*

---

[1] The accepted reading is 'flaw.' (*Coriolanus*, v. iii. 74-5.)

upon that gentleman to verify the fact here, for he is now made a peer himself.' But the Opposition had no such recompense in prospect.

After 1789 Sheridan's speeches gain notably in force and conviction, and after 1792—that is, after the outbreak of war—they become denunciatory and provocative to a very marked degree. Not even the most inadequate report can hide his qualities. The subjects of debate were now momentous, and the difference of opinion went too deep for merely factious opposition. What Sheridan urged was what he took to be right, and what an enormous and unshakable majority were convinced was wrong and dangerous. Allowing for the fact that he was in opposition it is not too much to say that he generally was right—that is to say, his wit and eloquence were nearly always employed on the side of justice and humanity. Members of the Opposition, of course, often find generous views profitable, as well as easily come by. They cost them nothing. But Sheridan, it must be remembered, had nothing to gain by his.

Like Fox, he held that the war could, and should, have been avoided, and he suspected the motives behind it. Burke, he said, had declared that the actual occasions of the war were too mean to inquire into—it was a war against the principles of the French. That doctrine Sheridan considered 'wild and detestable.' He distrusted our allies: 'We took the field against the excesses and licentiousness of liberty; they against liberty itself.' Why had Burke never come to 'brandish in that House a Russian dagger red in the heart's blood of the free constitution of Poland?' Nevertheless, as he—Sheridan—had declared before, 'the war once entered into, he should look to nothing but the defence of the country and its interests.' For nobody could be more patriotic than Richard Brinsley.

A year later (21st January 1794) on the address on the king's speech at the opening of the session, Lord Mornington maintained that the principles adopted by the French made it essential to continue the war until they had relinquished them. Sheridan replied in an elaborate speech, highly characteristic both in style and matter. The real grounds of the war, he said, had never yet been explained. They had just heard a laborious farrago of extracts and anecdotes—extracts from a book which the noble lord allowed every one to have read, and anecdotes of which no man who saw the newspapers could be ignorant—merely designed to rouse passion against France. If the madness of the French was not confined to their own country it was the fault of their enemies. . . . 'The noble lord had quoted from Brissot the author's recommendation to the English reformers to read a pamphlet of Condorcet's encouraging them to proceed, regardless of the smallness of their numbers, since revolution must always be the work of a minority. If that were true it was a most ominous thing for the enemies of reform in England. In what a dreadful situation must the noble lord be, and all the alarmists, for never, surely, was the minority so small as at present.'

After disposing of the argument that no peace could be made with the present Government of France, and remarking on the uncomfortable fact that, contrary to all calculation, the French armies continued 'vigorous and united,' Sheridan, warming to his work, observed that the noble lord had proved that the French ought not to be able to resist them—which reminded him of the man who 'made a clock which went excellently, but which a watchmaker declared had no right to go like other clocks, for it was not made upon sound principles.' It was argued that the French were in an unsound state because of their enormous taxes—nevertheless, they paid those taxes. 'Have we,' asked Sheridan, now approaching a subject dear to his heart, 'made any such exertions? Suppose the Chancellor of the Exchequer'—this, of course, was Pitt—'were to come down and propose such sacrifices—for example, that persons enjoying incomes from the bounty of the State should refund them, or that men of fortune should reserve to themselves only the bare means of subsistence and give up the rest to the country. No—he was far more likely to say something like the following: "Do I demand of you, wealthy citizens, to lend your hoards to the Government without interest? On the contrary, when I shall come down to propose a loan there is not a man of you to whom I shall not hold out at least a job in every part of the subscription, and an usurious profit upon every pound you devote to the necessities of your country. Do I demand of you, my fellow placemen and brother pensioners, that you should sacrifice any part of your stipends to the public exigency? On the contrary, am I not daily increasing your emoluments and your numbers in proportion as the country becomes unable to provide for you? Do I require of you, my latest and most zealous proselytes, of you who have come over to me for the special purpose of supporting the war—a war, on the success of which you solemnly protest that the salvation of Britain and of civil society itself depends— do I require of you that you should make a temporary sacrifice, in the cause of human nature, of the greater part of your private incomes? No, gentlemen, I scorn to take advantage of the eagerness of your zeal . . . I will quarter many of you on the public supply instead of asking you to contribute to it.'''

This curious digression Sheridan developed at such an inordinate length that one suspects him of regarding it as the main business of his speech—it was a performance of which he himself had a very high opinion. As to the war, he concluded that the reverses of the past year should be investigated by Parliament, and that 'our precipitate retreat from Dunkirk' had been hushed up 'between the Master-General of the Ordnance and the First Lord of the Admiralty, because one of them *was brother to the minister.*'

Neither Sheridan nor any one else could foresee that the war would last another twenty years: the rise of Napoleon and the menace of invasion were still hidden in the future. At present the war had very much the appearance of an attack by the strong against the weak, and an attempt to crush the infant liberties of France; and this was the view of it that Sheridan was putting forward in 1794. 'Any minister,' he exclaimed, 'ought to be impeached and lose his head who spilled the blood of his countrymen or expended the treasure of the nation to restore the ancient despotism of France.' He demanded to know 'in explicit terms what was the real object of this war on our part at this moment,' and thanked Pitt with grave irony for having, as he—Sheridan —declared, avowed that its object was the destruction of the Government of France.

Then the war was conducted with scandalous incompetence, and our allies were entirely unprincipled and unreliable. 'Ministers had not been denied a single man or single guinea.' They had been given the most ample resources; an enormous subsidy had been paid to the King of Prussia; they had been allowed to employ French emigrants. 'What had been the consequence of all this? Defeat, disaster, and disgrace, following each other in rapid succession. Had the King of Prussia fulfilled any articles of the treaty—except receiving our money? What had been done by him, the King of Sardinia, the King of Spain, or the Empress of Russia to prove that they could be depended on?' On the address on the king's speech at the end of October, Sheridan said he was astonished that the first noun substantive in that speech was 'satisfaction.' 'It was said to be the mark of a resigned and religious temper to be easily satisfied. *If that were true there were never ministers of more meek and primitive piety than the present.*'

As to the other matter which had bulked so largely in the reply to Lord Mornington, namely, the rewards enjoyed by Pitt's supporters, and particularly by his new adherents from the other side, Sheridan returned to it repeatedly, treating it with irony —sometimes fanciful and almost playful, sometimes savage— or with downright invective. He moved for an account of certain expenses and salaries, naming Mr. Anstruther, Mr. John Erskine, Mr. Dornford, Lord Yarmouth, Lord Malmesbury, and Sir Gilbert Elliot. This led to a sharp brush with Pitt, who permitted himself to doubt the sincerity of Sheridan's assurance that he had nothing but personal good-will towards those he had named. He also supported a motion for taxing placemen during the war, and took occasion to refer to the savings Burke had once made by his reform of the Civil List, 'though he now affects to consider a similar saving paltry.' Considerable sums, continued Sheridan insidiously, could be saved by the present proposal (which, of course, had no chance whatever of being adopted). 'For instance, if *a noble cousin of the minister's*'—the Marquis of Buckingham—'out of his place as teller of the exchequer were to give £8,000 a year, that, in four years, would

THE HOUSE OF COMMONS, 1793—*From the Painting by Karl Anton Hickel.*
(Pitt is addressing the House. On the opposite side is Fox, with Sheridan on his left.
Addington is in the Speaker's chair.)

make £32,000. *Another cousin, too'*—Grenville—'might apply £4,000, the amount of his place as ranger of the park. . . . The other Secretary of State'—Dundas—'out of his multiplied places of Treasurer of the Navy, President of the Board of Control, etc., might devote the profits of at least one of those places to the same patriotic purpose.'

It is unlikely that any one else felt such zeal as Sheridan on this subject: it has always been considered far less indelicate to accept large sums of public money in times of distress than to denounce others for doing so. The salaries and pensions continued to be paid, and honours and titles to be bestowed; and the war went on.

§

But besides the war there was the burning question of reform. Sober men with a stake in the country regarded reform with profound distrust. It was only the prelude to revolution, as the example of France showed all too clearly. Shorter Parliaments, more equal representation—these things would inevitably lead to all the horrors that had been perpetrated across the Channel. The Government could take no risks. Pitt himself, as Sheridan frequently reminded the House, had once been an advocate for reform; so had the Duke of Richmond. But times were altered now. The alarm had been given and the fear of revolution grew.

Sheridan had always favoured reform: as long ago as 1783 he had warmly supported a motion brought forward by Pitt. It was an unpopular cause now, and even a dangerous one, but he stood by it with disinterested zeal, speaking for it repeatedly, and presenting and supporting petitions. He denied the existence of any serious sedition and accused the Government of spreading panic for their own purposes. No plots or conspiracies had been proved, and the minister himself did not seem to think the danger very great, for in the course of the summer 'he proceeded with due solemnity to take the weight on himself of the laborious office of Warden of the Cinque Ports.'

Speaking on the same subject in March 1793, he said that 'the alarm had been brought forward in great pomp and form on

Saturday morning. At night all the mail-coaches were stopped; the Duke of Richmond stationed himself among the other curiosities in the Tower; a great municipal officer, too'—the Lord Mayor—'had made a discovery exceedingly beneficial to the people of this country—he had discovered that, at the 'King's Arms' in Cornhill, was a debating society where principles of the most dangerous tendency were propagated; where people went to buy treason at sixpence a head, and where it was retailed to them by the glimmering of an inch of candle, and five minutes, to be measured by the glass, were allowed to each traitor to perform his part in overturning the State.'

The Government, he continued, had offered £100 reward for the capture of two delinquents, Frost and Perry, though the former was at that moment under bail and ready for trial ('if he is to be tried'), and the only crime of the latter was to have printed in the *Argus* what Pitt had himself once delivered in a speech on parliamentary reform. These two men were labelled traitors, and in this way alarm was caused. There was even a trumped-up story of a plan for taking the Tower; and another of an attempt made to poison the New River, which obliged the proprietors to advertise in all newspapers that there was no truth in the report. If Pitt were not so 'stiffnecked and lofty'—if he condescended to mix in public meetings—he would see things as they were.

Addresses were said to have been transmitted 'from patriots in pot-houses to the National Convention'—one was signed by Mr. Hardy, 'an honest shoemaker, who little dreamt, God help him, how near he had been to overturning the constitution.' Hardy, it should be said, was the founder of the London Corresponding Society. He was brought to trial in October 1794, with others, and Sheridan gave evidence in his defence. He was acquitted, but after his arrest his house had been attacked by a mob, and as a result his wife, who was pregnant, died.

Sheridan declared there were many cases of hardship—he had meant to bring them to the notice of the House, but had been so occupied with the trial of Hastings that he could not do so. At the opening of the session the Attorney-General had said he had great numbers for prosecution, but very few had actually been brought forward, and most of those were only 'booksellers who had sold Paine's *Rights of Man*—omitting all the parts objected to by the Attorney-General at the trial of Mr. Paine.' Before concluding he spared a moment for Burke—'carrying about with him knives and daggers to assist him in his efforts of description.'

Not content with attacking the harsh measures of the Government, Sheridan gave hearty support to individual sufferers. The case of Muir and Palmer, sentenced in Scotland by Lord Braxfield to transportation for fourteen years and five years respectively, is well known. Sheridan presented a petition from Palmer against the sentence and spoke earnestly on the unhappy plight of the two men. The sentences, he said truly enough, would not have been tolerated in England. He had seen the prisoners—'seen them associated with convicts of the most worthless and despicable description; seen them, not indeed loaded with irons, but with those irons freshly taken off. He had seen them separated from one another—surely an unnecessary addition to their sufferings —thus wantonly depriving them of that last of all consolations, the society of affliction.'

The Lord Advocate attempted to justify the Scottish law under which the prisoners had been sentenced. 'Would the learned lord or any other person,' replied Sheridan, 'dare to attempt the introduction of a bill for transporting persons convicted of libels in England to Botany Bay?' (Muir and Palmer were convicted of *leasing-making*.) 'Mr. Palmer had been accused of inciting poor people to insist on a parliamentary reform. If the Lord Advocate had not been as ignorant of English history as of English law he would have found some resemblance to Mr. Palmer's conduct: he would have found a resolution signed "Pitt" and "Richmond," from which every word and statement used by Mr. Palmer had been stolen. . . . Good God, sir!' he concluded, 'is it possible this can be the law of Scotland? If it be, it ought not to continue an hour longer.'

In January 1795 he brought forward a motion for the repeal of the Bill for suspending the Habeas Corpus Act. This was a matter of principle, there being no hope of carrying the motion,

G

which got, in fact, only forty-one votes. In the course of his speech Sheridan dealt at some length with 'the late trials' (those of Hardy, Horne Tooke, and others) and remarked on the extraordinary pains taken—in vain—by the Government to secure convictions.

He was quite prepared to admit that there were 'many gross and scandalous libels brought to light, and mischievous men in in the societies. Others were actuated by enthusiasm such as had actuated men of the purest minds.' He added some effective touches of ridicule. 'On the first trial one pike was produced, and afterwards withdrawn from mere shame. A formidable instrument was talked of to be employed against the cavalry: it appeared upon evidence to be a teetotum in a window at Sheffield. There was a camp in a back shop, an arsenal provided with nine muskets, and an exchequer containing £9 and one bad shilling— all to be directed against the whole armed force and established Government of Great Britain.'

The alarms and plots, in short, were factitious, and even such evidence of sedition as had been produced ought to be regarded with suspicion: 'it was obtained by a system of spies and informers.'

Here Sheridan—not to omit altogether a favourite subject— devoted a few sentences to the emoluments of ministers, and reminded the House that a noble marquis (Buckingham) would that year derive £15,000 from his place as teller of the exchequer. He then declared that England was not to be judged by the example of France. 'The example of kings, as shown by the shameless and perfidious despots of Prussia and Russia, would be just as good an argument on the other side. The only king whose example he would accept would be one who felt the true security of his power to be the people's love. He'—Sheridan— 'disclaimed the servile cant of adulation, but felt sentiments of unabated attachment to the person of their present monarch, and an unshaken adherence to the principles of hereditary Government.'

Lady Holland noted in her Journal that he had got great credit as a witness in the State trials for his wit and repartee—with the result that he became so eager for further applause that he could never bring himself to give a plain and direct answer. To this failing her ladyship attributed (with more malice than truth) the conviction of Lord Thanet, who was implicated in the attempted escape of Arthur O'Connor after his trial at Maidstone for high treason. The question put to Sheridan was, 'Do you believe Lord Thanet meant to favour the escape of O'Connor?' He parried it several times and at last succeeded in evading it. It is hard to see what more he could have done.[1] Lord Thanet was sentenced to a year's imprisonment and a fine of £1,000. Sheridan himself had been a witness for O'Connor, and it was he who had written the note urging the prisoner to jump over the bar and escape. But this fact was not divulged in court and he was thanked by the judge for helping to quell the disturbance.

§

Sheridan undeniably deserves the fullest credit for his liberal and humane views, and it should be added that, as far as treason and sedition are concerned, his judgment of the situation was almost certainly much nearer the truth than Pitt's. The line he took was, of course, generally the same as that taken by Fox, but his opinions were his own, and so was his way of expressing them. Nobody else could use ridicule so effectively, and nobody else was the master of such a play of fancy or such keen and flexible irony. In a sense these very qualities were against him, a steady dullness being more highly esteemed in Parliament than wit. Irony, too, is liable to be regarded with suspicion, and a play of fancy can be easily dismissed as a sign of light-mindedness. Even among his friends Sheridan's peculiar gifts were not invariably felt to inspire complete confidence. If he happened to speak earnestly, as well as eloquently, members could always remind themselves of his character, and reflect that, if he were not in Parliament, he would most likely be in prison for debt.

By this time he might very well have concluded that he had nothing to expect from politics. Another election was at hand

[1] His fencing, of course, led to the natural conclusion that Lord Thanet did mean to favour the escape.

and the loyalty of the burgesses of Stafford would, of course, have to be stimulated in the usual way. At the end of 1796 he had been sixteen years in Parliament and fifteen in opposition, and the prospect was not encouraging.

But to Sheridan the situation appeared otherwise. He had his own scale of values and on that scale fame ranked more highly than solid interests. It hardly occurred to him to regard his career as a failure, or even as a disappointment. Next to Fox he was now the ablest and most distinguished of the Opposition. He loved to consider himself Fox's right-hand man. The day might come when he would succeed him—surely not too extravagant a hope. He might live to be the hero of a Westminster election. No honours could appeal more strongly to Richard Brinsley—in office or out.

Besides, he was a public figure, a celebrity. Fox and Pitt themselves were not better known. When he complained in the House that the newspapers accused him of being in correspondence with a person 'outlawed by the laws of his country,' Burke replied that 'any one as prominent as he, and possessing, as he unquestionably did, uncommon genius and activity, must naturally expect to be drawn before the scrutinizing tribunal of the newspapers.' He attacked Pitt as an equal, neither giving nor expecting quarter. One might have supposed that it was he, and not Fox, who had the chief interest in defeating the minister, and that he was the rival whom Pitt had supplanted. All weapons were good in this fight. If Pitt was absent there was no need to postpone the debate—the Government lost nothing. 'What exertion that the minister could have furnished had been unsupplied? Had there been any want of splendid and sonorous declamation to cover a meagreness of argument? Any want of virulence or invective to supply the place of proof in accusation? Any want of inflammatory appeals to the passions where reason and judgment were unsafe to be resorted to?' If the Habeas Corpus Act was suspended, Sheridan was ready with an anecdote which placed the minister in a ridiculous light: A certain Patterson had a shop in Manchester and kept a tilted cart on which he inscribed the names 'Pitt and Patterson.' He was known to have no partner, and the question was asked: 'Why Pitt?' He replied: 'If he has no share in the business he has a large share in the profit of it.' For this piece of pleasantry he was taken up and committed to Coldbath Fields prison. He was eventually set free with the strict order not to go within thirty miles of Manchester—which ruined his business. If it could be said that Pitt was guided either by ambition and love of power, or by feelings of patriotism and virtue, Sheridan 'would not hesitate to ascribe the former to a minister whose whole life had marked the same total disregard for the one as implicit devotion to the other.'

And yet there was a curious strain of simplicity in Sheridan— a soft core inside this wit and his worldliness. It can be found in his speeches and in his plays, and, indeed, in the whole of his life. It appears in his singular notion that gentlemen who exerted themselves in Parliament should blush to be found accepting places, pensions, and titles; and that it was an effective stroke in debate to suggest that Windham might give up his official salary and 'live contented on his own splendid income,' and that Pitt ought to renounce his salary from the Cinque Ports and be satisfied with 'the £6,000 a year attached to his other appointments.' It appears in his enthusiam for the French Revolution and in his uncomplicated patriotism. It appears also in his ingenuous belief that ability, unassisted by prudent calculation or interest, would make his way for him; and that in a system based solidly on party, an ostentatious independence would be highly valued—all of which means that, improbable as it may seem, he cherished a simple faith in human virtue.

The fact is significant. It explains many things in his life, and is not altogether without a bearing on the chief problem of his political career, namely, how it was that a man of his *uncommon genius and activity* could spend thirty years in Parliament without ever getting a leading part, or any of those other rewards by which the toils of politicians are so often sweetened.

CHAPTER FOURTEEN

Difficult Times at Drury Lane

A S MANAGER OF Drury Lane Sheridan was obliged to find new attractions—a task continually renewed, after the fashion of the toil of Sisyphus, and one on which the success of the theatre, and his own prosperity, largely depended. In this matter he was enterprising and skilful. Nobody could be more ready than Richard Brinsley to give the public what it wanted, and there were few shrewder judges of popular taste. He was fully alive to the value of novelty, and quite prepared to turn national occasions and emotions to account, as he did, for instance, in *The Camp*, *The Glorious First of June*,[1] and *Pizarro*. But besides all this, unremitting attention was needed, and unremitting attention, unfortunately, was what he was unable or unwilling to give. Even a successful play would not run very long, and new attractions were not to be had for the asking. The manuscripts which were heaped so high on the manager's table, like those that Rich used to stuff in his drawer (from which he would coolly invite an importunate author to take any one he liked if he could not find his own), and the dreary pile which accumulated at the next Drury Lane, when Byron was a member of the committee and the theatre knew Sheridan no more, rarely contained anything worth reading. The theatre offered its patrons a rich variety of fare—operas, dramas, comedies, farces, spectacles, and pantomimes all went to make up the bill —but though the stock pieces (among which, of course, the manager's own plays were now included) could be relied on to show a modest return, and there was a comfortable following for Kemble's beloved Shakespeare, it was only to something new that the public would flock in the large numbers that meant handsome profits. And the new attraction might prove to be no attraction at all and be damned out of hand or languish miserably for two or three nights.

On 2nd April 1796 Sheridan presented *Vortigern* to an expectant

[1] Here the purpose was charitable: see p. 75.

SHERIDAN'S DRURY
(Opened in 1794; destroyed by fire in 1809.)

public. This was certainly something to stir curiosity—nothing less than a play by Shakespeare recently brought to light. It seems almost incredible that such a forgery should have got as far as the stage, but Shakespearian scholarship was neither very widespread, nor, as a rule, very thorough in those days, and Shakespeare, though admired, was not regarded with much of that superstitious reverence which the next century accorded him. Nobody saw, for instance, any reason why his plays should not be altered and improved: indeed, they always were altered; and Kemble was considered to be indulging an odd and somewhat expensive whim when he paid £12 4s. for a quarto.

Before the performance opinion about *Vortigern* was divided. Kemble never believed in it and he had the support of his friend Malone.[1] Porson likewise declared it was not authentic, and it is unlikely that Sheridan himself put entire faith in it. He regarded the business mainly as a speculation, and did not profess to be a judge. He never troubled himself much about Shakespeare, said Kemble; but he often quoted from him very effectively—as he did, for example, when he compared Burke and Windham taking refuge with Pitt from the French Revolution, to Trinculo creeping under Caliban's gaberdine to shelter from the storm. He bought *Vortigern* for £300 and half the profits for the first sixty nights. It died on the first night.

At just after half-past six the prologue [2] was spoken to a crowded house, and the play then struggled through three acts, supported noisily by a party apparently brought in for the purpose of applauding it. From that point onwards it proceeded to the accompaniment of laughter and groans. A drunken gentleman in a stage box, who expressed loud approval of the performance, was, says Farington—an eye-witness of the scene— pelted with oranges. Kemble, whose opinion could be guessed by the discerning from the way in which he delivered some of his lines, had to address the audience, at the end of the fourth

[1] On the night of the performance a handbill was distributed at the doors of Drury Lane, promising an immediate and satisfactory reply to the objections published by Malone.
[2] It was written by Sir James Bland Burges, and began:
'No common cause your verdict now demands,
Before the court immortal Shakespeare stands.'

act, asking them to hear the play through. It was finished accordingly, the last curtain descending at ten o'clock. When Mrs. Jordan spoke the epilogue she tactfully left out a passage which referred to Shakespeare as the author. Barrymore then tried to announce that the play would be given again on Monday next, but the audience would not have it and he was hissed and hooted off the stage. The management could do no more: *Vortigern* had to be abandoned to its well-deserved fate. Kemble came forward to say that *The School for Scandal* would be given instead, and the audience graciously signified its approval by clapping.

Sheridan lost no money by this fiasco, for the house brought in about £800, but he was disappointed in his expectation of large profits, and the reputation of the theatre was not improved. New attractions were not forthcoming and Drury Lane was, says Boaden, 'in low water.' At the end of 1797, however, the prospect was brightened by 'Monk' Lewis's *Castle Spectre*, which, according to Michael Kelly, had 'a prodigious run.' Lady Holland tells a good story of the author and the manager, between whom some dispute arose when they were at supper at Burlington House. Lewis proposed a wager, and offered to lay Sheridan the profits of the play—which, he observed, Sheridan had not yet paid him. Sheridan, perhaps nettled by this reminder, replied that he did not care for high wagers, but was willing to bet *what the play was worth*.

In the following March the theatre found another success in *The Stranger*, translated and adapted from a play by Kotzebue.[1] How much Sheridan had to do with the acting version is uncertain, but he contributed the song 'I have a silent sorrow here.'[2] *The Stranger* provided Mrs. Siddons with one of her most effective parts—as Mrs. Haller she was overpowering—and she was admirably supported by Kemble. German drama having proved so popular, Kotzebue was again laid under contribution: in the spring of 1799 his *Spaniards in Peru*, 'adapted to the English stage by Richard Brinsley Sheridan,' was presented at Drury Lane under

---

[1] *The Stranger* long continued to be popular. The reader will remember Thackeray's account, in *Pendennis*, of Miss Fotheringay in the part of Mrs. Haller.

[2] The music of this song was written by the Duchess of Devonshire.

the title of *Pizarro, a Tragedy in Five Acts.* It was received, says Michael Kelly, 'with the greatest approbation, and though brought out so late in the season, was played thirty-one nights, and for years afterwards proved a mine of wealth to the Drury Lane treasury, and indeed to all the theatres in the United Kingdom.' This does not by any means overstate its success. During the short remainder of the season it earned some £15,000, and edition after edition came out in the course of the year. It eventually enjoyed the singular honour of being translated *into German*, and, on the whole, is as good an example as any one could desire of Sheridan's natural turn for popularity—a gift by which he was in a position to profit largely, both as author and as manager.

§

George III, who once confided to Miss Burney his opinion of Shakespeare ('Was there ever such stuff as great part of Shakespeare? only one must not say so!—What?—Is there not sad stuff?—What—What?') told Lord Harcourt that he thought *Pizarro* a very poor composition. Fox, likewise, had no great opinion of it.

The royal judgment on this occasion was perfectly correct: *Pizarro* is a very poor composition indeed—it is hard to see how it could have been much worse. It belongs to the same general class as Mr. Puff's *Spanish Armada*, of which it reminds us strongly at times. Echoes of that immortal work can surely be heard in the following dialogue:

> *Elvira.* One only passion else could urge such generous rashness.
> *Rolla.* And that is——
> *Elvira.* Love!
> *Rolla.* True!

And again in this:

> *Rolla.* There is in language now no word but battle.
> *Alonzo.* Yes, one word more—Cora!
> *Rolla.* Cora! Speak!
> *Alonzo.* The next hour brings us——
> *Rolla.* Death or victory.

* G

The plot is unblushing melodrama, but for this, of course, Sheridan was not responsible. The style, however, is his, or at least he did nothing to improve it, and it has the dubious merit of suiting the plot exactly. It is prose stuffed with false sublimities, and with such an unnatural hankering after poetic effect as to suggest that it should have been clad in the comparative decency of blank verse. Here again it may be said that Sheridan was only doing what the case demanded, and the success of the piece certainly seemed to prove that he understood perfectly what the case did demand. It was very odd employment for the author of *The School for Scandal*—but not so odd, perhaps, for the manager of Drury Lane.

There is not much mystery about the popularity of *Pizarro*: the play has all the necessary ingredients—sublime sentiments and high-flown heroics such as would have done honour to Amadis of Gaul; fervent patriotism, love, repentance, devotion, self-sacrifice, suspense, battle, heroic death, and the triumph of right. On the stage the rapid succession of incidents must have gone far to hide the wild improbabilities of the story; just as the over-simplified and incredibly exaggerated qualities of the characters left little room for anything but admiration. The audiences that applauded *Pizarro*; felt the 'throbbing fear' of Suspense; shed the 'grateful tear' of Melancholy; and 'with kindred zeal approved Maternal feeling and heroic love,' as the Epilogue has it, differed from those of our own day much more in fashion than in taste and judgment. The fashion of Pizarro is long outworn, and the tawdry finery can only be left to moulder in the attic.

The play had every advantage that acting could give it. The spectators saw Kemble as Rolla, Barrymore as Pizarro, Mrs. Jordan (with her child duly stolen by two Spanish soldiers) as Cora, and Mrs. Siddons as Elvira. They saw the heroic and devoted Rolla, with Cora's child in his arms, escape across the wooden bridge over the cataract, and, mortally wounded, restore the cherished infant to its distracted mother and immediately die. They heard Elvira, Pizarro's mistress, upbraid her lover and defy the worst torments he could devise for her: 'Yes, bid the minions of thy fury wrench forth the sinews of those arms that have caressed and—even have defended thee! Bid them pour burning metal into the bleeding cases of these eyes that so oft—O God!—have hung with love and homage on thy looks; then approach me bound on the abhorred wheel—there glut thy savage eyes with the convulsive spasms of that dishonoured bosom which was once thy pillow!' They heard her speak her bitter farewell: 'Farewell, thou condemned of heaven!—for repentance and remorse, I know, will never touch thy heart. We shall meet again. Ha! be it thy horror here to know we shall meet hereafter! And when thy parting hour approaches, hark to the knell whose dreadful beat will strike to thy despairing soul. Then will vibrate on thy ear the curses of the cloistered saint from whom you stole me. Then the last shrieks which burst from my mother's breaking heart as she died, appealing to her God against the seducer of her child! Then the blood-stifled groan of my murdered brother—murdered by thee, fell monster!—seeking atonement for his sister's ruined honour. I hear them now! To me the recollection's madness! At such an hour what will it be to thee!' And they discovered with sighs of relief, that, at the end of Act Five, she was safe and sound and, 'humbled in penitence,' was resolved to 'atone the guilty errors which, however masked by shallow cheerfulness,' had long consumed her secret heart.

They saw, moreover, the Temple of the Sun, representing 'the magnificence of Peruvian idolatry'; the procession 'from the recess of the temple above the altar'; the priests and virgins of the sun ranging themselves on either side; the offering made after the invocation of the high priest; and 'fire from above' lighting upon the altar. They heard the choruses of the priests and virgins, and the thanksgiving in which the whole assembly joined—Sheridan had dined with Michael Kelly and discussed the important question of the music with him. They saw Alonzo and Pizarro engage in single combat; Alonzo, his shield broken, 'beat down'; Pizarro stagger back appalled at the appearance of Elvira 'habited as when Pizarro first beheld her';[1] and Alonzo renew the fight and slay him.

[1] That is, as a nun.

This rich fare was a fashionable as well as a popular success. Every one went to see *Pizarro*. Pitt went, and was observed to smile significantly when he recognized in a speech of Rolla 'some favourite figures that he had before admired at the trial of Mr. Hastings.' He declared, however, that Kemble in this part was the noblest actor he had ever seen. The epilogue was written by the Hon. William Lamb, who was to marry the hapless Caroline, and, in the fullness of time, become Queen Victoria's Lord Melbourne.

But nobody approved of the play more highly than Sheridan. It was only an adaptation, but, says Boaden, 'he felt entire paternal solicitude for it.' He could hardly have been more anxious, restless, and irritable on the first night of *The Rivals*. Lady Holland observed his eagerness with surprise, but was glad to see that he was not so besotted with drinking as to be insensible, even now, to fame. He was critical of the actors, and altogether, 'querulous to the last degree.' Mrs. Jordan, in his opinion, 'could not speak a line of Cora'; and even with Mrs. Siddons he was not wholly satisfied—she had not 'fallen in with his notion of Elvira.' Only with Kemble was he entirely pleased: 'Beautiful!' he was heard to exclaim. 'Sublime! perfection! Nothing ever equalled that!'

In spite of all this concern, however, he did not put himself to the trouble of writing a new prologue for the play, but used an old one which was by no means in keeping with the drama, and fitted the occasion only because it happened to refer to the lateness of the season. Kemble, moreover, recorded in his journal that he was obliged to stay at home in order to receive his lines as they came in, and, if Fanny Kemble may be believed, the last scenes of the piece were being hastily completed as the beginning was being acted—but this, perhaps, is an exaggeration.[1]

To a certain extent Sheridan's delight in this success is understandable: he was nearly fifty, and it was twenty years since he had written a play. The piece was not original, but he had, after all, put his name to it, and an author is rarely indifferent to popular applause. The crowded theatre, the book in every one's

---

[1] The statement probably refers to the rehearsal.

hand, the name on every one's lips—these are lively gratifications which it would be churlish to despise. They are also assurances that fortune is merry and in a giving mood. Like Lady Holland, Sheridan might very well allow himself to think of them as fame. And it was so long since he had earned that particular kind of fame. Here was a proof that those who imagined he would never earn it again were wrong: he could still command success whenever he cared to take the trouble. Besides, the profit to the theatre was important. He was the manager, and the time had been when he had shown his worth with *The School for Scandal*. His hand had not lost its cunning: one day, perhaps, he would astonish the world with a new play of his own. Nine years later he was making that very possibility the subject of a bet.

But there is still something left to be explained, for it is hard to resist the conclusion that Sheridan really thought *Pizarro* an admirable piece of work. He was perpetually alluding to it and quoting from it in his talk that summer, and to the published version he prefixed both a dedication and an advertisement. The former runs thus: 'To her, whose approbation of this drama, and whose peculiar delight in the applause it has received from the public, have been to *me* the highest gratification derived from its success—I dedicate this play'; and the latter: 'As the two translations which have been published of Kotzebue's *Spaniards in Peru* have, I understand, been very generally read, the public are in possession of all the materials necessary to form a judgment on the merits and defects of the play performed at Drury Lane Theatre.'

Now it is unnecessary to inquire which particular lady Sheridan had in mind in the delightfully ambiguous dedication,[1] or whether (as may very likely have been the case) he meant to gratify more than one, but it is clear that in both passages he was taking credit to himself for the most shining qualities of the play, though not, of course, for the whole of it. The dedication would otherwise have been a very poor compliment, and there could be no point in inviting the public to judge the merits and defects of the piece if those merits and defects were essentially those of

[1] The most obvious conclusion, of course, is that it refers to his wife.

the original. Sheridan did, in fact, contribute some passages of his own. One of them is Rolla's address to the soldiers, which made Pitt smile significantly, and contains not only an echo of his speech at the trial of Hastings, but also sentences strongly reminiscent of his speeches in Parliament in 1798 on the subject of invasion from France. 'Be our plain answer thus,' it concludes: 'The throne *we* honour is the *people's choice*—the laws we reverence are our brave fathers' legacy—the faith we follow teaches us to live in bonds of charity with all mankind, and die with hope of bliss beyond the grave. Tell your invaders this, and tell them, too, we seek no change; and, least of all, such change as they would bring us. [*Loud shouts of the soldiery.*]'

According to Boaden he was responsible for Cora's description of the 'three holidays allowed by Nature's sanction to the fond anxious mother's heart,' but the 'embroidery' of it, observes Moore, was already in the paraphrase he used. Most of the scene between Alonzo and Pizarro (Act III, scene iii) was his, and so was Rolla's apostrophe to Nature: 'O holy Nature! thou dost never plead in vain. . . .' It is strange to find the author of *The Critic* turning out these pieces of claptrap, but far more strange to find him regarding them with serious admiration. It is true, of course, that an author is often a disconcertingly bad judge of his own work, but such an explanation hardly seems sufficient here. The truth is, Sheridan's taste in the sublime was uncertain—he could not be trusted to distinguish the true from the false. As long as his wit had the upper hand he was safe, but when his heart took charge the case was very different. Passages in his opening speech at the trial of Hastings point clearly enough to this conclusion—the peroration, for instance, is in the same style as that of Burke, but in Burke's passionate climax the sincerity is as unmistakable as the magnificence: Sheridan's is strained and artificial. But after all, this is not so very surprising: it means no more than that Sheridan's artistry was limited—for which it is no more reasonable to reproach him than it would be to reproach Wordsworth for deficiency in a sense of humour.

A further conclusion can be drawn from Sheridan's curious

concern with *Pizarro*. It is almost certain that the high-flown sentiments, the heroic virtues, and the overdone passions appealed strongly to him. They went naturally to his heart and therefore he was not critical of them. They represented the good he believed in and (after his fashion) cherished, but did not do. They touched the vein of Irish sentiment in him, and the simplicity which has already been noticed; they appeared in a different guise in the genial spirit of frankness and generosity which Hazlitt found in *The School for Scandal*, and in the good-natured malice of all his comedies. This was one side of Sheridan: opposed to it was his wit (which could be savage) and the artistic power which gave it form. Between the two lay his love affairs, his drinking, his vanity, his loyalty, his occasional indifference to the truth, his fondness for practical joking—a strange medley of things which could never resemble one side without conflicting with the other.

§

The success of *Pizarro* brought no more than a temporary relief to the troubles of Drury Lane. Ever since the building of the new theatre Sheridan had made heavy demands on it. A certain amount of new capital was provided by two new partners, of whom Joseph Richardson was one. Richardson, a Whig, and the author of a comedy, *The Fugitive*, successfully produced during the exile in the Haymarket, bought, according to Boaden, a quarter of the concern—'a bad speculation.' He had only £2,000 to dispose of, and could hardly have found a worse investment for it.

In 1800 Kemble again took over the management, and for a time thought seriously of becoming one of the proprietors—an idea which Sheridan, of course, did everything in his power to encourage. He drew up a memorandum setting forth the situation in terms that had all the appearance of strict moderation and yet seemed uncommonly attractive. He pointed out that the dormant patent, 'formerly such a terror to Drury Lane,' had now been secured and the fear of further competition thereby removed. He referred to the fortune that Garrick had made (which he put at £140,000) and estimated that Kemble might expect an income of at least £4,690, of which about £1,900 would come from his salary as actor and manager, and his payment 'in lieu of benefit.' Kemble, who could have produced £10,000 in ready money—the rest of the purchase price would have had to come out of his profits—naturally felt inclined to turn his talents to further account by owning a share in the enterprise which benefited by them, and he saw no reason why the theatre should not pay well enough if the necessary reforms were made. But then, what reforms could do any good while Sheridan was in control? At this very time Kemble was writing such notes to the treasurer as the following:

'MY DEAR PEAKE,

'We are all at a stand for want of colours. . . .'

'MY DEAR PEAKE,

'Let me remind you that you are to send me £50 for Mrs. Siddons to-day, or we shall have no *King John* on Saturday.'

'MY DEAR PEAKE,

'It is now two days since my necessity made me send to you for £60. My request has been treated with a disregard that I am at a loss how to account for.

'I shall certainly go and act my part to-night—but unless you send me £100 before Thursday I will not act on Thursday, and if you make me come a-begging again it will be for £200 before I set my foot in the theatre.

'I am, dear Peake, yours,

'J. P. KEMBLE.'

Kemble did not buy a share in Drury Lane: on 24th June 1802, when the theatre closed for the season, he left it for good, taking his talents and his money to Covent Garden, where he bought one-sixth of the property for £22,000. There were times when he professed to be dissatisfied with the profits at that house, but before he died his holding was reckoned to be worth £45,000.

The loss of Kemble and Mrs. Siddons was a severe blow to Drury Lane, and the superiority now passed decidedly to its rival. In this year, says Michael Kelly, Drury Lane was in 'a very bad way.' The salaries were greatly in arrear, and so were other payments. 'Mr. Grubb, one of the proprietors, and Messrs. Hammersley, applied to the Lord Chancellor praying that their demands on the theatre, with those of the old and new renters, might be taken out of the receipts before the performers were paid.'

Matters, in short, had come to a crisis. The debts of the theatre were owed not only to actors, stage hands, stage furnishers, and so forth, but to the holders of shares—that is to say, the 'renters'—for interest. Sheridan's readiest way of raising money was by selling such shares: as long ago as 1780, when he first entered Parliament, he was supposed to have paid his election bill by this means. It was almost inevitable that he should find it highly inconvenient to pay the interest on them punctually. Shaw's remark in his preface to Frank Harris's book on Oscar Wilde, that Sheridan may not have sponged on his friends but he sold them debentures in his theatre, has a good deal of truth in it, but Richard Brinsley was, no doubt, aware of a distinction, more easily perceptible to himself (with his unfailing optimism) than to others.

If this Chancery suit had succeeded, Sheridan must have found himself in serious difficulties. The actors threatened to strike if their salaries were endangered by such an order, and Sheridan's own name, according to Boaden, stood on the weekly pay-list for £31 10s., Richardson's for £15 15s., Tom Sheridan's for £6 10s., and Grubb's for £9. He appeared in person before the Chancellor and stated the case for the theatre (which is as much as to say, for himself) with great ability and complete success. As for his own irregularities, which were undeniable, he attributed them to the uncertainty of his income, and this, no doubt, did go some part of the way towards explaining them, though it could hardly be considered a sufficient excuse.[1] The Lord

---

[1] 'It is a great disadvantage, relatively speaking, to any man, and especially to a very careless and a very sanguine man, to have possessed an uncertain and fluctuating income. That disadvantage is greatly increased if the person so circumstanced has conceived himself to be in some degree entitled to presume that, by the exertion of his own talents, he may at pleasure increase that income—thereby becoming induced to make promises to himself which he may afterwards fail to fulfil.'

Chancellor administered a grave and telling rebuke, and the occasion must have borne a slight resemblance to that on which the Lord Chief Justice admonished Falstaff.

After this there seems to have been an improvement—not, of course, in the burden of debt which the theatre was destined to carry as long as it lasted, but at least in the payment of salaries and wages. The black Saturdays when the poorer actors, actresses, and workpeople thronged about the manager for their sorely needed money belonged to the past. No longer did Sheridan make his way through the clamouring crowd with bland assurances, pocket all the contents of the treasury except what had to be left to satisfy the important people, and take his departure by another door. Heath, the engraver, told Joseph Farington in 1804 that matters at Drury Lane were much improved, and payments were now made with great regularity. Sheridan himself drew a salary of £5 a night when the theatre was open, which meant £1,000 a year, on which the 'renters' had now no hope of making any claim. His son Tom was quartered on the concern for £2 a night: something had to be done for him, and as yet nothing better could be found. Wealth was no longer to be expected from Drury Lane—the stream still flowed, but it was running low.

Another episode belonging to this period deserves to be recorded: in 1800 the theatre was the scene of an attempt on the king's life—a shot was fired from the pit into the royal box. Sheridan, who, as the friend of Fox, could hardly expect to be regarded very graciously by his sovereign, might well have exclaimed like Lady Macbeth: 'Woe, alas! What, in our house?' The royal favour had been inclining of late towards Covent Garden, and it was to be feared that it would henceforth incline still more in that direction.

The shot, however, did no harm, and the king, whose courage was proof against all trials, went to the front of the box so that the audience could see he was unhurt. He was greeted with an enthusiastic demonstration of loyalty, and Sheridan, who was in the box at the time, had the tact and presence of mind to keep the queen and the princesses from entering until the disturbance had calmed down. He explained it, with his usual readiness, by saying that a pickpocket had been taken in the pit. The king assured the queen that the noise was 'only a squib.' He was delighted with the behaviour of Sheridan, who was to go to court to-morrow with Mrs. Sheridan and Tom. When the National Anthem was sung it was found to be embellished with an additional stanza, which had been. dashed off by Richard Brinsley himself for the occasion:

> From every latent foe,
> From the assassin's blow,
>   God save the King!
> O'er him Thy arm extend,
> O Lord our God defend
> Our Father, Prince, and Friend,
>   God save the King!

It is hard to read this effusion without a smile, and it was not likely to be much admired by Fox, who spoke with distaste of Sheridan's 'Pizarro rants.' But though well timed, it was no mere piece of sycophancy. Sheridan was perfectly sincere when he declared that he 'disclaimed the servile cant of adulation, but felt sentiments of unabated attachment to the person of the present monarch.' The writing of the verse was a gesture expressive of these sentiments, and it was prompted by the general excitement. The thing was as natural to him as the hanging out of flags at times of national rejoicing is to the dweller in the back streets of a London slum; for Sheridan, like Johnson walking with Savage round St. James's Square at night for want of a lodging, was resolved to *stand by his country*.

CHAPTER FIFTEEN

Patriotism and Party

AFTER 1796 a significant change came over Sheridan's political position— a change which made his relations with Fox and his friends increasingly uneasy and complicated. On certain points he differed with them sharply, and now and then —when he considered the national emergency demanded it—he even went so far as to lend support to the Government. To tell the truth, he was too big for the boots of a Foxite to fit him comfortably, and lacked some of the qualities which go to make a good party man. It seemed to him that what he was doing was right. He had no intention of leaving Opposition, and he maintained his feud with Pitt with all his customary zeal. But at the time of the mutiny of the Channel fleet he spoke earnestly and helpfully, instead of making party capital out of the crisis, and Pitt complimented him on 'the fair, candid, and liberal conduct he had adopted in that business.' Shortly afterwards Sheridan replied. 'He was not,' he said, 'much of an egotist, nor was he, out of that House, an arrogant man. He was almost ashamed of the praise the minister had bestowed upon him that day, merely for doing his duty when he spoke of the sailors. He hoped and trusted that, much calamity as the country felt, they would never bend their necks to an insolent foe, but would, if necessary, to a man, defend their rights with their lives.'

Such sentiments found very little favour with his political friends. It was too much to expect that Sheridan, of all people, should be given credit for disinterested patriotism—a different and much easier explanation suggested itself. Nobody could be more sensitive on this point than Richard Brinsley, and at the close of a patriotic speech in 1798 he took the House into his confidence in a style more common in those days than it is now.

'I am ashamed to say anything concerning myself,' he declared. . . . 'I am sorry, also, that it is hardly possible for any man to speak in this House and to obtain credit for speaking from a principle of public spirit; that no man can oppose a minister without being accused of faction, and none, who usually opposed, can support a minister or lend him assistance in anything without being accused of doing so from interested motives. I am not such a coxcomb as to say that it is of much importance what part I may take, or that it is essential that I should divide a little popularity, or some emolument, with the ministers of the Crown; nor am I so vain as to imagine that my services might be solicited. Certainly they have not been.' Whether, he continued, this was because he was not important enough, or because it was well known that he would never change sides, was of no consequence, but he thought it right to declare that his political enmity to the present ministers was irreconcilable, and his attachment to Fox unaltered and unalterable—in saying which he was, no doubt, thinking of his friends rather than of his enemies.

Now Sheridan was perfectly sincere in this profession of loyalty (and the best proof is that he stood by it to his own loss) but the fact remained that there were two matters on which he differed with Fox and took his own line. In 1797 the party seceded from Parliament as a protest against their failure to carry a motion for reform. Grey was the prime mover in this business, for which he afterwards blamed himself; but the final responsibility lay, of course, with Fox. In 1795 Fox had married Mrs. Armistead. Having lived comfortably with her in an unhallowed state for years, he proceeded to disconcert conventional prudence and morality by living with her as her lawful husband in complete happiness for the rest of his life. He had given up dissipation, the gaming-table claimed him no longer, his creditors were appeased, and he grew more and more attached to a quiet rural existence at St. Anne's Hill, which he left with increasing reluctance to come up to town. On one occasion, indeed, he was so vexed at losing a day owing to a postponed debate, that he was observed to shed tears. All this was not without its effect on his decision in the present question.

Secession, said Lansdowne (the Shelburne of old), was either rebellion or nonsense. It did not succeed in drawing attention to the need for reform, and had no good effect whatever. The party was too small for the gesture to be impressive, even if it had been defensible on other grounds. Sheridan opposed it, but reluctantly followed the rest at first—much as a poor but proud man might come forward with as handsome a subscription as any of his richer friends. Honour pricked him on. He had no rural retreat to console him—Polesden was not purchased until the following year—and he never acquired a taste for a calm, retired life. His place in Parliament meant too much to him to be given up without a pang. To make matters worse, Tierney, whose seat had cost him much trouble,[1] firmly objected to the plan and continued to attend the House, where, having the field almost entirely to himself, he made a considerable reputation by his opposition to Pitt, with whom, a year later, he fought a bloodless duel on Putney Heath.

The spectacle of Tierney stealing his thunder in this way was too much for Sheridan. He began to be seen in the House again—attending, observed Lady Holland (with a shrewdness, which, as usual with her ladyship, was slightly tinged with malice), more against Tierney than against Pitt. It is hard to blame him. The chance of distinguishing himself in debate was all he had for his election bills and his long years of brilliant service. His objections were as reasonable as Tierney's, and what he had to say was important. The secession was a blunder: it was incomplete and little short of ridiculous. . . . But these arguments, even if he had been able to urge them, would have done nothing to lessen the suspicions of his friends, who regarded his conduct as disingenuous and disloyal—a not uncommon result (as he had good reason to know) of trying to reconcile two opposites. His itch for acting differently from those to whom he declared himself attached, was, complained Fox, 'incurable.'

The other matter was still more serious: it concerned the war, which had now been going on for four years. Sheridan's attitude towards it had changed somewhat—but then, the war had changed likewise. France had become the aggressor, and once more the

[1] George Tierney (1761–1830) had been returned for Southwark in 1796, after two petitions against his opponent.

threat of invasion hung over Britain. The country was in danger; flat-bottomed boats were talked of again, and memories of the camp at Coxheath were revived. Moreover, the war had brought much distress; cash payments at the Bank were stopped; dangerous mutinies broke out in the navy; and Ireland was in rebellion.

These things stirred Sheridan's natural patriotism. He was as ready as ever to denounce the ministers, with all his force and wit, for their misconduct of the war, as well as for their other misdeeds and shortcomings. It was to their charge that he laid 'the blood shed; the 250 millions of debt; the honour and credit of the country ruined; the stoppage of payments at the Bank; the loss of the people's attachment to their constitution; the kingdom of Ireland endangered by a cruel system of military coercion.' . . . It was a comprehensive list, and he rounded it off with the assertion that 'all the pretended successes of the war were losses.'

But when it was a question of national danger, Sheridan forgot party and would think only of the country. On the address in reply to a message from the king concerning 'traitorous correspondence' and preparations against invasion (April 1798—four months after the previous speech) he said that he would not retract the sentiments with which he rejoiced at the establishment of the French republic, though he deplored 'the scenes of blood which stained its glorious efforts to be free.' But he thought the country had more to dread from France now than ever before. No preparation ought to be neglected, for the French, if they came, would come 'for the sinews and the bones, for the marrow and the very heart's blood of Great Britain.'

Here he reached the point which galled his friends: 'If there are any who say: "Ministers have brought on us our present calamities, they ought to be first removed," I will grant them that there is justice and logic in the argument, but its policy I am at a loss to discover. . . . Indeed, there are some gentlemen *who seem to divide their enmity and opposition between the ministers and the French*; but must they not see that the inevitable consequence of this division must be the conquest of the country by the French? . . . Can there be anything more childish than to say: "I will wait till the enemy have landed and then I will resist them"?—as if preparation were not part of effectual resistance.'

It was at the conclusion of this speech that Sheridan declared his unalterable attachment to Fox, but Fox was not likely to be placated by it, or even to put much faith in it. His own patriotism was of a different sort from Sheridan's. He had been accused by the Hon. Dudley Ryder of making a speech such as might have served as a manifesto for a French general after invading Ireland; just as, at the time of the American war, he had been accused of supporting the enemies of his country. If the French once landed, he told Grey, while the present Government was in power, slavery was inevitable; the only question was, under which tyrant—George III or the French. On the whole, he preferred the former, but not enthusiastically. His views on the war had undergone no change: he was one of those who, as Sheridan said, divided their enmity between the ministers and the French—and it was the former who got the larger share of it.

In the main, Sheridan was right. He had opposed the war originally, and though perhaps it had to come sooner or later, the opposition was none the less just. But when the country was threatened by an *insolent foe* it was time to unite in its defence. He was no friend to the ministers—'on the contrary, I think there is not a more determined, irreconcilable, and inflexible enemy to them and their system than myself.' But in a national emergency 'no party feelings could operate.' Nevertheless, he was anxious for peace: 'If the ministers cannot obtain a peace' —an unsuccessful attempt had been made—'they should be removed.' This was at the end of 1797: three years later he declared that ministers had 'never sincerely wished for peace or lamented the want of it.' He had been accused of favouring revolution, but 'what provocation had he to excite any opposition against the aristocracy of the land or against its monarchy? He had possessed at one time some confidence from the monarch, during the time he filled an office of considerable trust. He had been treated with civility by many of the first families in the country.' . . . There is something a little pathetic in this list of benefits.

But the more he tried to make his position plain, the more questionable it seemed, and he himself must have felt at times as if he were trying to ride two horses at once. He had nothing to hope for except from the Whigs. The first families in the country, where he had been treated with such gratifying civility, were Whig families, and to set up his own opinions instead of following Fox was to get himself looked at askance in that society. Neither then nor afterwards were the Whigs disposed to give him credit for good motives. Fox dined with him and found him full of *absurd notions*. The least uncharitable view was that he was led on by his excessive vanity. Ever since the regency crisis he had been thought unreliable, and, of course, every one knew there was no believing anything he said. He was suspected of wanting Fox to retire altogether, and the reason could easily be guessed—and yet nothing is more certain than that he had very little to hope for in such a case. In the summer of 1797 Fox thought that if there were a change of Government, Lauderdale, Bedford, and Grey would do better if he himself stood aside. He observed that he had not mentioned Sheridan —but admitted reluctantly that he could hardly be left out altogether. This expressed to a nicety—as the event was to show nearly nine years later—what Sheridan's position really was, and what he had to expect from his friends.

It is plain that, whatever he did, he took care not to gain anything by it. If anything could make his political prospects worse than they were before, it was what he was doing now. But his loyalty, as he saw it, was irreproachable: no Foxite was a more determined martyr to the cause, and certainly none was less able to afford such a luxury. He was like a woman who has painfully preserved her virtue and lost her reputation—a case which was so brilliantly analysed in *The School for Scandal*. Indeed, he might well have recollected the words of Joseph Surface: 'When a scandalous story is believed against one, there certainly is no comfort like the consciousness of having deserved it.' At one time there was an idea of forming an administration without either Fox or Pitt. Sheridan would have nothing to do with it. 'Mr. Sheridan,' wrote Lord Moira, 'has been traduced as wishing to abandon Mr. Fox.' In spite of all his arguments he had 'gained nothing upon Mr. Sheridan, to whose uprightness in that respect I can therefore bear the most decisive testimony.'

In this odd situation Sheridan continued, his proceedings comprehensible to himself, but not to any one else. He attacked Pitt; twitted Windham ('I can see that a right hon. gentleman trembles at the very idea of peace with the French republic'); found time for a thrust now and then at the Marquis of Buckingham for the £10,000 or £12,000 a year which he got from his place; and enlivened his oratory with sallies of wit and gaiety. The Bank of England, where cash payments had been stopped, was 'an elderly lady in the City, of great credit and long standing, who had lately made a *faux pas* which was not altogether inexcusable—she had unfortunately fallen into bad company.' A secret committee was appointed to examine the situation. 'They were not even apprised whether it was the wish of the Bank that the measure should be adopted. The Chancellor of the Exchequer said it was, but he took nothing upon his word.' On a motion for the reduction of useless places he had another brush with Rose, whose places, according to Sheridan, brought him in upwards of £10,000 a year. Rose was well able to take care of himself and replied suitably. Sheridan rejoined with suavity—but not without alluding to the fact that Rose had secured the reversion of the place of Clerk of the House of Lords 'to his own relation, for no service whatever.'

He spoke feelingly on the subject of Ireland. The rebellion there was attributed in a message from the king to the 'machinations of wicked men.' Sheridan took exception to the statement. On second thoughts, however, he did not disagree with that assertion—it was true. 'It is, indeed, to the measures of wicked men that the deplorable state of Ireland is to be attributed.' The wicked men, in short, were the ministers, who had broken their promises and abandoned Ireland to 'every species of

RICHARD BRINSLEY SHERIDAN
From the Pastel by John Russell.

oppression by which a country was ever overwhelmed or the spirit of a people insulted.'

He opposed Pitt's Act of Union, and declared that Ireland had no wish to unite, and that the union would be effected, if at all, by 'surprise, fraud, and corruption'—which was not far from the truth. He also urged that a measure of Catholic emancipation should be passed, on which point Pitt was so far in agreement with him as to feel morally bound to do something for the Catholics now that the union was carried. But here the king's scruples proved insurmountable, and accordingly Pitt resigned—a thing which Fox could hardly bring himself to believe when he heard of it. The king had another attack of madness and thoughtfully attributed it to Pitt. Once again it seemed that there might be a regency. The prince expressed a wish to consult the same friends as in 1788-9, and a messenger was sent post-haste to St. Anne's Hill for Fox, who came up early next morning. Old memories and hopes began to stir. Pitt, not having been able to resign the seals of office, found himself obliged to call on the prince to inform him that, in the event of a regency, the former conditions would be imposed. But the king recovered and no regency was necessary. Pitt was out of office and the mediocre Addington reigned in his stead.

Here ended a long and eventful chapter which reached back over seventeen years to the time when the Coalition, of unhappy memory, was overthrown, and Fox and Sheridan began their seemingly interminable course of opposition to Pitt. It was the spring of 1801, and Sheridan was going on for fifty. The war continued; bread was seventeen pence the quartern loaf, and coal six guineas a chaldron; and the income tax was found *dreadfully* oppressive.

There was a general election in 1802, and for the last time Sheridan was returned by the free and independent burgesses of Stafford. It was in this year that Creevey entered Parliament, as member for Thetford—a pocket borough. His admiration of Fox was unbounded, and he was correspondingly suspicious of Sheridan—but then, he could not help admiring Sheridan also, and for the life of him could not help enjoying his company as well.

Peace had now been made, and Fox went off to France, where he saw Napoleon, who considered it desirable to show attention to so eminent and reasonable a member of the Opposition. For a short while the vexed question of war ceased to trouble politics. Throughout 1801 Sheridan made no speech important enough to be worth recording—as if, now that Pitt was out, he hardly thought it worth while to waste his blows on inferior adversaries. Indeed, he was not ill disposed towards the undistinguished and self-sufficient Addington, and reflected that, as long as Addington remained in, Pitt would necessarily remain out, which seemed to him to outweigh the fact that Addington inherited the worst features of Pitt's Government, and would never have found himself in his present position if he had not been a determined opponent of Catholic emancipation. He even came to think that some sort of arrangement might be made between Addington and the Whigs—in pursuit of which idea he lost most of what remained of his credit with his party.

This did not prevent him, however, from ridiculing Addington unmercifully. In May 1802 he gave his opinion of the peace treaty in an admirable speech, in which he included some choice observations on the seemingly ambiguous position which Pitt now occupied. He supported the peace because he thought it the best that could be got, but he drew attention to the consistency of those who had opposed the war from the first. 'It is natural to every person to have pleasure in voting in a majority —though to that pleasure I have long been a stranger.' The previous Government had left the present one only the choice between an expensive, bloody, and fruitless war, and a perilous and hollow peace. 'The right hon. gentleman says we have preserved our honour. . . . "This," says he, "is a peace in which we relinquish nothing and gain much." Will any man of common sense undertake to prove that? . . . What did we go to war for? Why, to prevent French aggrandizement. Have we done that? No. Then we were to rescue Holland. Is that accomplished? No. Brabant was a *sine qua non*. Is it gained?

No. Then come security and indemnity. Are they obtained?
No.'

Echoes of Falstaff's catechism on honour are to be heard here.
'But,' continued Sheridan, 'let the French have colonies! Oh,
yes. "Let them have a good trade that they may be afraid of
war," says the learned member, "that's the way to make
Bonaparte love peace." He has had, to be sure, a sort of
military education. He has been abroad and is rather rough
company, but if you put him behind the counter a little he will
mend exceedingly. . . .'

Here Sheridan left the Treaty of Amiens—somewhat sore but
not seriously hurt—and went on to his next subject. 'One cannot
walk along the streets without hearing doubts expressed of the
nature and security of the peace. And the next great inquiry is,
"Pray, who is minister now?" Is there, then, an interior and
an exterior prime minister?—one who appears to the world, and
another, secret, irresponsible, directing minister. Certainly in
several respects I have given my testimony on behalf of the
present ministers. . . . But the present ministers continue to
identify themselves with the former. . . . The ex-ministers are
quite separate and distinct, and yet they and the new ministers
are all honourable friends! . . . I should like to support the
present minister on fair grounds, but what is he? a sort of outside passenger, or rather, a man leading the horses round a
corner, while reins, whip, and all are in the hands of the coachman on the box. (*Looks at Pitt, seated three or four benches above
that of the Treasury.*) Why not have a union of the two ministers,
or at least some intelligible connection? When the ex-minister
quitted office almost all the subordinate ministers kept their
places. How was it that the whole family did not move together?
Had he only one covered wagon to carry friends and goods? Or
has he left directions behind him that they may know where to
call? I remember a fable of Aristophanes: it is translated from
Greek into decent English—I mention this for the country gentlemen. It is of a man that sat so long on a seat (about as long,
perhaps, as the ex-minister did on the Treasury bench) that he
grew to it. When Hercules pulled him off he left all the sitting

part of the man behind him. The House can take the allusion.'
When Sheridan came later to visit Addington at his house in
Richmond Park, his host, no doubt, occasionally recollected this
anecdote, and reminded himself that, after all, he was Prime
Minister and his visitor, for all his wit, was nothing.

'Of the ex-minister,' went on Sheridan more soberly, 'I would
just say that no man admires his splendid talents more than I do.
If ever there was a man formed and fitted by nature to benefit
his country and to give it lustre, he is such a man. He has no
low, little, mean, petty vices. He has too much good sense,
taste, and talent to set his mind upon ribands, stars, titles, and
other appendages and idols of rank. He is of a nature not at all
suited to be the creature or tool of any court.' (Here Pitt bowed
repeatedly, and perhaps remembered times when Sheridan had
expressed a different opinion on the last point.) 'But while I
thus say of him no more than I think his character and great
talents deserve, I must tell him how grossly he has misapplied
them in the politics of this country.'

It was Sheridan who described the peace as one of which
every one was glad and nobody was proud—an epigram which, according
to Lord Holland, he had heard two hours before and borrowed
without leave.

§

All this while he was a prominent public figure, and his
patriotic views made him popular—which, of course, did nothing
to reassure his friends. It was rumoured that he was going over
to Addington, and in 1803 Farington heard that he was to be
Secretary of War. A little later, however, he corrected the report
—Sheridan had declared that he would never leave Fox. He
himself accounted for his support of Addington on the simple
(and, to him, entirely sufficient) ground that he considered him
a security against Pitt's return to power, 'which he regarded as
a national calamity.'

In the meantime he was suspected of using his influence with
the prince to support his own views: he was doing his best, said
Creevey, to separate the prince from Fox and bring him over to

Addington—conduct which Creevey considered nothing short of diabolical. Even where the prince's wishes were concerned, Sheridan would not, apparently, risk offending Addington. This symptom Fox thought *deadly*: he indulged the hope that the prince was out of humour with Sheridan, but a little later he heard that they were getting drunk together, and that Sheridan was boasting that he had persuaded His Royal Highness that everything he had done was right. Sheridan's influence at Carlton House—never much relished by his political friends—was clearly to be deplored. It might turn out to be important. The king was growing old, and even if he did not die for some years yet, there was always the chance that he might go mad. In 1804, indeed, he had another illness, and Creevey reported gleefully that four physicians were in attendance at Buckingham House, and that the king was certainly in a very bad way—in which case the Whigs would have the game in their hands.

Sheridan's visits to Addington (which, he observed, might perhaps be misconstrued by his friends, though, as Addington knew, he was not to be bought) produced no result. He met Fox and the prince at Lord Moira's, and undertook to see whether any arrangement could be made with 'the doctor' on fair and honourable terms; but nothing came of it, and he afterwards shuffled and prevaricated so lamentably, said Fox, that it was suspected he had never approached Addington on the subject at all. Such conduct, sighed Fox, was insane: it was nothing but vanity and folly. For the life of him he could not tell what Sheridan was driving at—nor, he believed, could Sheridan himself. In society he was as delightful as ever, even when he said nothing that was particularly witty or striking. It was about this time that Moore 'first had the gratification of meeting Mr. Sheridan,' and the company was distinguished. But these social pleasures were apt to be clouded by political distrust. Lady Holland, while confessing that she could never resist Sheridan's charm, was obliged to remind herself that his conduct was open to the gravest doubts. At Devonshire House every one was against him. He stayed at Stanmore Priory with the Marquis of Abercorn, and the guests included the Prince of

Wales and the Duke and Duchess of Devonshire; but at Woburn he was actually challenged by Adair for abusing Fox, and a meeting was only averted by the influence of Whitbread. He had been damning Fox, remarked Creevey, for months past—not only to Fox's enemies, but (when he was drunk) to his friends. Creevey himself would put no trust in what Sheridan said: he was far too clever at scene-shifting.

Sheridan did not go over to Addington: he might damn Fox, but he would not quit him. His loyalty was fantastic, but it answered his own simple test that whatever course he took should never be attended with the odium of gain. However, as nobody but himself could feel sure of this, it did nothing for his reputation—except with his enemies.

Fox allied himself with Grenville (who had come out of office with Pitt) and thus sowed the seeds of another coalition. The war broke out again, and Sheridan, who had uttered a warning some months before against the designs of Napoleon, moved that 'the thanks of this House be given to the volunteer and yeomanry corps for the zeal and promptitude with which they associated for the defence of the country in this important and dangerous crisis.' Pitt informed the king that he now found it his duty to oppose the Government. He was requested to form a ministry, and proposed to include Fox and Grenville. But the king would not have Fox, and Pitt, it was suspected, did not press the matter with much vigour. Fox was prepared to stand aside and let his friends and the Grenvillites take office without him, but not a man of them would agree. Sheridan, after attending a meeting of the party, where he was a good deal *badgered* and had a downcast and somewhat sheepish look, seemed anxious to get right with his friends again, but Fox confessed to Grey that he felt no great confidence in him. All through this business he had been in a false position, and had suffered accordingly; and he was still at variance with the party on the subject of the war.

But in Parliament he was as confident and brilliant as ever. The situation was the familiar one—Pitt at the head of the Government and Sheridan in opposition. Before long he was explaining to the House his views on the late Government and the present one. 'Some parts of the administration of the right hon. gentleman on the lower bench'—Addington—'I most cordially approved,' he declared. 'My right hon. friend'—this was Canning—'has given credit to him for retiring from office before he was forced out. . . . If he be serious in pronouncing this laudable, what can he think of the six members of the late Cabinet who still continue in office and consent to act with, and even subordinate to, the very right hon. gentleman'—Pitt—'who so lately treated them with contumely and contempt?' The new Cabinet had six old and six new members—'*the six new nags will have to draw not only the carriage but those six heavy cast-off blacks along with it.*' Canning had been well known to Sheridan before he was old enough to enter Parliament, and had been expected, as a matter of course, to take his place among the Whigs. He had chosen instead to enlist under Pitt. The younger generation was gaining on the old: Canning was in office and Sheridan, for all his brilliance, had been out of it for twenty years.

It was in the following year—the year of Austerlitz and Trafalgar —that Sheridan made the last and the most remarkable of all his speeches against Pitt. Never, thought Creevey, had it fallen to his lot to hear such words used by one man to another. Pitt's eyes seemed to start from their sockets, and it might have been supposed that he was warning Sheridan that he would have his life if he ventured any further.

The subject was the Additional Force Bill, which, Sheridan contended, had not brought in, and could not bring in, the necessary recruits. He read the full title of the Bill, observing that he did so rather than give it its general denomination— *Mr. Pitt's Parish Bill.*

It had failed ludicrously in its object. 'What is the case with respect to Kent, where the right hon. gentleman's influence, one would suppose, must be powerful? Why, it has furnished eleven men, all of whom deserted. But I would beg the particular attention of the House to the Cinque Ports, with which the right hon. gentleman is so particularly connected; where he has so much weight both in his civil and *military capacity*; where he is said to be so much adored *as a general* and as a man. The

H

Cinque Ports have produced one man; and no doubt he is an extra-ordinary man, if one could see him. He is, perhaps, a Milo or a Hercules, and might be equal to the numerous produce of another district; as in the fable of the lioness and the sow, where the lioness said to the latter, "What signifies your numerous brood? I have but one—*but he is a lion!*"'

Here he shifted his ground. 'We have heard much of the inefficient administration of the right hon. gentleman's predecessor, but I cannot perceive any particular difference that has arisen. . . . At the time the right hon. gentleman's predecessor was on the decline, the general voice was for what was called a broad-bottomed administration. My right hon. friend on the opposite side'—Canning—'expressed a particular wish for such an administration, and I firmly believe he was sincere in that wish. Perhaps *others* were equally sincere upon that point, but not being acquainted with them I cannot say positively. However, the wish . . . was disappointed. The right hon. gentle-man went into office alone—but lest the Government should appear too full of vigour from his support, he thought proper to beckon back some of the weakness of the former administration. He, I suppose, thought that the administration became, from his support, like spirits above proof, and required to be diluted; that like gold refined to a certain degree, it would be unfit for use without a certain mixture of alloy; that the administration would be too brilliant, and dazzle the House, unless he called back a certain part of the mist and fog of the last administration to render it tolerable to the eye.

'As to the great change made by the introduction of the right hon. gentleman himself, I would ask, does he imagine that he came back to office with the same estimation that he left it? . . . He retired from office because, as was stated, he could not carry an important question which he deemed necessary to satisfy the just claims of the Catholics; and in going out he did not hesitate to tear off the sacred veil of majesty, describing his sovereign as the only person who stood in the way of this desirable object. After the right hon. gentleman's retirement he advised the Catholics to look to no one but him for the attainment of their rights. . . . But how does it appear now that he is returned to office? He declines to perform his promise, and has received as his colleagues those who are pledged to resist the measure. Does not the right hon. gentleman then feel that he comes back to office with a character degraded by the violation of a solemn pledge?'

After this Sheridan reviewed the ministers in the present Cabinet: There was Lord Hawkesbury, who, after being highly praised by Pitt, was cashiered and made Secretary for Home Affairs after being Secretary for Foreign Affairs. There was Lord Castlereagh, from whom the Cabinet could derive no brilliancy. There was Lord Mulgrave, who had nothing in his favour except that Pitt had not given him a character. There was a noble duke, who seemed to have been introduced as an ornament. The Lord Chancellor was unchanged—Sheridan presumed that Pitt had not yet discovered that the noble lord was ignorant of law. Altogether, the present Cabinet was, if anything, inferior to its feeble predecessor.

This brought Sheridan to Dundas, now Viscount Melville and head of the Admiralty. Dundas had been one of the earliest of Pitt's supporters, and when, in this same year, he was impeached on the charge of misapplying public money, Pitt was seen to press down his little cocked hat over his eyes to hide his tears.

'But then I am told,' continued Sheridan, in his best vein of grim drollery, '"There 's the First Lord of the Admiralty—do you forget the leader of the grand Catamaran project?"[1] . . . Why, I answer that I do not know of any peculiar qualifications the noble lord has to preside over the Admiralty; but I do know that if I were to judge of him from the kind of capacity he evinced while minister of war, I should entertain little hopes of him. If, however, the right hon. gentleman should say to me: "Where else would you put that noble lord? Would you have him appointed War Minister again?" I should say: "Oh, no; by no means—I remember too well the expeditions to Toulon,

[1] A catamaran was a craft filled with explosives—a sort of primitive torpedo. It was intended for use against the French invasion flotilla.

to Quiberon, to Corsica, and to Holland. . . ." It may be said that, as the noble lord was so unfit for the military depart-ment, the naval was the proper place for him'—which reminded Sheridan of the story of Garrick and Johnny McCree. Johnny, having brought Garrick a tragedy which was judged useless, tried his hand at a comedy, which proved equally unacceptable.

'Nay, now, David,' said he, 'did you not tell me that my talents did not lie in tragedy?'

'Yes,' replied Garrick, 'but I did not tell you that they lay in comedy.'

'Then,' exclaimed Johnny, 'gin they dinna lie there, where the deil dithae lie, mon?'

'Perhaps his lordship, if told that his talents did not lie in the direction of naval affairs, and that his incapacity for the military department did not necessarily qualify him for the naval, would exclaim with honest Johnny, "Then where the deil dithae lie, mon?"'

Pitt and Castlereagh replied, and Sheridan rose once more. 'The right hon. gentleman has thought fit to charge me with insincerity in the support I gave to the late administration. I say that this charge is contrary to the fact. . . . If, indeed, I had, like him, recommended Mr. Addington to His Majesty and the public as the fittest person to fill his high station, because it was a convenient step to my own safety in retiring from a position which I could no longer fill with honour and security; if, having done so from such unwarrantable motives, I should have tapered off by degrees from a promised support, when I saw the minister of my own choice was acquiring a greater stability and popularity than I wished for; and if, when I saw an opening to my own return to power at a safer period than when I had left it, I had entered into a combination with others'—Fox and Grenville and their friends—'whom I meant also to betray, from the sole lust of power and office, in order to remove him; and if, under the dominion of these base appetites, I had then treated with ridicule and contempt the very man whom I had just before held up to the choice of my sovereign and the approbation of this House and the public, I should indeed have deserved the contempt of all sound politicians, and the execration of every honest private man; I should indeed have deserved to be told, not merely that I was hollow and insincere in my support, but that I was mean, base, and perfidious.'

Nearly four hundred members were present at this extraordinary performance, which brought to an end a series of onslaughts only wanting the highest kind of seriousness to be the most memorable set of philippics in the language. Ever since Fox quarrelled with Shelburne and resigned, Pitt had been, to Sheridan, the one great foe, to be opposed and attacked on every possible occasion and with every possible weapon. It amounted with him to a principle of political conduct, so that when, for instance, he said he supported Addington as the best means of keeping Pitt out of office, he was giving what seemed to him a completely satisfactory explanation of his behaviour.

But though he never spared Pitt in any of these encounters, there was nothing petty or ungenerous in his antagonism. Pitt was not an enemy to be lightly attacked, and few were equal to sustaining a regular warfare with him. But that haughty and withering glance could not quell Sheridan: he was as ready to take blows as to give them. When Pitt spoke of 'Mr. Sheridan, in most of whose speeches there was much fancy; in many, shining wit; in others, very ingenious argument; in all, great eloquence—and in some few, truth and justice,' Sheridan 'rejected such compliments with scorn. The right hon. gentleman might himself advance the most unquestionable claim to them. No man could be more clear and eloquent when he pleased; no man, when he wished to conceal his meaning, could veil it in greater elegance of language; or involve his sentences in a finer disguise of obscurity when he wished to conceal that he had no meaning at all.' [1]

But Pitt was now near his end. His health had greatly deteriorated, and as far back as 1803 Creevey noted with satisfaction that his face was not red but yellow, and that he was troubled by a hollow cough. The news of Austerlitz was a

[1] A good stroke. Macaulay also remarks on this characteristic in Pitt.

deadly blow. He died in January 1806; and nearly two months later Sheridan paid his tribute to him with dignity, simplicity, and sincerity. The motion, appropriately enough, was for the repeal of the Additional Force Bill.

'As for me,' he said, 'there were many who flattered him more than I, and some who feared him more; but there was no man who had a higher respect for his transcendent talents, his matchless eloquence, and the greatness of his soul; and yet it has often been my fate to have opposed his measures. I may have considered that there was somewhat too much of loftiness in his mind which could not bend to advice, or scarcely bear co-operation. I might have considered that, as a statesman, his measures were not adequate to the situation of his country in the present times; but I always thought his purpose and his hope were for the greatness and security of the empire.'

§

When he made this speech Sheridan was in office—for the first time since 1783. At last the turn of the Whigs had come after their long sojourn in the wilderness. Fox and Grenville formed the ministry hopefully nicknamed *of All the Talents*. It was another coalition and the spoils had to be shared with Grenville, who got, it was thought, more than his proper share. So Sheridan once more was honoured with 'some confidence from the monarch,' and 'filled an office of considerable trust.' Now was the time when he reaped the reward of his twenty-five years of service— and now was the time when he learned the price of independence. He was made Treasurer of the Navy.

There was room in the Cabinet for Windham and Fitzwilliam (whom he used to describe as deserters from Opposition, and proselytes of Pitt); there was room for Addington (now Viscount Sidmouth). But there was no room for Sheridan. Treasurer of the Navy—it was the post Addington had given Tierney; the post Pitt had given Canning. It was the post Sheridan himself was to have had seventeen years ago, at the time of the regency crisis. What had he to show for those seventeen long years—

he, who had shone so brilliantly with his *uncommon genius and activity*? Nothing . . . less than nothing. The prospect then had been bright enough—Chancellor of the Exchequer . . . Cabinet rank. . . . There was no talk of such things now. It was a painful blow to his pride, as well as to his hopes. He told Fox bitterly that though he accepted the office he felt no obligation of gratitude to *any one* for it—he had been led to believe seventeen years ago that he could count on very different treatment.

Moore was told that Sheridan's wife and some of his nearest friends urged him not to accept office in the circumstances, and particularly an office of so much 'responsibility and business.' His habits they thought, unfitted him for it in any case, and he would do better to take his chance in a position of honourable independence. But the time was past, observes Moore, when he could afford to adopt this policy—'the emoluments of a place were too necessary to him to be rejected.' Besides, in Parliament there was no chance in a position of honourable independence: Sheridan's chance lay in changing sides—but that he would have died rather than do.

He did not give up his independence, however. Still nursing it, he moved into the official apartments in Somerset House and began to consider the question of clearing off his most pressing debts. And in spite of the emoluments it must have seemed to him now and then that the best days were over.

CHAPTER SIXTEEN

Irregularities—A Place from the Prince—The Theatre burnt down

IT WAS THIRTY years since Sheridan had set out to make a living for himself and his lovely young wife, and to astonish the world. It had been a brilliant career in many ways, but then, it had never been quite safe. His position, which often seemed so enviable, had something flimsy about it, after the style of the scenery at Drury Lane. Still, whatever shifts he was put to, and whatever difficulties and disappointments he met, he was always somebody—a man of consequence, of whom the world had to take note, generally with admiration though not entirely with approval. He used his talents, thought Farington, to keep a position of considerable importance in spite of a life of profligacy which would have sunk any one else; and if only he had used them to good purpose he would certainly have found himself at the head of affairs. This was in 1806: he was not at the head of affairs then, and there was no chance that he ever would be. He was past the height of fortune and already on the decline. What ordinarily passes for success was not for him: nor was security. He was getting on in middle age, and the pattern of his life was shaped out. There was no likelihood that it would be much changed. The moralist was now safe in regarding him as an impressive example by which to take warning.

Sheridan, however, had an infallible charm against disillusion and regret. Reynolds's well-known portrait of him shows an unexpectedly heavy and serious face; but though it does not, at first, suggest quickness, irresponsibility, gaiety, or wit, it speaks eloquently of a strong zest and appetite for life. That appetite, parent of hope and illusion, and of much else, Sheridan never lost.[1]

His habits did not improve as he grew older, and there never was any probability that he would be seen in the character of a

[1] Reynolds's portrait was painted in 1789. The drawing by John Russell (in the National Portrait Gallery) shows the same appetite for life, and more charm and liveliness. It also does full justice to his neatness, and to the fineness of his eyes.

reformed rake. In his last illness the Bishop of London attended him and read prayers, but though poor Esther Jane declared that her dying husband expressed deep repentance for his sins, the bishop could not conscientiously bear out this statement. About Sheridan's sins there was, unfortunately, no doubt at all. They were the unmistakable ones that lend themselves to easy and hearty reprobation—especially when, as in his case, they are accompanied by imprudence. They concerned women, money, and wine, and thus were certain to be damned, not only by those who had no mind to them, but also (and even more zealously) by those whose inclination ran that way but was baulked by want of courage or opportunity. Lady Bessborough—formerly Duncannon—reproached him on his death-bed for having persecuted her all his life; and she told Lord Broughton that no other man ever had so much of the devil in him as Sheridan. Lady Holland felt she ought to despise him for his private life, and spoke of his habitual debauchery and profligacy. Her husband thought that his intemperance and dissipation were carried to such lengths that they would, by themselves, have disqualified him for the leadership of an English political party—though he went on to observe that his vanity and want of veracity were even more serious drawbacks. His intrigues were notorious, though not, as Byron protested, more so than those of some of his contemporaries. However, his reputation was certainly much blown upon. In 1807 Lawrence told Farington that he had dined at Sir H. Englefield's with Mrs. William Spencer, Sotheby, Rogers, and Francis Horner, in which sober and respectable society Sheridan's profligacy with women was talked of and many examples of it were mentioned. It was even said, among other things, that at one time a woman with any character to lose hardly dared to be left alone in a room with him. This, of course, is hearsay evidence, but though it is not to be relied on against Sheridan (for which reason some details have been omitted here) it shows very clearly what sort of reputation he enjoyed. Lawrence, it should be observed, was an enthusiastic admirer of his.

More mentioned in his Journal the story of a bag of love-letters,

* H

lost and recovered, but in his *Life of Sheridan*, which amounted
to an authorized biography and was written within nine years of
the death of its subject, he handled all such matters with the
nicest tact and discretion; and though he did not conceal Sheridan's
infidelities, refrained from dwelling on them or entering into
details.

Something, no doubt, must be allowed for the fact that the
society in which Sheridan loved so much to mix, was one in
which the ordinary writ of morality hardly ran. In that distinguished company he found not only temptations, but also a
high-spirited freedom of conduct which seemed to have a natural
connection with high birth and position, and which was therefore sure to appeal to his vanity. Besides this, his unsettled life
and the general uncertainty of his affairs encouraged dissipation,
and these things grew worse, instead of mending, as the years
went by. The success he had expected never came, and if he
drank his three to six bottles a day and in later years fortified
himself in addition with brandy, it must be admitted that he
had plenty of cares to drown. When he was carried home and
put to bed, it was, very likely, to a house where the bailiffs
were below stairs; and when he woke in the morning it was to
the knowledge that a heap of unpleasant business and an assiduous
crowd of duns awaited him as usual. In such circumstances it
was hardly to be expected that he would ever *purge and live
cleanly*.

He had a strong constitution which resisted these relentless
attacks remarkably well, but in the course of time dropsy, which
lay in wait for excessive drinkers, threatened him, and he suffered
from disorders of the stomach. He lost his appetite and would
only pick at his food, or at most take a grill. He had a *brandy*
appearance. His face and figure alike began to show unmistakable
signs of degradation, but he never became unwieldy, or developed
a prominent belly like Fox's, whose devoted wife used to refer
to it as his 'box.' The degeneration in Sheridan went far, but
was never complete: the thought of him might occasion a pitying
'Poor Brinsley!' but his dregs, said Byron, were better than the
first sprightly runnings of others; and his intoxication was that

JOHN PHILIP KEMBLE
From the Portrait by Gilbert Stuart.

of Bacchus and not of Silenus. To the end there was something of the archangel ruined about him.

His faults were like those of his own Charles Surface—warm-blooded and generous in their manner. Old Thomas Sheridan once said, in a moment of bitterness, that his celebrated son had not far to go for the characters of Charles and Joseph Surface—he could find them both in his own heart. He could have found Charles there, undoubtedly. The Charles Surfaces of the world have a great deal of charm and their gaiety lightens many an hour which would have been dull enough without it. People may shake their heads over them, but they are generally liked, and as long as they are young it seems very unreasonable to call their vices by harsh names. But when they grow older it is another matter: they lose their graces, their failings begin to have an ugly look, and they break the hearts of their fond Marias.

Something of this was to be seen in Sheridan's case. His second wife talked of leaving him. The poor lady had all Elizabeth's sorrows to bear, together with others which Elizabeth never suffered. Her comfort and happiness, she lamented, had been thrown away. The hope that everything would come right faded until, in spite of her husband's assurances, it vanished altogether. But Sheridan never could understand the natural result of his vagaries. He begged Esther Jane not to talk of leaving him—if she did, she would *destroy* him. He persuaded her that all would be well: difficulties about money would be overcome and he would 'bring his affairs into order.' The smallest cheerful event stirred his hopes. In 1810 he reckoned, for her benefit, that he would now be able to expect an income of £4,000 a year—having, no doubt, entirely convinced himself that this really was the case.

His irregularities did not destroy his natural generosity of mind, and very likely, except when their effects happened to be distressing, did not much disturb his conscience—a case which is less uncommon than might be supposed. He was particularly anxious to do well for Tom, who, as his step-mother sensibly observed, ought to have something settled to rely on. Drury

Lane was not the right kind of provision for an aspiring young man. As long as Sheridan was out of office he could not, of course, expect any favours from the Government, though in Addington's time an offer was made of the post (very profitable during a war) of Registrar of the Vice-Admiralty Court at Malta. But Sheridan felt obliged to refuse it: his position was somewhat delicate at the time and the thing might be misinterpreted —it might have the appearance of a bribe.

In 1804 Tom went to Edinburgh as aide-de-camp to Lord Moira. Here he had an affair with a Mrs. Campbell, the result of which was that damages to the tune of £1,500 for crim. con. were given against him three years later in the Sheriff's Court. In 1805 he ran off with, and married, Miss Caroline Callander —a bride whom his delighted father received with joy and thought immeasurably lovely and engaging. Miss Callander was described as an heiress (otherwise, of course, there would have been no need to run away with her), but Tom still had hardly enough to keep himself. In the following year, the Whigs being now in office, Sheridan approached Fox on the subject. His pride must have suffered, but where Tom was concerned he would never let pride stand in the way. Fox obligingly wrote a letter for him to take to Lord Grenville: 'Mr. Sheridan, who will deliver this . . .' It was in the usual form, and not at all the kind of document that the bearer would, in the ordinary way, have consented either to ask for or to present. Grenville was stiff and haughty in his manner, and Sheridan, who had opposed the alliance between him and Fox, must have found the interview trying. However, it bore fruit: in April Tom was appointed Joint Muster Master-General in Ireland.

Sheridan's efforts did not end here. When he was given the receivership of the Duchy of Cornwall by the prince he tried hard to get the place transferred to his son; and he told Esther Jane that, though he had always firmly refused to accept even the most trifling loan from the prince for himself, he had taken large sums from him in vainly endeavouring to get Tom into Parliament. In 1807 he was trying to arrange that Tom should be associated in the management of Drury Lane with a new partner—Tom's salary to be £1,000 a year. The theatre, indeed (from which Richard Brinsley himself needed every penny that could be got), was fated to provide Tom's patrimony: at the time of the fire he owned a quarter of the patent.

In the midst of all these attempts to fix his hopeful son in a noble independence, Sheridan (who never had any patrimony at all) entertained Creevey to dinner, where, as the latter observed, all sorts of odd characters, including sheriff's officers and employees at the theatre, officiated as servants out of livery.[1] It was about this time, too (to take a view of him in yet another light), that, in the disguise of a police officer, he appeared at Lady Sefton's and arrested her for unlawful gaming; and, as a guest at the Pavilion, took advantage of the darkness during a 'phantasmagoria' to sit on the lap of a haughty Russian lady, whose screams were loud enough to be heard from one end of Brighton to the other.

Tom, whose pleasant, easy-going ways were not compatible with his doing anything for himself (he should have been advised, thought Fox, to enter a profession), had in him unhappily the seeds of the disease which killed his mother. He was sent to the Cape as Colonial Treasurer in the hope that the change of climate would save him, and there he died in 1817, having outlived his father by little more than a year. Esther Jane's son, Charles, who could expect some help from his mother's family, was educated at Winchester and Cambridge. He inherited Polesden, and lived until 1843.

§

It was in 1804, when Sheridan had been living for twenty-one years (that is to say, since his brief term of office in the time of the coalition) solely upon the resources provided by Drury Lane, that the Prince of Wales offered him the receivership of the Duchy of Cornwall, which had become vacant by the death of Lord Elliot. The offer was made with the utmost graciousness: there was no reason why it should not be accepted, and nobody

---

[1] A similar tale is related of Sir Richard Steele, and it is not the only one which he shares with Sheridan.

but Sheridan would have thought it necessary to point out that it was not the price of baseness or servility. Its value fluctuated from year to year, but on average was not much short of £1,000. To Richard Brinsley, who, besides his debts, had a son to provide for, it was a godsend.

Unfortunately it soon appeared that the place had already been promised to General (afterwards Lord) Lake. The general was in India, but his friends were determined to look after his interests; and his brother had actually lent him money on the strength of his expectations. There was a strong protest from this quarter against Sheridan's appointment, and it was even suggested that the general's claim might be enforced as a matter of right.

This put the prince in an embarrassing position. The promise had certainly been given, and to have the affair made the subject of a contest would be extremely unpleasant. The general and his friends showed no great delicacy in their proceedings, and were not much concerned to spare the feelings of His Royal Highness. They took the simple view that a promise had been given and must be kept. It was left for Sheridan, whose needs were notoriously pressing, to show that generosity and fine sense of honour which would have been so much in keeping with a large independent income. 'Nothing on earth,' he wrote, 'shall make me risk the possibility of the prince's goodness to me furnishing an opportunity for a single scurrilous fool's presuming to hint even that he had, in the slightest manner, departed from the slightest engagement.' In short, his great anxiety was to guard everybody's interest but his own. He announced his determination to resign the profits of the place to Lake—and he did so. In 1808 Lord Lake died, and the income became Sheridan's for the rest of his life. It was contended at the time of the dispute that some of the duties of the place could not be performed by a deputy; but it does not appear that Sheridan was ever troubled with any such duties. It was in connection with this place that the story was told of his calling at the bank and being most agreeably surprised at the unusual compliance of the clerk, who showed an unaccountable willingness to let him draw a sum far beyond the trifling amount which Sheridan had hoped to wheedle out of him. The mystery was explained by the fact that a considerable payment had come in: the letter informing him of it had, of course, been left unopened with the rest.

This was the only place he ever got, apart from three short terms of office when his ill-starred party happened to be in power. If he pilloried Rose and the Marquis of Buckingham; if he made pointed allusions to the situation of Pitt as Warden of the Cinque Ports, and that of Grenville as Ranger of the Park, he did so at least with a clear conscience. Grenville, indeed, so stiff and haughty—that 'direct man,' as Fox called him—obtained the lucrative post of auditor of the Exchequer, and when, in 1810, he expected to come into office with Grey, he showed the utmost anxiety to keep it in addition to being First Lord of the Treasury. To Grey's objections he pleaded poverty, and finally agreed, though very reluctantly, that the place should be held in trust for him. Sheridan's views, like his conduct, must have seemed very odd to him—but then, they seemed odd and, indeed, incomprehensible, to most people. In a review of Moore's Life, the writer, entirely oblivious of what Hazlitt called Sheridan's 'honourable firmness,' dismissed him airily as 'an unsuccessful adventurer.'

§

Meanwhile his career was still being carried on the back of Drury Lane Theatre. The loss of Kemble and Mrs. Siddons was a severe blow to the company. The management was undistinguished, new attractions were harder than ever to find, and the income for the 1803-4 season fell a little below £50,000.

The star of Master Betty rose and for a while caused that of Kemble himself to pale by comparison. Sheridan did not think much of Master Betty, but he engaged him, the popular enthusiasm for the youthful prodigy being undeniable. Besides, he had already appeared with great success at Covent Garden. At Drury Lane he acted twenty-eight nights. The receipts were extremely gratifying (they averaged over £600 a night) but the expense was heavy, for a high value was set on the talents of the young Roscius. Altogether, Drury Lane continued to be in low water, and it seemed that its best days were over.

In 1807 the manager's hopes were cheered by the possibility that Jones, the Dublin theatre proprietor, might be induced to come into the concern. Sheridan displayed all the advantages of the scheme with his usual optimism, which deceived himself as much as anybody else. Drury Lane, he argued, wanted nothing but proper management to be prosperous. He suggested that Jones should take a quarter share and manage the theatre at a salary of £1,000 a year, together with an agreed percentage of the net profit. Tom Sheridan would be associated with him in the management, and would likewise receive £1,000 a year.

This hopeful plan would have given Tom a suitable income and provided his father with new capital, which would have afforded him some relief in his difficulties and ultimately have gone the way of all the rest. The negotiation languished, but was stimulated in the following year by a curious bet, recorded and witnessed at the One Tun Tavern, St. James's Market: 'In the presence of Messrs. G. Ponsonby, R. Power, and Mr. Becher, Mr. Jones bets Mr. Sheridan 500 guineas that he, Mr. Sheridan, does not write and produce under his own name a play of five acts or a first piece of three, within the term of three years from 15th September next.' To this was added a rider, which, in Sheridan's view, must have been the essence of the matter: 'It is distinctly to be understood that this bet is not valid unless Mr. Jones becomes a partner in Drury Lane Theatre before the commencement of the ensuing session.'

The pathetic idea that Sheridan (whose last original piece was nearly thirty years old) might yet write another play was, therefore, still being entertained, though very likely he himself had no longer any great faith in it. But ready money was urgently needed and the play might serve as a bait to catch it. So might the touch of magnificence in the thumping amount of 500 guineas. The financial reputation of the theatre was too bad for there to be the slightest hope now of raising money by selling shares—a partnership was the only chance. The proposals made to Jones were much the same as those formerly made to Kemble. The result, likewise, was the same. Jones did not become a partner before the commencement of the ensuing session, or at any other time; Sheridan did not write a play; the 500 guineas remained a mere figure on a scrap of paper; and before the end of the following season Drury Lane Theatre was a heap of blackened rubble and ashes.

In September 1808 Covent Garden Theatre was burnt down, and the company was forced to betake itself to the Opera House in the Haymarket. It was an omen. Five months later— 24th February 1809—when the House of Commons was debating a motion on the subject of the war in Spain, a vivid red glow lit up the windows. Drury Lane was on fire. A motion was made to adjourn, but Sheridan rose and said that 'whatever might be the extent of his private calamity, he hoped it would not interfere with the public business of the country.' He was reported to be not completely sober at the time. He went out and the debate continued.

At the Piazza Coffee-house he took a bottle of wine and watched the progress of the fire with a calmness which surprised his friends. 'Cannot a man,' he replied when they commented on it, 'take a glass of wine by his own fireside?' The joke, thought Moore, was perhaps not new; but he was quite as capable of inventing it as of borrowing it.

The destruction was complete. The iron curtain and the reservoir of water—those much-vaunted safeguards—had no effect. A fire left burning in a shoddily constructed fire-place sufficed to put an end to Sheridan's theatre. A harpsichord which had belonged to Elizabeth and had been moved from Somerset House when the late Treasurer of the Navy went out of residence, was lost with the rest. The insurance, which in any case covered only a small part of the value, was swallowed up at once by demands. Another of Sheridan's careers had come to an end. He had long since ceased to be a dramatist: he now ceased to be the manager of a theatre. Never again was a sneering reference to that occupation to be made by any hon. gentleman in the House.

For all that, he was not altogether done with the theatre, and, in fact, it was some time before he clearly understood what the situation was. Covent Garden had been burnt down and was now being rebuilt with an increased number of private boxes. This very year it was to reopen with Madame Catalani, the celebrated soprano, engaged at no less than £75 a night. Sheridan's own theatre—Garrick's, that is to say—had been pulled down and a new one built in its place. The debts of the old one had not been settled, as they should have been, on that occasion; but things could be managed better this time. Sheridan met the performers, says Michael Kelly, and 'exhorted them to stand together for the good of all.' The patent was still valid, and they could act as his company somewhere else. It had been done before and could be done again.

The plight of the company—to say nothing of the unfortunate stage-hands, box-keepers, and other employees—was worse than the manager's. They were allowed to act six nights for their own benefit at the Opera House, Taylor, the manager, taking only his bare expenses; and the Lord Chamberlain graciously permitted them to appear at the Lyceum until June—the end of the ordinary winter season. Sheridan himself could do nothing for them. The case, after all, was not the same as that of Covent Garden; and it was not the same as it had been when the old theatre was pulled down. The difference lay in the fact that no new theatre was being built. Holders of £500 shares got rid of them at any price they would fetch, and a very low price it proved to be. It was gradually borne in on Sheridan that something really had come to an end—something on which he had relied for more than thirty years. Nobody would invest a penny in another theatre of his. To be sure, he still had the patent— or, to be exact, half of it—and a patent was a valuable thing which could be bought and sold like any other commodity. But what was its value when there was no theatre to go with it?

§

The only income he now had was what he got from his place as receiver of the Duchy of Cornwall, for by this time he had been out of office nearly two years—the Ministry of All the Talents having ended its short and not particularly distinguished career in March 1807. The prince's gift, and the death of Lord Lake, were therefore providential. An income for life of about £1,000 a year should, one would suppose, have been quite enough to keep him and his family in comfort. His father had rarely enjoyed as much even in his palmiest days, and the time had been when Richard Brinsley himself thought £500 a great sum. If he had never been economical before, he could begin now.

But the thing was not so simple: his difficulties had been accumulating far too long for mere economy to get rid of them. The best he could hope for was to go on making head against them somehow or other. His unquestionable debts at this time were about £10,000. There were others amounting to upwards of £50,000, and though many of these were probably fraudulent, owing to his easy habit of disregarding such things as accounts and receipts, some, at all events, must have been genuine. The whole of his income for the rest of his life would not have paid off half of what he owed. The style in which he lived, therefore, could hardly make much difference except so far as it concerned the circumstances in which the bailiffs were likely to find him. As long as the debts remained unpaid the interest on them grew—in some cases, according to Moore, it came in the end to more than the original sum. Nothing but a large supply of ready money could cure this disease, and where was he to look for such a fortune now? Drury Lane, with all its encumbrances, had represented a large sum of money, but Drury Lane was gone. Nothing was left—except the patent.

In these circumstances it is easy to believe that some of the stories of 'poor Sheridan' were substantially true. 'Possibly he had little appetite for breakfast himself, but the servants complained bitterly on this head, and said that Mrs. Sheridan was sometimes kept waiting for a couple of hours while they had to hunt through the neighbourhood and beat up for coffee, eggs, and French rolls. The same perplexity in this instance appears to have extended to the providing for the dinner; for so sharp-set were they, that to cut short a debate with a butcher's apprentice about leaving a leg of mutton without the money, the cook clapped it into the pot: the butcher's boy, probably used to such encounters, with equal coolness took it out again, and marched off with it in his tray in triumph.'[1]

'It has been a principle of my life,' wrote Sheridan to Whitbread, 'persevered in through great difficulties, never to borrow money of a private friend; and this resolution I would starve rather than violate.' Tradesmen, of course, did not rank as private 'friends: besides, they were all to be paid some day. However, he told Esther Jane that he had at last broken this proud rule (which would, apparently, have doomed her to starve with him) and asked and accepted the 'pecuniary assistance of private friendship.'

A ray of light cheered this desolate scene: the theatre might be rebuilt. A committee could undertake the task and Sheridan had friends who were willing to serve his interests in this way if the difficulties could be overcome. The difficulties were formidable, for Drury Lane had become a byword. Everybody knew that the outstanding claims were heavy—and then there was Sheridan himself, whose name, unfortunately, inspired the deepest distrust. It needed a man of substance and well-known integrity to give the undertaking any chance of success. The man was found—it was Whitbread, the trustee, with Grey, of Sheridan's marriage settlement. 'Nothing short of the high character of Mr. Whitbread,' observed Boaden, 'could have raised the necessary funds and inspired confidence.'

Having gathered that Whitbread would not be unwilling to 'assist a committee for rebuilding Drury Lane,' Sheridan wrote to him accepting his informal offer with gratitude, and expressing his high opinion of Whitbread's ability. He referred to his own 'private difficulties,' which, he was sure, Whitbread, and others in prosperous plight, could never understand. But his mind had

[1] Hazlitt: *On the Want of Money.*

not been 'subdued by the late calamity,' nor had it lost its 'resolute independence,' though he admitted that he had been greatly 'embarrassed.' However, all would now be well, and he saw clearly how the thing could be managed—'I have worked out the whole subject in my mind.' And no doubt he had, for he was always very good at making plans.

The cloud had passed. This was the time when he assured Esther Jane that his affairs would soon be brought into order, and that he could look forward to an entirely satisfactory income for the future. He was getting on for sixty. Things had certainly been very hard of late, but that was all over now.

CHAPTER SEVENTEEN

The Price of Independence—Last Career ended

WHERE, SAYS BYRON mockingly in the eleventh canto of *Don Juan*, are

'My friends the Whigs?   Exactly where they were.'

That is to say, they were in opposition.   Sheridan was then lying in the Abbey, and the Whigs were in their customary plight, as they had been ever since the fall of the Ministry of All the Talents.   He might never have quarrelled with them; he might have followed Fox with the most complete docility—and he would not have been a day longer in office.

As long as he was Treasurer of the Navy, his income was quite large enough to cover his expenses and pay off some of his debts into the bargain.   That happy state of affairs lasted just over a year.   One would have supposed that, having accepted the place, he would have taken reasonable care not to risk losing it; but before many months were out he was informing the House that the Cabinet must not expect him to sacrifice his independence of opinion for the sake of his office—if they did, they would be disappointed.   To Creevey, who had managed to get a place as Secretary to the Board of Control, such behaviour seemed nothing less than infamous.

This was in July 1806.   Two months later Fox died.   Sheridan expressed the deepest grief, and was reported to be 'very low.' Nobody must expect to see him for a month.   Apart from the prince, he declared, Fox had been his only friend.   However, it was well known that relations between them had been strained for some time.   Fox never understood Sheridan's divided loyalties, and never sympathized with the complicated impulses which he described as his vanity.   Still, they had known each other intimately for thirty years, and for twenty-five of those years Sheridan had followed, sometimes against his better judgment, Fox's deplorable political fortunes.   It was now said that when he lay dying at the Duke of Devonshire's villa at Chiswick, Fox would

CHARLES JAMES FOX
From the Portrait by Karl Anton Hickel.

not see Sheridan; but this was not true, though it was true that
he did not see him alone.

Sheridan, however, was given the charge of the funeral arrangements, and he appeared among the distinguished mourners—the
Duke of Norfolk, Lords Holland, Howick (Grey), Fitzwilliam,
Grenville, Carlisle, and the rest. It was observed that they were
all in tears. The grave was in the Abbey, near those of Pitt and
Chatham; and perhaps Sheridan indulged a vain hope that one
day he himself would be buried in that august company. A doctor
who was present shook his head professionally over his altered looks
and thought they betokened an inflamed liver. Dropsy, which
had killed Fox, would carry him off, too, he feared, before long.

Sheridan's real position now became painfully clear. Grey was
at the head of the party and Grenville was First Lord of the
Treasury: neither of them had any love for him. The death of
Fox left a vacancy at Westminster, and it was no secret that
Sheridan was particularly anxious to be returned for that celebrated constituency as Fox's successor—a distinction quite free·
from sordid considerations of profit, and entirely to his taste.
But his chiefs had other views, and more important friends to
serve. He was bitterly mortified to find that they had already
decided to put forward Lord Percy. 'You must have seen by
my manner yesterday,' he wrote to a friend who was, apparently,
responsible for some misunderstanding on the subject, 'how
much I was surprised and hurt at learning, for the first time, tha℩
Lord Grenville had, many days previous to Mr. Fox's death.
decided to support Lord Percy.' He himself had resolved to
make no move while life remained in Mr. Fox, and he had been
led to believe that Grenville would not come to any decision
without first seeing him. He now found himself in 'a very
unpleasant dilemma.'

To Grenville he wrote that, if he had been asked to stand
aside and leave the field to Lord Percy, he would have done so
'cheerfully,' but as it was he felt bitterly that if no satisfactory
explanation were to be given, he would be left 'under an un-
merited degree of disgrace and discredit.' But no explanation
could possibly save him from humiliation: he had begun his

campaign, and now had to back out with the best grace he could find. Whatever misunderstanding there may have been, he had no sympathy to expect from Grenville, who was sure to attend to the wishes of the Duke of Northumberland (Lord Percy's father) in preference to those of Richard Brinsley Sheridan; and who was complaining that the Government was in a 'strange state' with its Treasurer of the Navy opposing it both in Parliament and at Westminster. He even thought it advisable to bring the matter to the notice of the prince, saying how concerned and mortified he was to learn that Lord Percy might be opposed by Mr. Sheridan—though he trusted that this would not prove to be the case. The prince took the hint and reassured the anxious Grenville: he would use all his influence over Mr. Sheridan. . . .

There was no help for it: Sheridan had to swallow the pill. At the Crown and Anchor Tavern he gave an address to his supporters. He spoke of Fox: 'It is true that there have been occasions upon which I have differed with him—painful recollections of the most painful moments of my political life.' Endeavours had been made to represent these differences as a departure from loyalty to Fox, but he knew that '*nothing on earth could detach me from him.*' If he—Sheridan—had to choose again, he would still choose to be an exile from power, distinction, and emolument, rather than 'a splendid example of successful servility or prosperous apostasy.'

There were, of course, awkward hints that his withdrawal was caused by the fear of offending the Government and losing his situation. 'One,' he said, 'who has struggled through such a portion of life as I have without obtaining an office, is not likely to abandon his principles to retain one when acquired.' He had not made an earlier move in the election because he could not bear to do it 'while one drop of life's blood beat in that heart, now cold for ever.' Finally, he confessed that it was with a 'very embarrassed feeling' that he announced his intention of retiring from the contest. On 7th October Lord Percy was returned.

Soon afterwards Parliament was dissolved and Sheridan, who had been brooding over his ill-treatment, immediately made it clear that he meant to stand this time, whatever came of it.

Lord Holland accused him of forcing himself on the constituency; Marquis Wellesley [1] complained that the seat was being sacrificed to his vanity; the Duke of Northumberland was deeply offended and withdrew Lord Percy, to the great distress of Lord Grenville; but the Duke of Bedford instructed his agent to give all possible support to Sheridan, as well as to Sir Samuel Hood. The Government found itself in the galling position of having to do likewise.

The contest was a violent one, and much enlivened by the candidature of Paull, the tailor, who stood for Liberty, Protection, and Peace. The ministers thought that the general opinion was against Sheridan, and that 'the tailor would beat him.' In point of character, they considered, there was nothing to choose between the two. Grenville declared that the expense of 'this horrible Westminster election' was beginning to distress Hood, and that something must be done to help him—as for Sheridan, he added callously, he took his expenses upon himself. Where he was to find the money was no concern of Grenville's. However, the Marquis of Buckingham went so far as to send £100, not to bring in Sheridan, as he was careful to explain, but to keep out Paull. The struggle ended half-way through November: Sheridan beat Paull by 277 votes and was returned with Hood. At last he had realized one of his great ambitions, but in the circumstances his satisfaction was not unalloyed: he could hardly consider himself Fox's successor, as he had so much wanted to do. As usual in his political life, his hopes were fated to be deceived. His expenses, fortunately, were met by a subscription.

Four months later the ministry fell, as a result of raising the Catholic question—a point on which it was sure to be faced with the hostility of the king. Sheridan's comment was in his best style: he had often heard of men running their heads against a wall, but he had never before heard of men *building a wall expressly for that purpose*.

He removed his belongings from Somerset House. Once more he was out of office, and so he remained for the rest of his life. He might get what comfort he could from the reflection that he was free from all reproach on the score of 'successful servility or prosperous apostasy.' Even the hollow satisfaction of representing

[1] Mentioned previously as Lord Mornington: created Marquis Wellesley in 1799.

Westminster, gained with so much recrimination and bitterness, was now lost. A dissolution followed almost at once, and he was beaten by Sir Francis Burdett. A seat was found for him, probably by the prince's influence, at Ilchester, and his cherished independence, like a too expensive establishment, was to that extent placed on a more modest footing by its impoverished owner. Grey succeeded to the earldom and took his seat in the House of Lords. The leadership of the party in the Commons thus became vacant, but it was not given to Sheridan. Nobody denied that, as far as experience and ability went, he had the best claim; but there was not the slightest chance that the claim would be allowed. His character had to be considered. . . . In short, he was not eligible. He was passed over, and the choice fell on George Ponsonby, ex-Chancellor of Ireland.

§

There was an autumnal touch in the air of these closing years of Sheridan's long political life—a touch suggesting, not so much mellowness, as the bleak approaches of winter. He could still make an excellent speech, though he was not invariably sober; but what were the Castlereaghs, Cannings, and Percevals to him? He had trod the stage with Burke, Fox, and Pitt, and was beginning to seem like a survivor from a bygone age. Napoleon bestrode Europe like a Colossus, and entertained hopes of the Whigs to the end. But he had nothing to hope for from Sheridan, who, in turn, had very little to hope for from the Whigs and nothing at all from the Tories. He supported the Government on the war, though he differed with them on other matters. He still considered that he belonged to the Whigs, but he kept up his independent style. As Johnny McCree might have said, 'If he didna belong to the Whigs, where the deil did he belong?' But Grenville never saw him, and Grey, if he did happen to speak to him, was barely civil. If, by any chance, the Whigs came into office again, they would, perhaps, feel that he could hardly be passed over altogether. They might give him something; but as to a leading position—Cabinet rank—those dreams were over for ever.

Still, there was one quarter in which he had influence: he continued to be on intimate terms with the prince, and the Whigs still had expectations from His Royal Highness. The time was at hand when Lord Holland would reflect that Grenville and Grey should have taken these things into consideration instead of neglecting Sheridan as they did. A very little would have sufficed to win him over—a cordial word, a sign of confidence, the merest civility would have been enough. He could always be soothed by the most trifling favour: indeed, his pride took offence at anything more.

Towards the end of 1810 the king went mad again. Twenty-two years had passed since the memorable regency crisis when Fox had hurried back from Italy, Sheridan had intrigued with Thurlow, and report had put it about that he was to be Chancellor of the Exchequer. Things had changed with him since then: Drury Lane was in ashes, he was cruelly embarrassed for money, the 'emoluments of office' must have seemed more desirable than ever before, and a little cordiality from Grey and Grenville would have been in season. They remained distant, however, and coldly refused his request for the Irish secretaryship when the party should come into office; though in all likelihood his chief motive in asking for the place was to avoid raising the question —a painful one to him—of a Cabinet appointment, which he knew they would never give him.

Once again a Regency Bill was brought in: it contained restrictions on the same lines as Pitt's, against which Fox, Burke, and Sheridan had long ago thundered so zealously. The prince consulted Sheridan. The time drew near when the address of the two Houses was to be presented. The prince requested Grey and Grenville to draw up his answer. They did so, and the day it was handed in Sheridan dined with him. He was shown the document and proceeded to find fault with the subject-matter and ridicule the style to such purpose that the prince desired the paper to be returned to the noble authors with directions to improve the wording and make the changes and additions he had indicated.

Such instructions were not likely in any case to be pleasing to the two lords, whose dignity adds considerably to the piquancy of the situation; but the thought that Sheridan, of all people, was the true source of them was unbearable. He was taken to task, and a painful scene, during which he twisted and turned in vain efforts to defend himself, ensued at Lord Holland's house in Pall Mall. According to Lady Holland he gave an incredible exhibition of jealousy and duplicity. Jealousy . . . it evidently did not occur to her ladyship that he had some cause to feel jealous. Twenty-two years ago the prince's advisers on this very subject had been Fox, Burke, Sir Gilbert Elliot, Lord Loughborough, and Sheridan—and nobody's influence had been greater than Sheridan's. He was generally believed to have written the prince's reply to the address of the Houses—the matter which was actually in question now—and though the belief was mistaken, it was perfectly natural. Who would seriously have considered Grey his equal at that time? As for Grenville, he had been on the other side and had approved of the restrictions: he was now giving the prince advice on that subject. And these were the men who had all the things that Sheridan was denied. They were to sit in the Cabinet, where there was no place for him; they had done their best to keep him out of Westminster; they looked down on him from immeasurable heights of superiority, and met his request for a place with a chilly refusal; he had nothing to expect except from them, and must be careful to give no offence. He, who had been advising the prince for more than twenty years, must say nothing now. It was too much.

But for all that, he was in a thoroughly false position, just as he had been so often before. The question was essentially one of loyalty, and on that point he was always sensitive. Hence his shuffling and prevaricating, which did him no good, the evidence being too strong and his reputation too well known. Still, the business hardly concerned the national welfare, however much it concerned the party; and, as usual, he had no personal gain to expect. On the contrary, he had everything to lose, which made his motives a puzzle even to his critics—as if he ever paid the least attention to such considerations.

The two lords declined to make the required changes in their paper, or to take any responsibility for a version inspired, as they had only too much reason to suspect, by Sheridan. As time was now pressing, the prince sent for Michael Angelo Taylor [1] at the unseasonable hour of three o'clock at night and gave him a draft of the answer to copy, saying that those 'd——d fellows' would be there in the morning. He then retired to bed and Taylor set about his copying. He noticed that the draft was partly in the prince's handwriting and partly in Sheridan's. Sheridan was present and so was Adam,[2] and both were still warm from the recriminations at Lord Holland's. Adam, disgusted at Sheridan's conduct, which, since he had brought the original answer from Grey and Grenville to the prince, he had seen at close quarters, was looking 'very black.' They were walking up and down the room but keeping to opposite sides. Presently Adam drifted up to Taylor and muttered, looking darkly at Sheridan, 'That's the d——dest rascal existing!' After a while Sheridan in his turn wandered up to Taylor and whispered, 'D——n them all!' —meaning, presumably, Adam, Grey, Grenville, and the rest.

The reply was copied and duly delivered. Grey and Grenville sent a remonstrance, in a somewhat lofty style, to the prince, who showed it to Sheridan. Sheridan ridiculed both the remonstrance and the haughty demeanour of the noble lords, who, he artfully suggested, intended to keep the prince in leading-strings. He even made satirical verses on this mischievous subject:

> In all humility we crave
> Our Regent may become our slave. . . .

This suggestion had a considerable effect on the prince, who disliked both the unbending Grenville and the 'high and mighty' Grey. In the sequel the Government remained in office, and the Whigs, who, ever since 1788, had built so many vain hopes on a regency, remained out. Sheridan, though not the only begetter of this unlucky consequence, could hardly have done more if his sole object had been to keep the Whigs—and consequently himself—from coming into power. He wrote a long letter to Lord

[1] Taylor was a friend of the prince and one of his council for the Duchy of Lancaster. It was he who was to have carried the bag for Sheridan when the latter was replying on the charge relating to the Begums.

[2] William Adam (1751–1839).

Holland to explain and justify his proceedings, but in spite of an engaging appearance of candour, it can hardly be said to explain them, or even to explain them away. It is fair to assume, however, that among his oddly mixed motives, was a genuine desire to serve the interests of the prince.

After this extraordinary performance it might have been thought that he would have been satisfied with what he had done in that line, and with easing his heart at whatever cost to himself. The event proved otherwise.

For some time it was uncertain whether the king would recover or not, and accordingly there was a makeshift look about the prince's arrangements. But the king did not recover: blind, and wandering in his wits, he made his way about the rooms and corridors at Windsor, or solaced himself with music. It was, as Burke had declared, prematurely, nearly a quarter of a century ago, 'total eclipse.' The regency continued and the Whigs still had expectations of coming in. Twice in 1812 it seemed that they were about to return to office; but on the first of these occasions they insisted on keeping to their policy over the Catholic question. It was in this connection that they were praised at dinner at 'Robins the auctioneer's' for their firmness in resisting the temptations of office and keeping to their principles—praise which caused Sheridan, who thought of his own firmness (which nobody troubled to praise) and its consequences, to shed tears. The second occasion was after the assassination of Perceval. This time the question of the control of the prince's household was a difficulty, but it was settled: Lord Yarmouth, the Vice-Chamberlain, informed Sheridan that the household were prepared to resign. Sheridan, who was opposed to the resignation, not only kept back this information, but went out of his way to convey the opposite impression. He even offered to bet on the subject. The Whigs remained in opposition, where they were still to be found long after Sheridan was in his grave. As Byron was to express it:

> Nought 's permanent among the human race
> Except the Whigs *not* getting into place.

Twice, observed Creevey, had Sheridan kept them out of

office. It was a strange, and yet not wholly inappropriate, end to his long and tormented relations with the party.

The truth about the affair of the household having been made known, he tried hard to justify himself in the House, where, as the prince told Croker, he made a 'strange figure' in the debate. A strange figure indeed. He spoke more than once, very painfully and with much wandering; and even with physical distress. His arguments, like the situation, were characteristic and almost pathetic: there was no possibility that they would convince anybody. However, he was still able to make a joke. He admitted having offered to bet Tierney that the household would not resign, and only wished he could have offered 'to *stake* the money as well as to lay it. (*Laughter.*)'

Once again he had been guilty of bad faith. It was the last time. Vanity, levity, subterfuge, artifice, want of veracity, an occasional indifference to the truth—the long indictment was complete. And what was the reason for such unspeakable perverseness? Like so many acts of his political career it could bring him no profit. Nobody, in fact, suffered by it more than himself. The case went beyond any mere matter of vanity: there was an accumulated bitterness in him. He had suffered too many disappointments, too many slights. What reward had he for all his exertions, and all his talents? It was easy for my Lord G., or Earl G., or the Marquis of B.; it was easy for Whitbread and Adam and scores of others to cut a noble and disinterested figure. But for him it was not easy, and never had been. Now he was old and in difficulties, and nobody thought he had suffered any hardship in a political life of thirty years and upwards, out of which he had been only two years in any kind of office. What did he owe the Whigs? If he had gone out of his way to remind Grey and Grenville that he was a man to be reckoned with, was it so very surprising? No one could say that he had ever changed sides, or spoken or voted against his conscience. Even in this last unfortunate affair he could, no doubt, in spite of all his shufflings in public, have explained matters to his own satisfaction. It was impossible for any one else to understand properly. Perhaps the account would not have come quite straight without a little adjusting, but that was the usual way with his accounts. After all, it is the common lot of man to stand in need of some such indulgence.

In 1830, Lord Holland, surveying Sheridan's character and career, found no difficulty in explaining why he had never been able to achieve such a position as, for instance, North, Fox, and Pitt. His remarks have an outward appearance of kindness, such as might be expected from one who had enjoyed Sheridan's society and friendship, and professed to feel a regard for his memory. But his indulgence does not go to the length of overlooking any of Sheridan's failings, or even of taking a sympathetic view of his circumstances. It was easy for my Lord H. 'with thousands upon thousands a year from the public money' to keep clear of temptation, but what of poor Sheridan? Had he no reason to chafe under the leadership which had kept him out of office half a lifetime and left him in the end poor and neglected? He was, admits Lord Holland, less jealous of Fox than of any one else—which is as much as to say he was given to jealousy. He was kind to inferiors; he took more offence at a slight than at a real injury, and most offence of all if anybody did him a great favour. And so forth. It is a case of damning with faint praise. Of all Sheridan endured during the long misfortunes of the Whigs; of his steady refusal to bring his political talents to market; of the bitterness and frustration which account so largely for his *vagaries*, even in their latest and most disquieting manifestations, not a word is said.

Though he did not know it, Sheridan's career in Parliament had now reached its end. On 21st July 1812 he spoke in his high patriotic style in support of the war with France: the House was never to hear him again.

The immediate question was, where was he to find a seat at the forthcoming elections? He could not keep Ilchester: the prince was now regent and Sheridan was in opposition. As for Grenville, after all that had come and gone it was impossible to expect anything from his influence. The prince thought he might, perhaps, try Westminster again. In that case he would need the support of the Government, but as far as His Royal

Highness was concerned there was no objection to his coming into office. Sheridan saw things differently. To the prince it might seem that he was on neither one side nor the other, but Sheridan had been on one side all his life and still felt he belonged there. Besides, he clung to his independence. He had already turned his eyes towards Stafford, as if he wanted to return at last to the place where he had begun. To contest that seat in his present circumstances was a desperate undertaking: still, the money might be found. 'Thousands and thousands' were due to him from the theatre. The money would certainly be found. . . . Before the end of 1811 he was writing hopefully to Sir Oswald Moseley to prepare the way: 'It will,' he concluded, 'I confess, be very gratifying to me to be again elected by the sons of those who chose me in the year eighty . . .'

§

He could not pay his debts, but he was, in his invariable style, still talking of 'thousands and thousands.' The source of this impressive but visionary wealth was, as of old, the patent which he had acquired with so much enterprise and resource some thirty-five years ago. That curious and apparently indestructible property, after surviving so many vicissitudes, was now valued, in the financial arrangements for the new theatre, at no less than £48,000. Sheridan, who owned half of it, was therefore to get £24,000, together with £4,000 for the 'property of the fruit offices and the reversion of boxes and shares.' Tom Sheridan, who owned a quarter, was to have £12,000. It had the gratifying sound of wealth—and, as usual, little more than the sound.

According to the prince, Sheridan disliked Whitbread, and indeed, had an 'actual hatred' of him. However that may have been, it is certain that the enthusiasm and gratitude with which he originally welcomed Whitbread's offer to help with the arrangements for the new theatre, soon gave way to very different feelings. In the circumstances this was almost inevitable. Whitbread considered, not unreasonably, that he was responsible in the first place to the subscribers, and bound to see that their

I

interests were properly safeguarded. Indeed, it was only on these terms that the undertaking could be carried through. That the building of a new theatre also concerned Sheridan's interests, was, in the nature of things, a secondary consideration. But Sheridan could never be brought to see the business in this light.[1]

Since nobody could be expected to subscribe to a theatre in which the late manager had any hand, it was important to keep him altogether out of the arrangements. He was quite ready to agree to this—indeed, he was ready to agree to anything—but he did not expect the agreement to be taken literally. Whitbread's idea of an agreement was of a less accommodating sort: he intended the terms to be strictly kept. Accordingly, when Sheridan manifested a desire to give the plans for the new building the benefit of his experience and advice, he was firmly reminded that it was no concern of his what sort of building was erected; and it was quite in vain that he expostulated warmly, urging that, on the contrary, it concerned him seriously, since the success of the undertaking, and therefore the prospects of his being paid, depended on it. He also spoke virtuously of the interests of the proprietors, but the truth is that, apart from these business-like considerations, he was a good deal hurt, as if he had not really understood that he and Drury Lane were to be separated for ever.

The prospects of his being paid. . . . There were heavy claims against the compensation due for the patent. He would take them all upon himself—Tom's share was not to be burdened with a penny of them. There were pressing debts of his own, too, and the news that he had a large sum in prospect stirred all his creditors into activity. He had agreed, and even volunteered, to wait for his money until the theatre should be built—a highly desirable arrangement in view of the difficulties with which the committee had to contend. But here again it seemed to him unreasonable to interpret the agreement with perfect strictness. Something, surely, could be advanced. After all, the money was his and he needed some immediately, as Whitbread knew perfectly well. But Whitbread, though he was sorry for Sheridan's

[1] A caricature of 1811 depicts Whitbread, in the guise of a brewer's man, wheeling off Sheridan in a barrow containing old bricks. Sheridan is flourishing a paper marked '£20,000.' (Wright: *Caricature History of the Georges*.)

distressed condition, and declared his readiness, as a private man, to contribute his 'mite' towards giving him relief, would allow no laxity in his accounts. Nothing could be advanced without the most careful arrangements: it was a matter of business, and the subscribers must be treated with scrupulous fairness. To Sheridan, on the other hand, business was never merely business —it was an adventure and left room for optimism. As he saw it, Whitbread was behaving not merely ungenerously, but unjustly; and was, in fact refusing him what was lawfully his.

Something far more important to him than his debts was now in question: he had to fight for his seat at Stafford. To his great distress he was defeated. The sons of those who chose him in 1780, however they may have been touched by the prospect of electing him, required the same sort of persuasion as their fathers had done, and it was not forthcoming in a sufficient amount. Nevertheless, the unlucky attempt must have cost him a considerable sum, and it is plain that he could not afford a shilling of it. He was beaten, he told Whitbread bitterly, for want of £2,000 which he—Whitbread—ought to have paid him. 'This, and this alone,' he declared, 'cost me my election.' He gave the same explanation to the prince, speaking with downright fury of Whitbread, and even going so far as to call him a *scoundrel*. The £2,000, he assured the prince—who was inclined to believe him—was his by right. He was convinced than Whitbread had acted with the deliberate intention of keeping him out of Parliament. It is possible that Whitbread may have thought, and said, that Sheridan could not afford the expense of an election; it is not likely that he was actuated by any ungenerous or unworthy motives. But Sheridan was too sore to judge fairly. His place in Parliament meant more to him than Whitbread could possibly understand. For thirty-two years it had given him his chief claim to importance; he had devoted to it his best energies, talents, and hopes; it was all he had left, and now it actually seemed as if it might be lost, and his occupation, like Othello's, gone.

CHAPTER EIGHTEEN

Poor Brinsley

IT WAS LORD MOIRA who remarked to the prince that it was a sad thing that poor Sheridan should be out of Parliament at the end of such a career as his had been. The prince considered that it was very largely Sheridan's own fault: his indolence and procrastination were to blame, and he would never have found himself in such a plight if he had placed himself squarely on one side or the other. However, he was willing to help, and, above all, not to expect Sheridan to sacrifice his independence in return. This implied that he was prepared to find a reasonable sum of money if a seat could be found. Long afterwards he told Croker these things, but it is proper to observe, in this case as in others, that the royal memory was not famous for accuracy, and, especially in awkward passages, was apt to call fancy to its aid.

The first suggestion, apparently, was that Sheridan might have a seat of the Duke of Norfolk's. The duke's price for it was £4,000, but he was willing to let Sheridan have it for £3,000. There was one objection, however: Sheridan would have to vote as the duke wished. This idea came to nothing.

The next plan seems to have been Sheridan's own. There was a seat at Wootton Bassett, held by a Mr. Attersoll, who, it appeared, was prepared to give it up for £3,000. It will be remembered that Sheridan had had thoughts of Wootton Bassett in 1780, before he settled on Stafford. If the money could be found this would be perfectly satisfactory. The money was forthcoming. It was paid, not to Sheridan himself—*we knew him too well for that,* said the prince—but to a Mr. Cocker, a solicitor. Cocker was to make the payment to Mr. Attersoll when the business was concluded. Here follows a story which could be told of no one but Sheridan.

He was to go down to Wootton Bassett. He made preparations for the journey—it was understood that he was about to set off —it was understood that he had actually gone. But he never did go. The prince was surprised to catch a glimpse of him by accident in town. Eventually he came to see Macmahon[1] and told him that the affair had fallen through. In the meantime, however, the £3,000 had disappeared. Cocker declared that Sheridan had told him that the money was to be placed to his account and instructed him to pay some urgent debts out of it. Accordingly he had done so. One of these debts, oddly enough, was to Cocker himself. It was an urgent debt, and he had been obliged to press Mr. Sheridan for it, and had been told to take it out of the £3,000. Such, according to the prince, was the solicitor's explanation.

The money, apparently, was actually Macmahon's and had been advanced out of a trust fund. The prince had to repay it. He saw nothing of Sheridan, and, indeed, never did see him again to speak to. However, Sheridan did make some attempt to account for what had happened: he paid another visit to Macmahon to try to explain the thing. He began by blaming Whitbread, whose fault, according to him, it all was. Whitbread had refused to give him his £2,000 except on condition that he stayed out of Parliament. This did nothing to clear up the matter of the £3,000, but he came to that eventually. The explanation was neither easy nor likely to be received with much satisfaction. He said he had called on Cocker to get the money and return it to Macmahon, but 'that fellow' had seen fit to appropriate it for the payment of his own debt, and consequently it was not to be had. That was all. After this he never came near Macmahon or the prince.

What is to be thought of this story? To suggest that Sheridan deliberately swindled the prince out of £3,000 is absurd. It would have been completely foreign to his nature, as well as against his own interests. There was nothing he prized more highly than the favour and confidence of the prince, which was nearly all he had nowadays to give him consequence; and there was nothing he wanted more eagerly at this moment than to be in Parliament. The transaction just narrated was bound to cost him both of these things. On the other hand, the story is

---

[1] Colonel Macmahon, a gentleman in the prince's service and confidence.

circumstantial, and it contains, no doubt, a fair reason for the break between him and the prince. Still, it is a very odd story, and obviously stands in need of explanation in more respects than one. In any case it does not require us to suppose that Sheridan was guilty of a deliberate fraud at the expense of his most gracious master. However, whether there was a misunderstanding, or whether Cocker paid himself and left Sheridan to get out of the scrape as best he could, it is certain that the latter found himself in an acutely embarrassing position. He had no hope of raising the money and therefore no possible way of escape. He was the chief sufferer by the affair, but the only explanation he could give had no chance of being considered acceptable, or even of being understood. On the whole, there was nothing for him to do but to keep away.

When the prince told Croker this story he had it thoroughly in mind that he was accused of having treated Sheridan very shabbily, and this made him anxious to display his own conduct in the best possible light, and Sheridan's in the worst. It was ungenerous of him, but human, and very much in his characteristic style. He was not unkindly, but he was selfish. He meant well enough—it was the difficulty of being selfish and kind at the same time that always troubled him. So, as has been already observed, he told Croker that, first and last, he had given Sheridan some £20,000, which was, very likely, not far from the truth, if the income from the receivership of the Duchy of Cornwall was included. And he remarked that, after all, Sheridan's conduct over this affair of Wootton Bassett was not much worse than some other things he had done. Besides, even though he never spoke to Sheridan again, he did not give any positive order that he should be refused admittance—as if that were much to his credit. It did not occur to him that a kindly word would have been a solace to the 'proud man' who had been devoted to him for thirty years and in whose company he had so often found pleasure. He might have known that Sheridan, of all people, would never come near him after what had happened, unless he himself first made some movement of sympathy and friendliness. What kept Sheridan away was not, as the prince evidently supposed, a sense of guilt, but a sense of bitter humiliation.

But by the time the story was told, Sheridan was dead and gone, and the prince, like all egoists, could take a curiously cool view of departed friends. He gave Croker a remarkably effective sketch—almost brutal in its artistic detachment—of Sheridan as he caught sight of him for the last time on 17th August 1815. The prince was driving, with his secretary, Sir Benjamin Bloomfield, to Brighton from Oatlands, where he had been visiting the Duke of York. Near Leatherhead he noticed a familiar figure walking along the footpath, and pointed him out to his companion. It was Sheridan. There he was, about thirty yards off, with his black stockings and blue coat with metal buttons. But he turned off into a lane without looking behind him, and the prince saw him no more. The details remained fixed in the prince's memory unaccompanied by any sympathetic ideas—it was only old Sheridan, now reduced to living in a very low and obscure way, and expecting nothing better than *brandy and water* from the company he kept.

In considering the prince's conduct it is fair to point out that he was now regent, and that Sheridan could be of no service to him, even in Parliament.[1] The friendship had once been creditable, but it could hardly be so any longer. Richard Brinsley's reputation had sunk and his financial troubles were notorious. The prince took the general view that his debts were enormous —*la mer à boire*; and he was uneasily conscious that he might be expected to help in undertaking that hopeless task. As a matter of prudence it was clearly better to have nothing more to do with a man in such a position, and it might even be said (as it has been said) that he did not give up Sheridan until Sheridan gave up himself. It was all very well for Moore to talk loftily about a prince's friendship as the frailest of sublunary treasures: such sentiments cost him nothing and took no account of the circumstances. The prince had been generous within reason, but unfortunately Sheridan's case required a degree of generosity which the nature of His Royal Highness was quite unable to afford.

[1] In 1812 Sheridan spoke several times in what he considered to be the prince's interest.

§

In the meantime Sheridan was out of Parliament. The third and last of his careers had come to an end, though he continued to delude himself with hopes of finding a seat. The spring that had sparkled so brilliantly in his comedies had long since run dry; the new theatre was completed, but he had no hand in it. Whitbread, as chairman of the committee, wrote kindly to Esther Jane, placing a box at her disposal. It was a thoughtful attention, but he received no reply. He wrote again, and again the letter remained unacknowledged. In the disputes with Whitbread Esther Jane stood loyally by her husband. In spite of all she had suffered, she told Lady Holland, she could never see him so hurt as he had been, without feeling for him with all her heart. And he had been hurt—so deeply that he could not be just to Whitbread: he could only see him as the source of all his misfortunes.

It was in vain that Whitbread assured him that he would be glad to agree to 'anything practicable,' and pointed out that 'without a clear arrangement nothing could be done.' If Sheridan would only look at the state of the account between him and the committee he would see for himself how many claims and engagements were entered against him. No doubt they still left a large balance, but then there were claims against that as well, and it was Sheridan's own desire that they should be satisfied out of it. Since it was uncertain at present how much they would amount to, the only satisfactory solution would be for him to agree to take a large part of the balance in bonds, and leave the bonds in trust to 'answer the events.' That done, it might be possible to arrange an advance.

But all Sheridan could think of was that the advance which would have saved him from losing his election—that parent of so many evils—had not been given him, and that a sum of £28,000, admittedly due to him, remained exasperatingly out of his reach. It was dangled before his eyes and he could not lay his hands on a shilling of it, even for his most desperate needs. Of course he wanted the claims to be settled. Had he not

always insisted on his concern for the interests of the proprietors?
It was well known that he had no intention of defrauding anybody: even Mr. Hammersley, the banker, was heard to acknowledge handsomely that he always meant fairly and honourably.

Remembering his way with sums of money which came into
his possession, we can hardly doubt what would have happened
to the £28,000 if it had been handed over to him. As it was,
he had the mortification of seeing many of his obligations settled
out of it by others, and everybody's demands preferred to his
own. The irony of circumstance had placed him at last in the
position, so desirable to the true economist and so peculiarly
painful to him, where his debts were actually being attended to
before his own needs. If it was true that only a small fortune
could clear off the debts, here the fortune was, and it was being
applied largely to that end. The debts never were cleared off
during his lifetime, but two years after he died they amounted
to no more than a few thousands of pounds.

One result of his not being in Parliament was particularly unfortunate: he was as liable now as any other unprivileged citizen
to be arrested for debt. In August 1813 this fate overtook him.
The arrest was for £600 and, from the creditor's point of view,
it produced the desired effect. Sheridan was still good for a
reasonable amount if pressed. He naturally turned to Whitbread,
who arranged for his release, but not without a short delay, during
which the sensitive prisoner, fretting bitterly, wrote him a
reproachful letter from 'Tooke's Court, Cursitor Street, past
two.' He protested hotly against being left in such a humiliating
predicament. There were still 'thousands and thousands' due
to him from the theatre 'legally and equitably.' Whitbread's
behaviour was ungenerous in the extreme: 'I shall only add that
I think, if I know myself, had our lots been reversed and I had
seen you in my situation, and had left Lady E. in that of my
wife, I would have risked £600 rather than have left you so.'
To do him justice he would certainly have risked that sum, and
even more—if he had had it.

The incident shook him more, perhaps, than those who thought
they knew him would have expected. He broke down, says

*I

Moore, when he got home, and shed tears at the *profanation* he had been forced to undergo. He never thought of his debts as being like those of other people. He was a man of honour as well as a man of fortune, and ought never to have been arrested like a common debtor. There was the sting—he had thousands and thousands due to him and he was carried off to a sponging house for want of a paltry £600 which he would have been sure to pay in due course. The £28,000 was like a mirage, it represented the value of a property which was lawfully his; but then, he might have reflected that he had come by that property without paying for it in quite the usual way. But however deeply this affair mortified him, it had no effect on his natural optimism. Whitbread found him calculating with great confidence on being returned for Westminster, where a vacancy was expected in consequence of the proceedings against Lord Cochrane. The thing was being talked of as a possibility, and Creevey reported that the Whigs were inclined to favour old Sherry in spite of all that had happened, and that he would even have the support of Carlton House and Lord Liverpool. But it came to nothing. Westminster had done with Sheridan, who had known the electors in that constituency thirty-three years ago—before he ever sat in Parliament. They had seen him, likewise, at the celebrated election of 1784, when the beautiful Duchess of Devonshire had exerted her charms in support of Fox; and they had seen him often enough since then at Fox's side on the hustings; and once they had actually elected him, not without some tumult and violence.

But times had changed and the world Sheridan had known was passing away. Fox and the duchess had now been seven years in their graves. Lady Bessborough, to be sure, was still living, but her affections had long since been transferred from Sheridan. On the Continent another and far more spectacular career was coming to an end. Napoleon had been to Moscow an come back without his army. Wellington had done great things in Spain, for victory, so constantly denied to the great Pitt, was vouchsafed to Perceval and Liverpool. Sheridan had seen the beginning of all that, and much more. He had seen the Americans win their independence, and before anything was heard of the French Revolution, while yet Louis XVI sat securely on his throne, he had held the House enthralled with what Fox judged to be the finest speech he had ever heard. By the time the prince saw him going along the pathway at Leatherhead in his blue coat and black stockings, the Allies were in Paris and Waterloo was two months old.

It had been a long career and a remarkable one. Lord Brougham, when he wrote his *Historical Sketches of Statesmen who flourished in the time of George III*, included Sheridan as a matter of course. And yet, when he had done justice to his qualities and spoken of his remarkable genius and power, he fell to reflecting that, after all, he could hardly be considered as a statesman, and even added that he 'did not seem to be ambitious for the character.' It would have been more to the point to say that he never had any opportunity of appearing in the character. He was thirty-two years in Parliament and never sat in a Cabinet. Whatever he got from the political life which he was so eager to take up, it was not office and it was not wealth. To account for this by his low birth, or his lack of fortune, or his dissipated habits, or his vanity, or his want of veracity, is to overlook the simple and sufficient explanation that he stood by the Whigs and took his full share of their political misfortunes. He did so with his eyes open, and out of a sense of loyalty. There were times when he could have gone over to the Government side with as clear a conscience as Windham or Burke. After 1797 it seemed to him that the most vital concern of the country was the war, and he would therefore have found himself far more happily placed in the ranks of the Government than in those of the Opposition. But he would *never quit Fox*. When Pitt came back to power he was not more convinced than Sheridan of the danger from France, or more anxious to confront it. But Fox's unhappy break with Pitt had long ago settled the issue for Sheridan—Pitt was his enemy likewise, and he would attack him, if only for not going efficiently about the business of raising men.

But though he remained loyal to the Whigs in the most essential article of all, he spoke and voted according to his own conscience—a proceeding which, in the latter part of his career, made it quite certain that he would get very little from his friends. Even the praise to which he is fully entitled for his disinterestedness and his just and public-spirited views, has been doled out to him with a niggardly hand. His private character has stood in the way of his public one; his wit has been set off against his seriousness; and since, politically speaking, he failed to *do well unto himself*, men have rarely seen occasion to *speak good of him*. It is a melancholy thought that his reputation would have stood far higher if he had died a quarter of a century earlier. And yet he won a certain kind of distinction, and it was always distinction that he wanted above all. There is no reason to think that, in spite of his disappointments, he ever regretted his political career, or agreed with the opinion that he would have done better to stick to his pen. He did not see himself as a failure; and we, likewise, feel that, though he may have made no great impression on the history of his time, he was far too gifted and conspicuous to be passed over or forgotten.

If his career was remarkable in itself, it was even more so as being his. Where Drury Lane was concerned it was easy to see him as an unscrupulous adventurer, but in politics it was far otherwise. There he was proof against all temptation, and whatever uneasiness he caused his friends, remained strictly 'exempt from all reproach.' His sympathies were with the unprivileged and the oppressed, and the words he used of Pitt might have been applied with equal justice to himself: his purpose and his hope were for the greatness and security of the empire.

Which of these two was the real Sheridan? The contradiction runs through his whole life. He was a poor man who was concerned with large sums of money. He ought to have had a fortune; he never had the least intention of swindling anybody, and always meant fairly and honourably; he would never have borrowed a shilling from a private friend—if he could have done without; he won the heart of Elizabeth Linley by his *delicacy*, and wounded it cruelly by his infidelity; he was a *friend to economy*, though the course of his own life was never regulated on that principle. His instincts were generous: he was an erring

THE RUINS OF DRURY LANE THEATRE AFTER THE FIRE

From a Water-colour by W. T. Sherlock.

mortal who saw the good very clearly and followed the bad all too often. He was careful of his honour. If he betted and lost he must pay promptly, whatever the inconvenience: if he owed money to a tradesman—why, the case was different, but he meant to pay. One of his creditors is said to have hit on the lucky idea of tearing up his bill, thus putting the business in the light of a debt of honour, and to have got his money on the spot. Parliament, in the same way, concerned his honour; but Drury Lane was another matter.

As to honours, the only public one he ever received was to be made a privy councillor and be called right honourable—a barren reward, but not less acceptable, to his way of thinking, on that account. It was said that he used to envy Burke that distinction long ago. The University of Oxford nearly conferred the degree of D.C.L. on him, but it was too much to expect that such an honour should fall to his lot. He went to Oxford when Grenville was made vice-chancellor, but two objectors proved implacable, and there was nothing for it but to withdraw his name. At the ceremony the undergraduates clamoured that he should sit among the doctors, and he did so. This circumstance, says Moore, gave him greater pleasure than any other event of his public life. He was close on sixty at the time, and had written *The School for Scandal* before the undergraduates were born.

§

The new theatre was completed by the autumn of 1812, and it occurred to Whitbread that it should be opened with a poetical address, spoken from the stage. Johnson had once written such a prologue for Garrick—the sonorous lines beginning:

> When learning's triumph o'er her barbarous foes
> First rear'd the stage, immortal Shakespeare rose. . . .

Whitbread's idea was to make the required address the subject of a competition, £100 being offered to the successful candidate. This had only one good result: it gave rise to the highly entertaining *Rejected Addresses* of Horace and James Smith. Numerous contributions were received, but not one proved acceptable. Whitbread himself, always conscientious, laboured to compose a set of verses for the occasion, and produced upwards of fifty lines. The new theatre being in place of one which had been destroyed by fire, the idea of the phoenix naturally suggested itself to the luckless poetasters. It suggested itself to Whitbread, and Sheridan, who had had a sight of his attempt as well as the others, declared that they had all used the phoenix, but that Whitbread had made more of that remarkable fowl than anybody else—he had entered into details, describing its wings, its beak, its tail, its feathers; in short, it was a regular *poulterer's bird.*

The address was eventually written, at Lord Holland's request, by Byron, who showed a good deal of self-consciousness over the task and positively refused to be present on the great occasion when his lines were recited. It was just as well, for they were spoken very badly. He began with the fire:

> In one dread night our city saw, and sigh'd,
> Bow'd to the dust, the Drama's tower of pride . . .

—continued with Shakespeare, Mrs. Siddons, and Garrick; expressed a hope that this 'fane' would 'emulate the last'; spoke of the bright days 'Ere Garrick fled or Brinsley ceased to write'; and, having carefully avoided any reference to the phoenix, arrived at last, doubtless with relief, at the point where

> The curtain rises—may our stage unfold
> Scenes not unworthy Drury's days of old;
> Britons our judges, Nature for our guide,
> Still may *we* please—long, long, may *you* preside.

But Sheridan was not present, and the thought of the theatre can have given him nothing but pain. Was he, whose theatre it had been for more than thirty years, to appear now in the character of a mere member of the public? It was not until a considerable time afterwards that he was induced to go there. In the course of the performance he slipped away and it was feared that he had found the experience too trying. However, he was discovered in the green-room, making himself extremely agreeable to the actors and actresses.

The mention of his joke about Whitbread and the phoenix

reminds us that the prince's picture of him as an unhappy out-cast reduced to living in poverty and obscurity, and condemned to the unspeakable degradation of having to get drunk on brandy and water, instead of on claret, gives a totally wrong impression. It suggests a beaten man, beyond the help of friends, no longer able to struggle against adverse circumstances—a victim of his own follies and vices. The truth is, he confronted the world with courage to the last, thought out schemes for making money and paying off his debts, and never lost his wit. Being found drunk in the gutter by the watchmen and asked his name, he hiccuped, ' *Wilberforce !* '

No doubt there were many things in his life on which he might have looked back with bitter regret, but it does not appear that he was ever much concerned with the past. He had, he thought, been too confiding—too ready to trust the good faith of others—and there was some truth in this idea: he had, for instance, expected too much from the sympathy and generosity of mind of those with whom he had to do. But if he had had his life to live over again, it is most likely that he would have lived it in the same way, for in the main it had given him what he wanted. Those who measured by the common standards could never understand him, and could find nothing but vanity in his curious ambitions. But it is not always easy to draw a firm line between vanity and ambition, and even if we feel that some of his desires lay in the province of the former, we shall still have to remember how many of them he had the satisfaction of gratifying, and how far out of his reach that satisfaction was at the outset. He walked into the great world, where he could show no passport but his own natural gifts; he stayed there, and he died there.

However, he had other and better claims to distinction. Whatever he tried, declared Byron, he did better than any one else. He had written the best comedy, *The School for Scandal*; the best opera, *The Duenna*; the best farce, *The Critic*; and the best address, the *Monologue on Garrick*. And to crown all, he had delivered the very best oration ever conceived or heard in this country, the famous Begum speech. When we have subtracted

as much as is proper from this panegyric, there is still enough
left for any man's fame. He himself was not insensible to it.
He was old by that time, and when somebody repeated it to
him he burst into tears.

Byron was always his enthusiastic admirer. He only once
heard him speak in Parliament, and then briefly, but he thought
him the only man there he ever wished to hear at greater length.
When Moore was writing the Life, Byron wrote to him from
Italy, urging him to remember the pleasant days they had had
with him, and to pay no attention to the lies of the 'humbug
Whigs'—there were worse people than Sheridan in 'that gang.'
Fox with his coalition, and Burke with his pension, had not half
Sheridan's principle, whatever men might say. He was too good
for them all, and though he had nothing to help him in the way
of family, influence, or fortune, he beat them *out and out* in
everything he tried.[1]

Moore did his best, but he was not likely to please everybody.
Sheridan's character, wrote Hazlitt handsomely in 1819, 'will
soon be drawn by one who has all the ability and every inclination to do him justice, who knows how to bestow praise and to
deserve it, by one who is himself an ornament of private and of
public life, a satirist beloved by his friends, a wit and a patriot
to boot; a poet and an honest man.'

But in 1827, the work having appeared in the meantime, he
expressed himself on the subject in a very different style, and
added the following observation to what he had been saying of
Sheridan in the essay *On the Want of Money*: 'There was one
comfort, however, that poor Sheridan had: he did not foresee
that Mr. Moore would write his life!'

§

Sheridan's accounts with the theatre were cleared up at last,
though not until a year or more after the opening. The balance
of what was due to him was paid, says Moore, in a 'certain
number of shares.' Even-handed justice could do no more. He,

---

[1] 'I do not know any good model for a life of Sheridan but that of Savage.' (*Byron to Moore*.)

who had been wont to dispose of shares to others, was now
fobbed off with them himself. Whatever their value may have
been, it was not enough to pay his debts. Moore relates, as an
instance of his lordly indifference in money matters, that he
would sometimes hand over shares to his creditors, leaving them
to pay themselves and return any surplus as they saw fit. The
truth is, however, that he had no other means of paying them.
The patent, which he had got by means of such curious transactions on paper, had left him in a similar way—as if the fortune
it represented never had been quite real, and the airy edifice
built on it nothing but a piece of enchantment. He had come
to the last stage of the long journey: he was the Right Honourable
Richard Brinsley Sheridan; he was the Receiver of the Duchy of
Lancaster (that appointment being for life)—and he was nothing
more. Rumour found a natural satisfaction in magnifying his
debts; and whatever their amount really was, they were so complicated that nobody knew the truth about them except himself.
Since he had no means of paying them off he had to deal with
demands as best he could—a business of which he had had a
vast experience. Such valuables as were left found their way to
the pawnbroker.

Byron records an instance of his attorney's scouting the idea
of taking proceedings against *old Sherry* as being quite useless.
The debt in question was owed, suitably enough, to a wine-
merchant. He was 'old Sheridan' now, and sometimes 'poor
Brinsley,' or 'poor Sherry.' The time had gone by when he
could proudly claim that he never borrowed from a private
friend. He had money from Canning, from the Duke of Bedford, and from Rogers. Doubtless there were others. The
house in which he died—17 Savile Row—was lent him by Lord
Wellesley. The amounts were not large, and the process bore
a certain resemblance to that of stopping up holes in a sieve.
Any idea that his wealthy and noble friends were prepared to
shoulder his liabilities would inevitably have brought the
creditors down on him more eagerly than ever.

Those friends were reproached by Moore for neglecting him,
and it is probable that they could now have made him easy at

no great expense. Lord Holland, however, thought the reproaches not altogether justified. Moreover, in his opinion, nothing really effective could have been done for want of Sheridan's co-operation. Very likely this objection was sound, for he was always sensitive, and in consequence inclined to be secretive. From first to last there had always been something to be covered up—something he did not want to appear in its true light. It began in his schooldays, and he never quite reached the point where he felt he could afford to be perfectly open. On the subject of money (like Napoleon with the numbers of his armies) he would never be entirely candid, even to himself. Nevertheless, Moore had some justification for his remarks. Sheridan in the great world was a stranger after all, and when it came to the point his claims were not allowed. He might think himself fortunate to pick up the crumbs that fell from the table.

CHAPTER NINETEEN

Closing Scenes

IN MARCH 1816 Sheridan was to have been present at the St. Patrick's Day dinner, at which the Duke of Kent took the chair; but he was too ill to come and was obliged to send an excuse. His health was broken: he was suffering from a diseased stomach, and had an abscess *distressingly situated*. Within four months he was dead.

News of his condition was brought to Carlton House by a Mr. Vaughan, who told Macmahon that Sheridan was dangerously ill and in a shocking state of want. Having heard this from Macmahon (who prefaced it with an apology for mentioning the name of Sheridan after his outrageous conduct in the matter of the £3,000) the prince, according to the account he gave to Croker, declared that something must be done. A sum of money was mentioned—£500—but he could not remember whether it was he or Macmahon who suggested it. However, no limit was actually fixed.

Here he paused in the story to explain that he did not want it to be known that the money came from him, partly because, if it were known, it might be thought that he was willing to discharge all Sheridan's debts; partly because he could not overlook the business of the £3,000; and partly because he felt it would be indelicate to let the name of the benefactor appear. He added that it would also be inconvenient—which spoilt the effect of the last observation.

Vaughan was given his instructions and £200, on the understanding that he would come back for more if necessary. However, when he did come back he said he had spent only £130 or so. He also said he had found Sheridan and his wife in their beds, both almost starving and apparently in a dying condition. Mrs. Sheridan was suffering from cancer of the womb: she could hardly leave her bed and was far too ill to look after her husband.

Scarcely a servant remained in the house; the reception rooms were bare of furniture, and the whole place was filthy and smelt intolerably. Mrs. Sheridan would have got rid of her maid, but it was impossible to raise the guinea or two needed to pay her wages. As for Sheridan, he lay in a garret, on a truckle-bed with a coarse red and blue covering like a horsecloth thrown over him. He had been unable to move from the bed for a week, even for the 'occasions of nature,' and in that state he had been left to wallow. Apparently none of his friends had done anything for him, except Lady Bessborough, who had sent £20, and Lord and Lady Holland, who had sent ice and currant water. He seemed to cheer up at the sight of Vaughan. He had eaten nothing for a week, but declared he was quite well and *talked of paying off all his debts.* Vaughan did what he could: he got a bed and some bedclothes, shirts, basins, towels, and other aids to cleanliness; had Sheridan washed and put into a clean bed; and had the rooms fumigated. He also paid a few pressing bills.

Two days later he returned the entire £200 to the prince. Some of Sheridan's friends, it appeared, had suspected where the money came from, and insisted that it should be given back. They repaid Vaughan, assuring him that the patient had everything he needed. This assistance, remarked Vaughan, came a little late. . . .

Such, in substance, was the prince's story, and, as before, it is necessary to remember that he had been pained by Moore's reflections on him. However, they were no more than might have been expected from that gentleman's ingratitude, for the prince had taken notice of him and got him a place in the Bermudas, and Moore's return, he complained, was to libel him in the *Penny Post-Bag.*

Nevertheless, the prince certainly did make a cautious offer of help through Vaughan. It was refused by Mrs. Sheridan after she had discussed it with some of her relatives. Dr. Bain attended Sheridan, and Vaughan wrote to him saying that *a friend of his* had employed him 'to convey a small sum for Sheridan's use.' The sum he mentioned was certainly small, but he added that

MRS. R. B. SHERIDAN (BORN OGLE) AND HER SON
After the Painting by Hoppner.

more might be forthcoming if any good could be done with it. The prince's anxiety not to be entangled in the debts had evidently been impressed upon him, for he was careful to add that of course the doctor would feel that the money was not intended for the purpose of 'satisfying troublesome people.'

It is hard to say how much truth there is in the prince's description of Vaughan's proceedings and of the plight in which the latter found Sheridan. The story was retailed to Croker at second hand and nine years after the event. But whether Sheridan was or was not lying helpless and neglected on a truckle-bed in a garret, with a red and blue covering that looked like a horsecloth thrown over him (the details are curiously striking), there is no doubt that he was in great distress. On 15th May he sent a desperate note to Rogers, which arrived after midnight: 'I find things settled so that £150 will remove all difficulty. I am absolutely undone and broken-hearted. I shall negotiate for the plays successfully in the course of a week, when all shall be returned. I have desired Fairbrother to get back the guarantee for thirty.

'They are going to put the carpets out of the window and break into Mrs. Sheridan's room and *take me*—for God's sake let me see you.'

The note, with its pathetic and characteristic mixture of optimism, despair, reassurance, and terror, gives a startlingly vivid picture of Sheridan during his last days. Moore, who was with Rogers when it arrived, walked down with him to Savile Row to make sure that the threatened arrest had not actually been carried out. A servant spoke to them from the area and told them that everything was safe for the night, but that bills were to be pasted over the front of the house next day. In the morning Moore took the £150 from Rogers, but it settled, of course, only one claim out of many. Lord Holland afterwards insisted on paying half of it.

Sheridan's dread of being *taken* was only too well founded, in spite of the fact that he was so ill that he could not get out of bed. A sheriff's officer was actually going to carry him off in his blankets, and only the stern representations of the doctor stopped him from doing it. Esther Jane, who, as her spirited refusal of the prince's help shows, had a pride not unlike her husband's, put the best face she could on the dismal situation. The poor woman was desperately ill, and if not actually dying, had no chance of being cured. The doctor had ordered her not to move from a sofa. Smyth, the former tutor, called, and she offered him some refreshment, saying painfully that the house could still afford something. He found strange-looking people in the hall, and seeing a piece of paper lying on a table, picked it up: it was a prescription, but only for a strengthening medicine. Michael Kelly sent for Sheridan's servant, who told him his master wanted for nothing. The *Morning Post* called for life and help, rather than Westminster Abbey and a funeral.

Three days before Sheridan died Lady Bessborough came to see him, making her way into the house in the wake of a bailiff. The bailiffs, indeed, she told Lord Broughton some two years later, were in possession, and had taken up their quarters downstairs, where they were smoking, and amusing themselves by playing cards. Sheridan lay dying above, and his wife was in little better case. She begged Lady Bessborough not to let him know that he could not recover. Sheridan made her sit on a trunk, there being nothing else in the room for the purpose. He asked her how she thought he looked. She could find nothing to say in reply except that his eyes were as brilliant as ever. He said they would soon be fixed eternally, which frightened her. Then he took her hand and, holding it tightly, said he was determined she should never forget him—if possible he would come back to her after death. She reproached him for persecuting her, and he said other terrifying things, so that she went away at last in great distress.

This story has been questioned, but it is not likely to have been invented. It is strange, and even grotesque; but it is never safe to try to confine Sheridan within the limits of the probable. Except in the plainest and most public concerns he generally contrived to elude close observation, just as he daily eluded duns and other troublesome people. Everybody knew Sheridan, and nobody knew him. He was seen dressed and ready, and to this day it is hard to say anything about him without finding something else which appears to qualify or even contradict it.

In this respect the close of his life was like the rest of it. To Lady Bessborough, sitting terrified on the trunk with Sheridan holding her hand, succeeds Dr. Howley, the Bishop of London, reading prayers to the dying man. To the bare rooms with their filth and stench, and the bailiffs downstairs with their cards and tobacco, succeeds Charles Sheridan's comforting letter to Tom at the Cape, assuring him that his father had received every possible care and comfort which could soothe his last hours. And to the sheriff's officer on the point of carrying him off in his blankets, succeed the imposing train of mourners and the grave in the Abbey.[1]

Out of these and so many other conflicting elements in his life, come—the grosser parts being purged away by some strong native virtue—the peculiar charm and distinction which are inseparable from his memory, and which the sight or sound of his name never fails to recall.

He died on Sunday, 7th July 1816. Ten days later, Byron, at Diodati, wrote his 'Monody on the Death of the Right Honourable Richard Brinsley Sheridan.'

> Even as the tenderness that hour instils
> When Summer's day declines along the hills,
> So feels the fulness of our heart and eyes
> When all of Genius which can perish dies.
> A mighty spirit is eclipsed—a Power
> Hath pass'd from day to darkness. . . .

In some ways Byron recognized a kindred spirit in Sheridan. But then, as he said himself, he could never write to order. He did what he could. He spoke of wit, intelligence, song, eloquence, which were only

> sparkling segments of that circling soul
> Which all embraced—and lighten'd over all.

He spoke of the 'loud cry of trampled Hindostan,' and reminded those who dwelt on Sheridan's failings

> That what to them seem'd Vice might be but Woe.

[1] According to Lord Broughton the burial service was not very impressively performed, and there was no great display of grief when the coffin was lowered.

But it is not here that we shall find Sheridan's proper epitaph: we shall do better to look for that in some less obvious and formal setting. 'Observe,' says Charles Lamb, 'who have been the greatest borrowers of all ages—Alcibiades—Falstaff—Sir Richard Steele. . . .' He adds a fourth to this high company, and it is pleasant, and not altogether fanciful, to think that he would gladly have allowed his words a far wider application— 'our late incomparable Brinsley.'

A SELECTION OF AUTHORITIES

(a) BIOGRAPHICAL

Thomas Moore: *Memoirs of the Life of the Right Honourable R. B. Sheridan* (1825); W. Fraser Rae: *Sheridan* (1896); Walter S. Sichel: *Sheridan* (1909). [These had the use of the papers left by Sheridan, which, unfortunately, included few intimate letters. Moore's publisher allowed him to take his own time over the work, and it did not appear until nine years after Sheridan's death. Fraser Rae wrote the article on Sheridan in the *Dictionary of National Biography*, in which, as in the two volumes of his full-length work, he took the position of an advocate for Sheridan more decidedly than is altogether desirable in a biographer. To his industry, and that of Walter Sichel, a great deal of interesting and significant information is due, but it has not seriously modified the account given by Moore. Moore's *Life*, in fact, remains the most distinguished, and, on the whole, the best. It is scholarly and urbane, and its chief defects, from the point of view of a modern reader, are due to the circumstances in which it was written. Like most official biographies it dutifully includes a certain amount of material of no great importance or interest; the author was obliged to bear in mind that persons concerned in the story of Sheridan were still living; and many of the events with which he had to deal were familiar to his generation, but are not so to ours.]

Other biographical works are J. Watkins: *Memoirs of the Public and Private Life of . . . Richard Brinsley Sheridan* [this was turned out for Colburn in 1817 to take advantage of the interest caused by Sheridan's death]; Mrs. Oliphant: *Sheridan* (English Men of Letters); L. C. Sanders: *Life of R. B. Sheridan* (Great Writers)—with bibliography by J. P. Anderson; *Sheridan and his Times* 'by an Octogenarian who stood by his knee in youth and sat at his table in manhood' [this appeared in 1859: Fraser Rae identified the author as William Earle]; P. H. Fitzgerald: *The Lives of the Sheridans*. To these should be added: William Smyth: *Memoir of Mr. Sheridan* (privately printed, 1840); and two comparatively recent studies, both able and well-informed—R. Crompton Rhodes: *Harlequin Sheridan* (1933); E. M. Butler: *Sheridan, a Ghost Story* (1931).

(b) DRAMATIC AND THEATRICAL

The Poems and Plays of Richard Brinsley Sheridan (ed. R. Crompton Rhodes, 1928); G. H. Nettleton: *The Major Dramas of Richard Brinsley Sheridan*; *Sheridan's Comedies* (*The Rivals* and *The School for Scandal*, ed.

Brander Matthews); J. Genest: *Some Account of the English Stage from . . . 1660 to 1830* (1832); Colley Cibber: *Apology for his Life*; Herschel Baker: *John Philip Kemble* (Harvard, 1942); Michael Kelly (see note, p. 15): *Reminiscences of M. K. of the King's Theatre, etc.*; P. H. Fitzgerald: *The Life of David Garrick*; James Boaden: *Memoirs of the Life of John Philip Kemble*; and *Memoirs of Mrs. Siddons*; *The Dramatic Works of Samuel Foote* (ed. Jon Bee—i.e. John Badcock, 1830); Vanbrugh: *The Relapse, or, Virtue in Danger*; *Memoirs of the Late Mrs. Robinson, 'written by herself'*; *Ketton MSS.*, Historical Manuscripts Commission; Allardyce Nicoll: *Eighteenth-Century Drama* (1750 to 1800).

(c) POLITICAL

The Speeches of the Right Honourable Richard Brinsley Sheridan, edited by a constitutional friend; Lord Holland: *Memoirs of the Whig Party*; and (ed. Lord Stavordale) *Further Memoirs of the Whig Party* (1807–21); *Life and Letters of Sir Gilbert Elliot, First Earl of Minto* (ed. Countess of Minto); Sir Nathaniel William Wraxall: *Historical Memoirs of my Own Time*; *Posthumous Memoirs of his Own Time*; *Memorials and Correspondence of Charles James Fox* (ed. Lord John Russell); Horace Walpole: *Journal of the Reign of George III from 1771 to 1783*; Sir Philip Magnus: *Edmund Burke*; Edward Lascelles: *Life of Charles James Fox*; J. Holland Rose: *Life of William Pitt*; A. Mervyn Davies: *Warren Hastings*; Michael T. H. Sadler: *The Political Career of Richard Brinsley Sheridan* (the chief interest in this short study lies in the fact that it includes previously unpublished letters from Mrs. Sheridan to Mrs. Canning—see Chapter IX); E. A. Bond: *Speeches of the Managers and Counsel in the Trial of Warren Hastings*; Historical Manuscripts Commission: *Dropmore Papers*, I, VII, VIII, X; *Rutland MSS.*, III; *Charlemont Papers*, II; *Carlisle MSS.*

(d) GENERAL

Alicia Lefanu: *Memoirs of the Life and Writings of Mrs. Frances Sheridan*, etc. ('with remarks upon a late Life of the Right Honourable R. B. Sheridan . . .'—i.e. that by John Watkins); *The Journal of Elizabeth, Lady Holland* (ed. Earl of Ilchester); J. C. Hobhouse (Lord Broughton): *Recollections of a Long Life*; *Memoirs, Journal, and Correspondence of Thomas Moore*; Horace Walpole: *Letters*; Madame D'Arblay: *Diary and Letters*; *The Creevey Papers* (ed. Sir H. Maxwell); Moore: *Life of Byron*; Byron: *Monody on the Death of the Right Honourable Richard Brinsley Sheridan*; *Address spoken at the Opening of Drury Lane Theatre*; *Letters and Journals*; Joseph Farington, R.A.: *The Farington Diary* (ed. James Greig); Leigh Hunt: *Autobiography*; Hazlitt: *Lectures on the English Comic Writers*; and *On the Want of Money* (*Monthly Magazine*); *Memoirs, Diaries, and Correspondence of the Right Hon. John Wilson Croker* (ed. Jennings).

INDEX